SOFTWARE MAINTENANCE
Concepts and Practice
Second Edition

SOFTWARE MAINTENANCE
Concepts and Practice
SECOND EDITION

Penny Grubb (University of Hull, UK) &
Armstrong A Takang (Software Systems Consultant, USA)

World Scientific
New Jersey • London • Singapore • Hong Kong

Published by
World Scientific Publishing Co. Pte. Ltd.
5 Toh Tuck Link, Singapore 596224
USA office: Suite 202, 1060 Main Street, River Edge, NJ 07661
UK office: 57 Shelton Street, Covent Garden, London WC2H 9HE

British Library Cataloguing-in-Publication Data
A catalogue record for this book is available from the British Library.

SOFTWARE MAINTENANCE: CONCEPTS AND PRACTICE (2nd Edition)
Copyright © 2003 by World Scientific Publishing Co. Pte. Ltd.
All rights reserved. This book, or parts thereof, may not be reproduced in any form or by any means, electronic or mechanical, including photocopying, recording or any information storage and retrieval system now known or to be invented, without written permission from the Publisher.

For photocopying of material in this volume, please pay a copying fee through the Copyright Clearance Center, Inc., 222 Rosewood Drive, Danvers, MA 01923, USA. In this case permission to photocopy is not required from the publisher.

ISBN 981-238-425-1
ISBN 981-238-426-X (pbk)

Printed in Singapore by World Scientific Printers (S) Pte Ltd

Acknowledgements

To our families, especially

- George and Danny (and thanks for all that proof-reading)
- Ayem, Bessem and Nyente.

The authors would like to thank colleagues and friends in the various health care facilities across the world whose software trials and tribulations have been amalgamated into the Acme Health Clinic case studies used in the book.

Thanks also to Steven Patt and his colleagues for editorial assistance.

Preface

Aims and Objectives

The purpose of this book is to explore the key issues underpinning software change and to discuss how these issues impact on the implementation of changes to software systems. The motivation for the book came from the need for texts dealing directly with challenges that software engineers face when modifying complex software systems. The extent of this challenge can be seen in the cost of modifying software. This cost can reach 70% of the total life-cycle cost [4, 36, 176]. Software maintenance is recognised as a key area in software engineering [9, 163]. Despite this, many mainstream software engineering courses are biased towards the development of new software systems at the expense of issues surrounding changes to these systems after they become operational [70].

Our intention is to produce a text that presents:

- a coherent and comprehensive coverage of software change concepts;
- a theoretical base for the skills required to effect, control and manage changes to evolving software systems;
- a framework for understanding and applying current maintenance techniques and methods to solve problems.

This is not a cookbook; there is no set of cut and dried rules for dealing with the problems of software maintenance. An elegant and workable solution in one situation may be completely inadequate for the same problem in a different environment. Nonetheless, it is essential for software engineers to have a sound understanding of software maintenance for several reasons. Firstly, it is common wisdom that a large part of finding a solution to a problem lies in understanding it. Secondly, an insight into the issues underpinning software maintenance can help in the formulation of an adequate framework that can be used to guide the development of appropriate support tools. This framework also enables researchers to identify potential research questions and compare research findings.

Target Audience

This book is aimed at students, academics and professionals who have an interest in the development and maintenance of software systems.

It is intended as a reference text and also as a course book for software maintenance, software evolution and general courses on advanced software engineering. It can also serve as an introductory text for those intending to engage in research into software maintenance.

For undergraduate study, the book aims to raise awareness of software maintenance issues, for example the need to develop programs that cater for the evolutionary tendency of software systems. This not only provides a grounding in the discipline, but is also a preparation for life in the commercial world. The first job of many graduates going into the software industry involves the maintenance of existing systems rather than the development of new systems [187, 282]. Additionally, the book is intended to complement other undergraduate software engineering and programming courses.

For software professionals, the text provides a collection of definitions for some of the commonly used terms. This is important because of the plethora of terms and jargon in use [211]. In addition, the case studies and real world examples provided should help during in-service training or refresher courses on software maintenance.

Structure and Organisation of this Book

The book is organised into five parts.

The first part looks at the context of software maintenance. It introduces the basic concepts and the framework within which maintenance operates. Underlying theory is introduced by looking at the fundamentals of software change, but real world considerations are also introduced at this stage. This part of the book concludes with a look at how software development and maintenance life-cycles are modelled.

The second part of the book goes through the activities that take place during maintenance, starting with understanding the system to be changed, through the specifics of making the change and testing the modified system, to the managerial issues and decision-making that accompanies the process.

The third part looks at means of measurement and assessment, both of the overall process and of the components of software and software maintenance, showing how to keep track and provide objective assessment.

These first three parts of the book look at what software maintenance is and how to do it. In total they build the case for maintainability in systems.

The fourth part looks at how these lessons can be used in the building of better systems.

The fifth and final part looks at research areas and the future for the discipline of software maintenance.

Each major section is preceded by a number of discussion points aimed at provoking thought about some of the fundamental issues.

Exercises throughout the book vary from straightforward questions on the details of the text, to more complex role-playing projects where the reader is asked to put themselves into a particular maintenance context and think through a specific problem.

Both minor and major case studies are used throughout to relate the material to what is happening at the coal face of software maintenance.

Contents

ACKNOWLEDGEMENTS V

PREFACE VII

PART I: THE CONTEXT OF MAINTENANCE 1
    OVERVIEW 1
    DISCUSSION POINTS 2

1. **INTRODUCTION TO THE BASIC CONCEPTS** 5
    1.1   INTRODUCTION 5
    1.2   DEFINITIONS 6
    1.3   THE BASICS 7
    1.4   HOW NEW DEVELOPMENT AND MAINTENANCE ACTIVITIES DIFFER 9
    1.5   WHY SOFTWARE MAINTENANCE IS NEEDED 10
    1.6   MAINTAINING SYSTEMS EFFECTIVELY 11
    1.7   CASE STUDY – AIR TRAFFIC CONTROL 12
    1.8   CATEGORISING SOFTWARE CHANGE 14
    1.9   SUMMARY 15

2. **THE MAINTENANCE FRAMEWORK** 17
    2.1   INTRODUCTION 17
    2.2   DEFINITIONS 17
    2.3   A SOFTWARE MAINTENANCE FRAMEWORK 18
        2.3.1   Components of the Framework 20
            2.3.1.1   User 20
            2.3.1.2   Environment 20
                            Operating environment 20
                            Organisational Environment 21
            2.3.1.3   Maintenance Process 23
            2.3.1.4   Software Product 25
            2.3.1.5   Maintenance Personnel 28
        2.3.2   Relations Between the Maintenance Factors 29
    2.4   SUMMARY 31

3. **FUNDAMENTALS OF SOFTWARE CHANGE** 33
    3.1   INTRODUCTION 33
    3.2   DEFINITIONS 33
    3.3   SOFTWARE CHANGE 34
        3.3.1   Classification of Changes 34
            3.3.1.1   Corrective Change 35

		3.3.1.2	Adaptive Change	36
		3.3.1.3	Perfective Change	36
		3.3.1.4	Preventive Change	39
	3.3.2	The Importance of Categorising Software Changes		40
	3.3.3	Case Study – The Need to Support an Obsolete System		40
	3.3.4	Incremental Release		41

3.4 ONGOING SUPPORT 42
3.5 LEHMAN'S LAWS 44
3.6 SUMMARY 46

4. LIMITATIONS AND ECONOMIC IMPLICATIONS TO SOFTWARE CHANGE 47

4.1 INTRODUCTION 47
4.2 DEFINITIONS 47
4.3 ECONOMIC IMPLICATIONS OF MODIFYING SOFTWARE 48
4.4 LIMITATIONS TO SOFTWARE CHANGE 50
    4.4.1 Resource Limitations 50
    4.4.2 Quality of the Existing System 51
    4.4.3 Organisational Strategy 51
    4.4.4 Inertia 51
    4.4.5 Attracting and Retaining Skilled Staff 52
4.5 THE NOMENCLATURE AND IMAGE PROBLEMS 52
4.6 POTENTIAL SOLUTIONS TO MAINTENANCE PROBLEMS 54
    4.6.1 Budget and Effort Reallocation 54
    4.6.2 Complete Replacement of the System 55
    4.6.3 Maintenance of the Existing System 56
4.7 SUMMARY 56

5. THE MAINTENANCE PROCESS 59

5.1 INTRODUCTION 59
5.2 DEFINITIONS 60
5.3 THE SOFTWARE PRODUCTION PROCESS 60
5.4 CRITICAL APPRAISAL OF TRADITIONAL PROCESS MODELS 65
    5.4.1 Code-and-Fix Model 66
    5.4.2 Waterfall Model 67
    5.4.3 Spiral Model 69
5.5 MAINTENANCE PROCESS MODELS 71
    5.5.1 Quick-Fix Model 76
        5.5.1.1 Case Study – Storage of Chronological Clinical Data 77
    5.5.2 Boehm's Model 80
    5.5.3 Osborne's Model 82
    5.5.4 Iterative Enhancement Model 84

	5.5.5 Reuse-Oriented Model 85
5.6	WHEN TO MAKE A CHANGE 86
5.7	PROCESS MATURITY 87
	5.7.1 Capability Maturity Model® for Software 88
	5.7.2 Software Experience Bases 88
5.8	SUMMARY 89

PART II: WHAT TAKES PLACE DURING MAINTENANCE 91

OVERVIEW 91
DISCUSSION POINTS 94

6. PROGRAM UNDERSTANDING 97

6.1	INTRODUCTION 98
6.2	DEFINITIONS 98
6.3	AIMS OF PROGRAM COMPREHENSION 100
	6.3.1 Problem Domain 100
	6.3.2 Execution Effect 101
	6.3.3 Cause-Effect Relation 101
	6.3.4 Product-Environment Relation 103
	6.3.5 Decision-Support Features 103
6.4	MAINTAINERS AND THEIR INFORMATION NEEDS 103
	6.4.1 Managers 104
	6.4.2 Analysts 104
	6.4.3 Designers 105
	6.4.4 Programmers 105
6.5	COMPREHENSION PROCESS MODELS 107
6.6	MENTAL MODELS 109
6.7	PROGRAM COMPREHENSION STRATEGIES 110
	6.7.1 Top-Down Model 111
	6.7.2 Bottom-Up / Chunking Model 113
	6.7.3 Opportunistic Model 115
6.8	READING TECHNIQUES 115
6.9	FACTORS THAT AFFECT UNDERSTANDING 116
	6.9.1 Expertise 118
	6.9.2 Implementation Issues 118
	6.9.2.1 Naming Style 118
	6.9.2.2 Comments 120
	6.9.2.3 Decomposition Mechanism 121
	6.9.3 Documentation 122
	6.9.4 Organisation and Presentation of Programs 122
	6.9.5 Comprehension Support Tools 125
	6.9.5.1 Book Paradigm 125
	6.9.6 Evolving Requirements 126

	6.10	IMPLICATIONS OF COMPREHENSION THEORIES AND STUDIES 128
		6.10.1 Knowledge Acquisition and Performance 128
		6.10.2 Education and Training.. 129
		6.10.3 Design Principles 129
		6.10.4 Guidelines and Recommendations................................ 129
	6.11	SUMMARY 130

7. REVERSE ENGINEERING 133

- 7.1 INTRODUCTION.. 133
- 7.2 DEFINITIONS 134
- 7.3 ABSTRACTION 134
  - 7.3.1 Function Abstraction 135
  - 7.3.2 Data Abstraction 135
  - 7.3.3 Process Abstraction 135
- 7.4 PURPOSE AND OBJECTIVES OF REVERSE ENGINEERING.................. 135
- 7.5 LEVELS OF REVERSE ENGINEERING 138
  - 7.5.1 Redocumentation 139
  - 7.5.2 Design Recovery.. 141
  - 7.5.3 Specification Recovery.. 142
  - 7.5.4 Conditions for Reverse Engineering 143
- 7.6 SUPPORTING TECHNIQUES.. 143
  - 7.6.1 Forward Engineering 144
  - 7.6.2 Restructuring 144
  - 7.6.3 Reengineering 146
- 7.7 BENEFITS 146
  - 7.7.1 Maintenance... 146
  - 7.7.2 Software Reuse 147
  - 7.7.3 Reverse Engineering and Associated Techniques in Practice 147
- 7.8 CASE STUDY: US DEPARTMENT OF DEFENSE INVENTORY............. 148
- 7.9 CURRENT PROBLEMS 149
- 7.10 SUMMARY.. 151

8. REUSE AND REUSABILITY.. 153

- 8.1 INTRODUCTION.. 154
- 8.2 DEFINITIONS 154
- 8.3 THE TARGETS FOR REUSE 155
  - 8.3.1 Process... 155
  - 8.3.2 Personnel 156
  - 8.3.3 Product... 156
  - 8.3.4 Data.. 156
    - 8.3.4.1 Design 156
    - 8.3.4.2 Program... 157

8.4	OBJECTIVES AND BENEFITS OF REUSE			158
8.5	APPROACHES TO REUSE			159
	8.5.1	Composition-Based Reuse		160
	8.5.2	Generation-Based Reuse		162
		8.5.2.1	Application Generator Systems	162
		8.5.2.2	Transformation-Based Systems	163
		8.5.2.3	Evaluation of the Generator-Based Systems	164
8.6	DOMAIN ANALYSIS			164
8.7	COMPONENTS ENGINEERING			166
	8.7.1	Design for Reuse		166
		8.7.1.1	Characteristics of Reusable Components	166
		8.7.1.2	Problems with Reuse Libraries	168
	8.7.2	Reverse Engineering		169
		8.7.2.1	Case Study – Patient Identification	170
	8.7.3	Components-Based Processes		171
8.8	REUSE PROCESS MODEL			172
	8.8.1	Generic Reuse/Reusability Model		173
	8.8.2	Accommodating a Reuse Process Model		176
8.9	FACTORS THAT IMPACT UPON REUSE			177
	8.9.1	Technical Factors		177
		8.9.1.1	Programming Languages	177
		8.9.1.2	Representation of Information	177
		8.9.1.3	Reuse Library	178
		8.9.1.4	Reuse-Maintenance Vicious Cycle	178
	8.9.2	Non-Technical Factors		178
		8.9.2.1	Initial Capital Outlay	178
		8.9.2.2	Not Invented Here Factor	179
		8.9.2.3	Commercial Interest	179
		8.9.2.4	Education	179
		8.9.2.5	Project Co-ordination	179
		8.9.2.6	Legal Issues	179
8.10	SUMMARY			181

9. TESTING 183

9.1	INTRODUCTION			183
9.2	DEFINITIONS			183
9.3	WHY TEST SOFTWARE			184
9.4	WHAT IS A SOFTWARE TESTER'S JOB			186
9.5	WHAT TO TEST AND HOW			187
	9.5.1	Who Chooses Test Data		187
9.6	CATEGORISING TESTS			189
	9.6.1	Testing Code		190
		9.6.1.1	Black Box and White Box Testing	190
		9.6.1.2	Structured Testing	190
		9.6.1.3	Integration Testing	191

		9.6.1.4	Regression Testing	191
9.7	VERIFICATION AND VALIDATION			192
9.8	TEST PLANS			192
	9.8.1	Points to Note		193
9.9	CASE STUDY – THERAC 25			194
9.10	SUMMARY			201

10. MANAGEMENT AND ORGANISATIONAL ISSUES 203

- 10.1 INTRODUCTION 204
- 10.2 DEFINITIONS 205
- 10.3 MANAGEMENT RESPONSIBILITIES 205
- 10.4 ENHANCING MAINTENANCE PRODUCTIVITY 206
  - 10.4.1 Choosing the Right People 206
  - 10.4.2 Motivating Maintenance Personnel 206
  - 10.4.3 Communication 208
    - 10.4.3.1 Adequate Resources 209
    - 10.4.3.2 Domain Knowledge 209
- 10.5 MAINTENANCE TEAMS 210
  - 10.5.1 Temporary Team 211
  - 10.5.2 Permanent Team 211
- 10.6 PERSONNEL EDUCATION AND TRAINING 211
  - 10.6.1 Objectives 212
    - 10.6.1.1 To Raise the Level of Awareness 212
    - 10.6.1.2 To Enhance Recognition 213
  - 10.6.2 Education and Training Strategies 213
- 10.7 ORGANISATIONAL MODES 214
  - 10.7.1 Combined Development and Maintenance 214
    - 10.7.1.1 Module Ownership 214
    - 10.7.1.2 Change Ownership 215
    - 10.7.1.3 Work-Type 215
    - 10.7.1.4 Application-Type 216
  - 10.7.2 Separate Maintenance Department 216
- 10.8 SUMMARY 217

PART III: KEEPING TRACK OF THE MAINTENANCE PROCESS 219

OVERVIEW 219
DISCUSSION POINTS 220

11. CONFIGURATION MANAGEMENT 223

- 11.1 INTRODUCTION 223
- 11.2 DEFINITIONS 225
- 11.3 CONFIGURATION MANAGEMENT 226
  - 11.3.1 A Specific View of Software Configuration Management 231

		11.3.1.1	Version Control	232
		11.3.1.2	Building	234
		11.3.1.3	Environment Management	234
		11.3.1.4	Process Control	235

11.4 CHANGE CONTROL 235
    11.4.1 The Responsibilities of Management in Change Control 236
11.5 DOCUMENTATION 238
    11.5.1 Categories of Software Documentation 238
    11.5.2 Role of Software Documentation 241
    11.5.3 Producing and Maintaining Quality Documentation 242
11.6 SUMMARY 245

12. MAINTENANCE MEASURES 247

12.1 INTRODUCTION 247
12.2 DEFINITIONS 248
12.3 THE IMPORTANCE OF INTEGRITY IN MEASUREMENT 249
    12.3.1 Software Measurement 250
    12.3.2 Software Measure and Software Metric 251
12.4 OBJECTIVES OF SOFTWARE MEASUREMENT 253
    12.4.1 Evaluation 253
    12.4.2 Control 253
    12.4.3 Assessment 253
    12.4.4 Improvement 254
    12.4.5 Prediction 254
12.5 EXAMPLE MEASURES 254
    12.5.1 Size 255
    12.5.2 Complexity 255
        12.5.2.1 McCabe's Cyclomatic Complexity 256
        12.5.2.2 Halstead's Measures 257
    12.5.3 Quality 259
        12.5.3.1 Product Quality 259
        12.5.3.2 Process Quality 259
    12.5.4 Understandability 260
    12.5.5 Maintainability 260
    12.5.6 Cost Estimation 261
12.6 GUIDELINES FOR SELECTING MAINTENANCE MEASURES 261
12.7 SUMMARY 263

PART IV: BUILDING BETTER SYSTEMS 265

OVERVIEW 265
DISCUSSION POINTS 266

13. BUILDING AND SUSTAINING MAINTAINABILITY 269

13.1 INTRODUCTION 270
13.2 DEFINITIONS 270
13.3 IMPACT ANALYSIS 271
    13.3.1 Models and Strategies 271
    13.3.2 Impact Analysis in Creating Maintainable Systems 272
13.4 QUALITY ASSURANCE 272
    13.4.1 Fitness for Purpose 273
    13.4.2 Correctness 274
    13.4.3 Portability 274
    13.4.4 Testability 275
    13.4.5 Usability 275
        13.4.5.1 Case Study – Usability 275
    13.4.6 Reliability 276
    13.4.7 Efficiency 277
    13.4.8 Integrity 277
    13.4.9 Reusability 278
    13.4.10 Interoperability 278
13.5 FOURTH-GENERATION LANGUAGES 279
    13.5.1 Properties of Fourth-Generation Languages 281
    13.5.2 Impact on Maintenance 282
        13.5.2.1 Increased Productivity 282
        13.5.2.2 Reduction in Cost 283
        13.5.2.3 Ease of Understanding 283
        13.5.2.4 Automatic Documentation 283
        13.5.2.5 Reduction in Workload 283
    13.5.3 Weaknesses of Fourth-Generation Languages 283
        13.5.3.1 Application-Specific 284
        13.5.3.2 Proprietary 284
        13.5.3.3 Hyped Ease of Use 284
        13.5.3.4 Poor Design 284
13.6 OBJECT-ORIENTED PARADIGMS 285
    13.6.1 Decomposition to Aid Comprehension 286
    13.6.2 Impact on Maintenance 288
    13.6.3 Migration to Object-Oriented Platforms 290
    13.6.4 Approaches 290
    13.6.5 Retraining Personnel 291
13.7 OBJECT-ORIENTED TECHNIQUES IN SOFTWARE MAINTENANCE 292
    13.7.1 Case Study – Mobile2OOO 292
    13.7.2 Case Study – Insight II 293
    13.7.3 Case Study – Image Filing System 295
13.8 SUMMARY 297

14. MAINTENANCE TOOLS 299

- 14.1 INTRODUCTION 299
- 14.2 DEFINITIONS 300
- 14.3 CRITERIA FOR SELECTING TOOLS 300
- 14.4 TAXONOMY OF TOOLS 302
- 14.5 TOOLS FOR COMPREHENSION AND REVERSE ENGINEERING 302
  - 14.5.1 Program Slicer 303
  - 14.5.2 Static Analyser 303
  - 14.5.3 Dynamic Analyser 304
  - 14.5.4 Data Flow Analyser 304
  - 14.5.5 Cross-Referencer 304
  - 14.5.6 Dependency Analyser 305
  - 14.5.7 Transformation Tool 305
- 14.6 TOOLS TO SUPPORT TESTING 305
  - 14.6.1 Simulator 305
  - 14.6.2 Test Case Generator 306
  - 14.6.3 Test Paths Generator 306
- 14.7 TOOLS TO SUPPORT CONFIGURATION MANAGEMENT 306
  - 14.7.1 Source Code Control System 307
  - 14.7.2 Other Utilities 308
- 14.8 OTHER TASKS 308
  - 14.8.1 Documentation 308
  - 14.8.2 Complexity Assessment 308
- 14.9 SUMMARY 309

PART V: LOOKING TO THE FUTURE 311

- OVERVIEW 311
- THE PAST AND PRESENT 312
- RESEARCH AREAS 313
  - Classification 313
  - Software Experience Bases 313
  - Software Reuse 313
  - Support Tools 314
  - Software Measurement 314
  - Program Comprehension 314
  - The Software Maintenance Process 315
  - The Threesome Marriage 315
- THE BEST OF BOTH WORLDS 316

REFERENCES 317

INDEX 341

PART I: The Context of Maintenance

Overview

This section of the book looks at software maintenance in context. It aims to set the scene for looking in detail at what happens during the maintenance process, and to provide a grounding in the subject that will support you in the building of better software systems.

As with any discipline, it is important to have a good understanding of the theoretical base and the context within which it operates, in order to understand the cutting edge and be able to take the discipline forward.

In this first part of the book, we will look at the basic concepts of software maintenance and the overall framework within which it operates. This includes a study of the fundamentals of software change, some of the limitations and constraints, and finally a look at the theory of maintenance process models.

- **Basic Concepts**

A study of the basic concepts shows where and how software maintenance fits within the discipline of software engineering. It highlights the aspects that make software maintenance a distinct discipline, whilst exploring why software maintenance is needed and how it can be carried out effectively.

- **Maintenance Framework**

A study of the framework within which software maintenance operates, roots the discipline firmly in the real world and gives a flavour for how many different elements must be taken into account during maintenance projects.

- **Software Change Fundamentals**

A study of the theory of software change leads to a deeper understanding of the types of change that are and are not possible within software systems. It allows for a more structured and effective approach to the whole issue of implementing change.

- **Limitations and Economic Implications**

Looking at the theory is useful, and you cannot be an effective software maintainer without it. However, it is no use seeing software maintenance as something that operates in a vacuum or always has unlimited resources at its disposal. Being aware of economic and other constraints is vital in making appropriate decisions.

- **Maintenance Process Models**

The process of carrying out software maintenance has evolved over many years, and the underlying processes can be modelled. An understanding of the models that you are working to when effecting software change leads to a far better grasp of the overall processes and thus aids good decision making.

Discussion Points

These points are intended to stimulate thinking and discussion on fundamental issues in software maintenance. The issues raised are explored in the chapters of this section, but it is beneficial to think around these areas and try to draw conclusions yourself, before looking for answers in the text.

- **When to Implement Change**

Imagine that you are in charge of a large software project. As well as a major upgrade that is being implemented, you have to support three different versions running on different Windows platforms and also a DOS version that is still in use by a small group of users. A number of different clients approach you over the course of a week to request the following changes:

- One of the DOS users has seen a colleague's Windows version. He doesn't wish to upgrade his system entirely, but he would like a specific functionality. Can you provide it?

- One of your more enthusiastic users has been experimenting with the latest functions in the latest Windows version. A problem has come to light whereby the database may be corrupted. Can you fix it?

- Another of your Windows clients has heard about the wonderful new upgrade that is coming on stream, but it seems a long time to wait. Could you provide one small extra function in the current version?

Discuss the issues raised above. What sorts of things should you think about when considering these requests? What considerations would persuade you to agree? What would persuade you to turn the request down? For each request, try to think of one scenario where you would agree and one where you would turn it down. In each case, which is the most likely – that you will or will not agree to make the change?

1

Introduction to the Basic Concepts

"There is no such thing as a 'finished' computer program"

Lehman [169 chapter 2]

> **This chapter aims to**
>
> 1. Define and introduce software maintenance and software evolution.
> 2. Show how these topics fit within the wider context.
> 3. Distinguish software maintenance from software development.
> 4. Outline why maintenance is needed.
> 5. Give a flavour of the theoretical background and key skills required to implement effective software change.
> 6. Introduce the specific activities that comprise software maintenance.

1.1 Introduction

The discipline concerned with changes related to a software system after delivery is traditionally known as **software maintenance**. This section of the book will examine software maintenance with a view to defining it, and exploring why it is needed. An appreciation of the discipline is important because costs are extremely high. Many issues, including safety and cost, mean there is an urgent need to find ways of reducing or eliminating maintenance problems [211].

During the past few decades, there has been a proliferation of software systems in a wide range of working environments. The sectors of society that have exploited these systems in their day-to-day operation are numerous and include manufacturing industries, financial institutions, information services, healthcare services and construction industries [176, 263]. There is an increasing reliance on software systems [69] and it is ever more important that such systems do the job they are intended to do, and do it well. In other words, it is vital that systems are useful. If they fail to be useful, they will not be accepted by users and will not be used.

In today's world, correct use and functioning of a software system can be a matter of life and death. Some of the factors that bear on the usefulness of software systems are functionality, flexibility, continuous availability and correct operation [170]. Changes will usually be required to support these factors during the lifetime of a system [256]. For example, changes may be necessary to satisfy requests for performance improvement, functional enhancement, or to deal with errors discovered in the system [176].

One of the greatest challenges facing software engineers is the management and control of these changes [131]. This is clearly demonstrated by the time spent and effort required to keep software systems operational after release. Results from studies undertaken to investigate the characteristics and costs of changes carried out on a system after delivery show estimated expenditure at 40-70% of the costs of the entire life-cycle of the software system [4, 33, 35, 176].

1.2 Definitions

Evolution – a process of continuous change from a lower, simpler, or worse to a higher, more complex, or better state.

Maintainability – the ease with which maintenance can be carried out.

Maintenance – the act of keeping an entity in an existing state of repair, efficiency, or validity; to preserve from failure or decline.

Software – the programs, documentation and operating procedures by which computers can be made useful to man [192 p.1].

Software maintenance – modification of a software product after delivery, to correct faults, to improve performance or other attributes, or to adapt the product to a modified environment [272 p.94].

1.3 The Basics

To understand software maintenance we need to be clear about what is meant by 'software'. It is a common misconception to believe that software is programs [184 p.4]. This can lead to a misunderstanding of terms that include the word 'software'. For instance, when thinking about software maintenance activities, there is a temptation to think of activities carried out exclusively on programs. This is because many software maintainers are more familiar with, or rather are more exposed to programs than other components of a software system. A more comprehensive view of software is the one given in the definitions section.

McDermid's definition [192 p.1] makes clear that software comprises not only programs - source and object code - but also documentation of any facet of the program, such as requirements analysis, specification, design, system and user manuals, and the procedures used to set up and operate the software system. Table 1.1 shows the components of a software system and some examples of each.

McDermid's is not the only definition of a software system [264] but it is a comprehensive and widely accepted one and is the one we shall use in this book.

The maintainability of a software system is something that is notoriously difficult to quantify. Certain aspects of systems can be measured. For example, there are several different ways of measuring complexity. Specific features such as interoperability or adherence to standards are also significant. However, there is no simple overall 'maintainability factor' that can be calculated. Nonetheless, recognising the features and traits that make a system easy to maintain is one of the major attributes of a good software maintenance engineer, and one of the things that makes such a person worth his/her weight in gold to a commercial enterprise. The true worth of software maintenance skills is being recognised more and more, and software maintainers are drawing level with software developers as the 'elite' of the software engineering team. The different factors that make up maintainability, and also the issue of the 'public face' of software maintenance are issues discussed in more depth later in the book.

Table 1.1 Components of a software system

Software Components					
			Examples		
Program	1	Source code			
	2	Object code			
Documentation	1	Analysis / specification:	(a)	Formal specification	
			(b)	Context diagram	
			(c)	Data flow diagrams	
	2	Design:	(a)	Flowcharts	
			(b)	Entity-relationship charts	
	3	Implementation:	(a)	Source code listings	
			(b)	Cross-reference listings	
	4	Testing:	(a)	Test data	
			(b)	Test results	
Operating procedures	1	Instructions to set up and use the software system			
	2	Instructions on how to react to system failures			

You will find many different definitions of software maintenance in the literature [209, 70, 6, 176]. Some take a focussed and specific view, and some take a more general view. The latter definitions e.g. defining maintenance as "any work that is undertaken after delivery of a software system" [70 p.233] encompass everything, but fail to indicate what maintenance entails. The former more specific definitions, whilst showing the activities of maintenance, tend to be too narrow. Typical amongst this set of definitions are

- the bug-fixing view – maintenance is the detection and correction of errors,
- the need-to-adapt view - maintenance is making changes to software when its operational environment or original requirement changes,
- the user-support view - maintenance is the provision of support to users.

The definition used in this book is from the IEEE software maintenance standard, IEEE STD 1219-1993. This (given in the previous section) draws on the different classifications, and provides a comprehensive definition.

1.4 How New Development and Maintenance Activities Differ

Although maintenance could be regarded as a continuation of new development [85, 108] (Figure 1.1), there is a fundamental difference between the two activities. New development is, within certain constraints, done on a green field site. Maintenance must work within the parameters and constraints of an existing system.

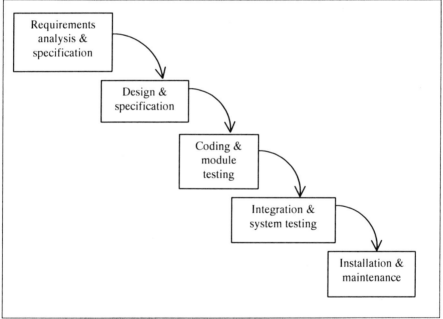

Figure 1.1 Waterfall model of a software life cycle

Before undertaking any system development or maintenance work, an *impact analysis* should be carried out to determine the ramifications of the new or modified system upon the environment into which it is to be introduced. This is discussed in more depth in Chapter 13. The impact of introducing a specific feature into a system will be very different if it is done as a maintenance activity, as opposed to a development activity. It is the constraints that the existing system imposes on maintenance that give rise to this difference. For example, in the course of designing an enhancement, the designer needs to investigate the current system to abstract the architectural and the low-level designs. The reasons for this are explored further in Chapter 6. This information is then used to:

(i) work out how the change can be accommodated;

(ii) predict the potential ripple effect of the change, and

(iii) determine the skills and knowledge required to do the job.

To explain the difference between new development and software maintenance, Jones [146] provides an interesting analogy where he likens the addition of functional requirements to a live system, to the addition of a new room to an existing building:

"The architect and the builders must take care not to weaken the existing structure when additions are made. Although the costs of the new room usually will be lower than the costs of constructing an entirely new building, the costs per square foot may be much higher because of the need to remove existing walls, reroute plumbing and electrical circuits and take special care to avoid disrupting the current site"

Jones (quoted in [69 p.295]).

A detailed comparison of the individual activities of software development and software maintenance can be found in [270].

Exercise 1.1 Define the term software maintenance and indicate the factors that initiate the modification of software.

Exercise 1.2 Compare and contrast software development and software maintenance.

1.5 Why Software Maintenance is Needed

Having looked at what software maintenance is, and briefly what it entails, it is important now to appreciate why it needs to be done. There are a number of factors [4, 33, 36, 35, 176] that provide the motivation for maintenance:

- *To provide continuity of service:* Systems need to keep running. For example, software controlling aeroplanes in flight or train signalling systems cannot be allowed just to stop if an error occurs. Unexpected failure of software can be life threatening. Many facets of daily life are now managed by computer. There can be severe consequences to system failure such as serious inconvenience or significant financial implications. Maintenance activities aimed at keeping a system operational include bug-fixing, recovering from failure, and accommodating changes in the operating system and hardware.

- *To support mandatory upgrades:* This type of change would be necessary because of such things as amendments to government regulations e.g. changes in tax laws will necessitate modifications in the software used by tax offices. Additionally, the need to maintain a competitive edge over rival products will trigger this kind of change.

- *To support user requests for improvements:* On the whole, the better a system is, the more it will be used and the more the users will request enhancements in functionality. There may also be requirements for better performance and customisation to local working patterns.

- *To facilitate future maintenance work:* It does not take long to learn that shortcuts at the software development stage are very costly in the long run. It is often financially and commercially justifiable to initiate change solely to make future maintenance easier. This would involve such things as code and database restructuring, and updating of documentation.

If a system is used, it is never finished [169 ch.2] because it will always need to evolve to meet the requirements of the changing world in which it operates.

1.6 Maintaining Systems Effectively

In order to maintain systems effectively, a good grounding in the relevant theory is essential and certain skills must be learnt. Software maintenance is a key discipline, because it is the means by which systems remain operational and cope efficiently in a world ever more reliant on software systems. Maintenance activities are far-reaching. The maintenance practitioner needs to understand the past and appreciate future impact. As a maintenance engineer, you need to know whether you are maintaining a system that must operate for the next five minutes or the next five decades. These problems were illustrated with the introduction of a new air traffic control system in the UK, where the deferring of the date of completion of the new system meant that the old system had to be supported long beyond its expected lifetime (see the case study below). The motivation to get it right comes from understanding the wider implications, which in turn comes from an understanding of the theories and complexities of the discipline of software maintenance.

- The maintenance engineer needs a far wider range of skills than just computer programming. Amongst other things, he / she needs comprehension skills and wide-ranging analytical powers

1.7 Case Study – Air Traffic Control

For many years, air traffic over England and Wales was handled by two centres run by National Air Traffic Services in West Drayton, Middlesex and in Manchester. These centres dealt with air traffic crossing British airspace and also with take-off and landing traffic at British airports.

However, with air traffic doubling every 15 years, (the 1.6 million flights a year in UK airspace in 1998, was predicted then to rise to 2 million by 2003) the centres were working at and beyond their planned capacity. Alarmingly, the number of in-flight near misses was also increasing.

It was clear that new centres were needed. Planning began in early 1990 and the decision was taken to build a brand new centre and air traffic control system to replace the control centres in London and Manchester. The aim was to increase the number of flights that controllers could handle. The new centre was to be staffed by 800 controllers. IBM was chosen to build a bespoke system. It would be based on a US system, but would require new hardware as well as new software. It was due for completion in 1996 at an estimated cost of £339 million.

In 1996, stability problems were found with the new software and the centre was not opened. Because of continued delays, an independent study was carried out in 1998. The option of scrapping the project altogether was considered and experts warned that the system might never work properly. Completion was rescheduled to between late 1999 and 2001 at a revised cost of £623 million.

An independent audit of the new software in 1999 found 1400 bugs in the two million lines of code. By August 2000, the number of bugs was reported to be down to 500, an estimated 200 of which were deemed to be serious. At this stage, 400 computer technicians were working on the system and managers were warning of possible failure to meet the new deadline.

Over a year was spent clearing the 1400 bugs found by the 1999 audit. Tony Collins of Computer Weekly reported "enormous success" at this stage i.e. in the latter months of 2000. He warned however that confidence in the plan to sort out the remaining serious bugs might be thrown into disarray if one of them turned out to be more serious than realised.

In the event, the new centre opened on Sunday, January 27th 2002, six years behind schedule and about £300 million over budget.

What went wrong with this project? The reasons were varied, and numerous, but stemmed from the initial decision to start from scratch. Mr Butterworth-Hayes, author of Jane's Air Traffic Control Special Report said this decision was "probably wrong" and that off-the-shelf components should have been used. He pointed out that the system needed to last 25 to 30 years, but software advances would be likely to outdate a new system in 18 months.

There were other problems. In 1994, IBM sold the project to another company, which was later taken over. This inevitably caused disruption to schedules and work plans.

Interestingly, in 1995, the US system that was the template, was scrapped.

In failing to meet both its deadlines and revised deadlines, the project was showing a classic early warning sign of serious problems.

> The new system was brought on-line, not without further teething problems, but to date has provided a safer, more efficient environment and has a lot of much-needed spare capacity.
>
> Was safety compromised by the delays? Almost certainly, yes. The controllers at the West Drayton centre had to cope with far more work than the old systems had been designed to handle. This compromised both the safety of air traffic and the health of the controllers themselves who were forced to work in high-stress conditions. It was during the most stressful period, towards the end of the new project, that staff had to be taken off live duties to be trained on the new system. This was a cause of further delay.
>
> It is interesting to compare this project with the European mainland, where less ambitious upgrades resulted in much earlier working versions. These may not have been the ideal solutions conceptually, but they worked in practice because they took better account of what could actually be delivered with the available technology. The new French system for example, used off-the-shelf software to be updated every year. It was introduced with far fewer problems and far more cheaply.
>
> The last word goes to Mr Butterworth-Hayes, speaking in 2002. "There are four major air traffic improvement programmes in Europe at the moment: France, Britain, Italy and Germany. Who has been the most successful? You have to say the UK is not in the top three."

1.8 Categorising Software Change

Software change may be needed, and initiated, for a number of reasons and can be categorised accordingly. In brief, software change may be classified under the following categories:

- Modification initiated by defects in the software.
- Change driven by the need to accommodate modifications in the environment of the software system.
- Change undertaken to expand the existing requirements of a system.
- Change undertaken to prevent malfunctions.

The categorising of software change is not simply an academic exercise. It is vital in understanding when and how to make changes, how to assign resources and how to prioritise requests for change. These areas are expanded and explained in more detail in the following chapters.

1.9 Summary

The key points covered in this chapter:

- The cost of maintaining systems in many organisations has been observed to range from 40% to 70% of resources allocated to the entire software life-cycle.
- It is important to understand what is meant by the basic terms that underlie the field, *software, maintenance, evolution* and *maintainability,* in order to understand the importance of software maintenance and how it fits into context in the modern world.
- Software maintenance and software development, although closely linked, are different. It is important for those involved in maintenance fully to appreciate the differences.
- In a world ever more reliant on software systems, the discipline of software maintenance is becoming more and more important.
- As with other fields, software maintenance is underpinned by a theoretical base. It is important to be aware of this in order to be an effective software maintainer.

Having introduced the basic concepts and given a broad overview of maintenance activities, the next chapter looks at the overall framework within which maintenance is carried out.

2

The Maintenance Framework

"Everything is connected to everything"

Mercury Rising: Film 1998

> **This chapter aims to**
> 1. Look in detail at the context in which software maintenance activities are carried out.
> 2. Discuss in depth the components of the maintenance framework and show how they interrelate.

2.1 Introduction

Software maintenance is not an activity carried out in a vacuum. It affects, and interacts with the environment within which it is carried out. Indeed, it is changes and interactions in the surrounding environment that bring about the need for change. Understanding the framework, and the relationship between the factors comprising this framework allows prediction of problem areas and the ability to avoid them.

2.2 Definitions

Environment – the totality of conditions and influences which act from outside upon an entity.

Environmental factor – an agent which acts upon the entity from without and influences its form or operation.

Framework – a set of ideas, conditions, or assumptions that determine how something will be approached, perceived, or understood.

Information gap – this is the discrepancy between the body of knowledge that system users and system maintainers possess and the body of knowledge that each needs to have in order to satisfy a request for change.

Maintenance challenge – the need to keep systems running. Historically the challenge has been to keep mechanical systems operational after physical wear and tear on components. Software is not subject to physical wear and tear, but to influences less easy to identify and address. Thus the maintenance challenge when applied to software is a far more complex beast than when applied to mechanical systems.

Maintenance personnel – the individuals involved in maintaining a software product.

Maintenance process – any activity carried out, or action taken, either by a machine or maintenance personnel during software maintenance.

Operating environment – all software and hardware systems that influence or act upon a software product in any way.

Organisational environment – all non-software- or non-hardware-related environmental factors.

Safety-critical – a system where failure could result in death, injury or illness, major economic loss, environmental or property damage.

Safety-related – a system where failure could significantly increase the risk of injury or damage.

Software maintenance framework – the context and environment in which software maintenance activities are carried out.

2.3 A Software Maintenance Framework

To a large extent the requirement for software systems to evolve in order to accommodate changing user needs contributes to the high maintenance costs. This is discussed further in chapter 4. Additionally, there are other factors which contribute indirectly by hindering maintenance activities. A Software Maintenance Framework (SMF)[1] will be used to discuss some of these factors. The elements of this framework are the user requirements, organisational and operational environments, maintenance process, software product, and the maintenance personnel (Table 2.1). To understand the sources of the software maintenance challenge, you need an understanding of these components, their characteristics and the effect of their interactions.

Table 2.1 Components of a software maintenance framework

Component	Feature
1. User requirements	<ul><li>Requests for additional functionality, error correction and improving maintainability</li><li>Request for non-programming-related support</li></ul>
2. Organisational environment	<ul><li>Change in policies</li><li>Competition in the market place</li></ul>
3. Operational environment	<ul><li>Hardware innovations</li><li>Software innovations</li></ul>
4. Maintenance process	<ul><li>Capturing requirements</li><li>Creativity and undocumented assumptions</li><li>Variation in programming practice</li><li>Paradigm shift</li><li>'Dead' paradigms for 'living' systems</li><li>Error detection and correction</li></ul>
5. Software product	<ul><li>Maturity and difficulty of application domain</li><li>Quality of documentation</li><li>Malleability of programs</li><li>Complexity of programs</li><li>Program structure</li><li>Inherent quality</li></ul>
6. Maintenance personnel	<ul><li>Staff turnover</li><li>Domain expertise</li></ul>

---

[1] This is a derivative of the Software Maintenance Framework proposed by Haworth *et al.* [126].

2.3.1 Components of the Framework

2.3.1.1 User

The user in this context refers to individuals who use the system, regardless of their involvement in its development or maintenance. As touched upon in chapter 1, there are several reasons why there could be requests for modification of a system after it becomes operational. The categorisation of software change is explored in detail in chapter 3. The implementation of such modifications may necessitate:

(i) 'progressive' work to refine existing functions or to introduce new features; and

(ii) 'anti-regressive' work to make programs well structured, better documented, more understandable and capable of further development [294].

Regardless of the degree of success of a system, it has a propensity to evolve (while it remains operational) in order to support users' changing needs.

2.3.1.2 Environment

Essentially, the environments affecting software systems are the operating environment and the organisational environment. Typical environmental factors within these are business rules, government regulations, work patterns, software and hardware operating platforms.

Operating environment

Examples of factors within the operating environment are innovations in hardware and software platforms:

- *Hardware innovations:* The hardware platform on which a software system runs may be subject to change during the lifetime of the software. Such a change tends to affect the software in a number of ways. For example, when a processor is upgraded, compilers that previously produced machine code for that processor may need to be modified.

- *Software innovations:* Like hardware, changes in the host software may warrant a corresponding modification in the software product. Operating systems, database management systems and compilers are examples of host software systems whose modification may affect other software products.

> ### *Mini Case Study – Upgrading an Operating System*
>
> At the research institute attached to the ACME Health Clinic[2] a Solaris 1.x[3] was upgraded to Solaris 2.x (Solaris is a UNIX-based operating system for SUN[4] machines). As a result of this change, many applications that previously ran on Solaris 1.x had to be modified in order to use Solaris 2.x. This also meant the users had to retrain and learn the use of new commands. Some administrative practices became out of date as a result of the upgrade.
>
> The end result was a more efficient and cost-effective system but the cost of accommodating the upgrade went well beyond the retail price of the new software.

Organisational Environment

Examples of the entities of the organisational environment are policies and imposed factors of business and taxation, and also competition in the market place:

- *Change in policies:* Many information systems have business rules [182] and taxation policies incorporated into their program code. A business rule refers to the procedures used by an organisation in its day-to-day operation [159]. A change in the business rule or taxation policy leads to a corresponding modification of the programs affected. For example, changes to Value Added Tax (VAT) rules necessitate modification of programs that use VAT rules in their computations.

- *Competition in the market place:* Organisations producing similar software products are usually in competition. From a commercial point of view, organisations strive towards having a competitive edge over their rivals (by securing a significant proportion of the market for that product). This can imply carrying out substantial modifications so as to maintain the status of the product [108] – reflected in the level of customer satisfaction – or to increase the existing 'client base'.

---

[2] The ACME Health Clinic is an amalgam of many healthcare facilities whose experiences pertaining to software maintenance have been used throughout the book.
[3] *Solaris*™ is a trademark of Sun Microsystems.
[4] *SUN*™ is a registered trademark of AT&T (Bell Laboratories).

The user may not be billed directly for maintenance costs arising from changes in the organisational environment motivated by the need to keep a competitive edge. However, despite no direct financial input from the user, resources (both machine and human) still need to be allocated.

Generalised Case Study – Maintainability and VAT Rules

Consider the evolution of a system that has accommodated VAT in buying and selling prices for many years.

The original system will have had to cater for a fixed VAT rate on a specific list of goods. Over time, both the VAT rate and the list of goods will change. The fixed rate will then become variable depending upon the class of goods. Further variations will occur such as different rates for the same goods depending upon how they are sold.

In an early system, both the VAT rate and the list of goods may have been "hard-wired" into the code. Updating would require tedious line-by-line checking and amendment with no guarantee that vital elements were not being missed. The code could have been improved by declaration of constants and the use of internal tables. This would allow updates to be made to one section of the code and once only, thus cutting down the room for error. However, it would still mean rewriting programs and would allow the misuse of values within the program.

Later modifications to produce modular code would address the latter problem.

Software engineering point: encapsulation of parts of the code means that execution of a particular part of a program cannot accidentally modify variables that have no relevance to that section of code.

A major step forward is to take the data out of the programs altogether, to store it in external tables or files. VAT upgrades can now be carried out by providing new data files and the programs need not be modified.

Software engineering point: proper separation of data from code avoids unnecessary code modification.

VAT rates and the eligibility of different goods in different contexts are in fact nothing to do with system developers and maintainers. They are set and amended by Government bodies. Even separation of the data as above will not prevent the need to modify programs. Suppose that a new factor enters the arena. VAT rates now depend on a specific selling context such that the same goods sold in different contexts attract different rates. Amending the data files will not be enough. The solution is that programs should not rely on their own internal calculations for things over which they have no control. They should access central data sources e.g. a central VAT server, which is essentially a black box that takes in information from the program and returns a current rate.

Software engineering point: true interoperability between software systems using properly researched and formulated interfaces is the route to real flexibility and is a quantum leap forward in building maintainable systems.

2.3.1.3 Maintenance Process

The maintenance process itself is a major player in the software maintenance framework. Significant factors are the capturing of change requirements, programming practice, 'dead' paradigms and error detection.

- *Capturing change requirements:* This is the process of finding out exactly what changes are required. It poses a lot of problems. Firstly, it is fundamentally difficult to capture all requirements *a priori* [27, 108]. Requirements and user problems only really become clear when a system is in use. Many users know what they want but lack the ability to express it in a form understandable to the analyst or programmer. This is due to the 'information gap' [210] defined earlier.

- *Variation in programming practice:* This refers to differences in approach used for writing and maintaining programs. It involves the use of features or operations which impose a particular program structure. This tends to vary between individuals and organisations and may present difficulties if there is no consistency. Basic guidelines on good programming practice have been available for decades and aim to minimise future difficulties. Traditional guidelines would include: avoiding the use of 'GOTOs', the use of meaningful identifier names, logical program layout, and use of program commentary to document design and implementation rationale. There exist psychological arguments and empirical evidence, albeit sparse, which suggest that these features impact on program comprehension [48, 247, 293] and hence can influence the amount of time required for effecting change.

- *Paradigm shift:* This refers to an alteration in the way we develop and maintain software [34]. Despite the enormous strides made in structure and reliability of programming languages, there still exists a large number of systems developed using inadequate software tools. As well as the many systems still in use that were developed using low-level programming languages [211] and those developed prior to the advent of structured programming techniques, there are many programs in operation and in need of maintenance that were developed without the means to take advantage of the more advanced and more recently developed techniques.

    Such programs inherit a number of characteristics [69]:

    (i) They were designed using techniques and methods that fail to communicate essential features such as program structure, data abstractions and function abstractions.

    (ii) The programming languages and techniques used to write the code did not make visible and obvious the program structure, program interfaces, data structures and types, and functions of the system.

    (iii) The constraints that affected their design no longer present a problem today.

    (iv) The code can sometimes be riddled with non-standard or unorthodox constructs that make the programs difficult to understand, the classic example being the use of GOTOs.

    In order to address these weaknesses and reap the benefits of modern development practices and the latest programming languages, existing programs may be restructured or completely rewritten. Examples of techniques and tools that can be used for this include: structured programming, object orientation, hierarchical program decomposition, reformatters and pretty-printers, automated code upgrading. It must be noted however that even programs developed using state of the art programming methods gradually lose their structure after being subjected to a series of unplanned and *ad hoc* 'quick fixes' (see chapter 5). This continues until preventive maintenance is carried out to restore order to their structure.

- *'Dead' paradigms for 'living' systems:* Many 'living systems' are developed using 'dead paradigms' [216], that is, using the Fixed Point Theorem of Information Systems [*op. cit.*]. Based on this theorem, there exists some point in time when everyone involved in the system thinks they know what they want and agree with everyone else. The resulting system is satisfactory only at the point at which it is delivered to the user. Thereafter, it becomes difficult – with few exceptions – to accommodate the changing needs of the users and their organisations. The extra flexibility to evolve that is provided by interoperability goes some way towards alleviating this problem, but does not solve it. However, it should be noted that in order for a system to be built at all, it is essential that requirements are agreed – this is not the same as agreeing what the "finished" product is.

- *Error detection and correction:* 'Error-free' software is non-existent. Software products have 'residual' errors which are difficult to detect even with the most powerful testing techniques and tools. The later these errors are discovered during the life-cycle of a software product, the more expensive they are to correct. The cost gets even higher if the errors are detected during the maintenance phase (Figure 2.1).

2.3.1.4 Software Product

There is a tendency to assume that computer programs are static artefacts that do not change once they correctly implement the agreed system specification [273]. However, this is far from the case and the evolving programs themselves contribute to the maintenance challenge. Programs are seldom static and can never be so when they implement large systems that are in continuous use. Lehman compares this phenomenon to the evolution of biological organisms and of social groupings [168]. Remember however, that it is not just the programs themselves but also the accompanying documentation and operating procedures that are subject to such changes. Aspects of a software product that contribute to the maintenance challenge include:

- *Maturity and difficulty of the application domain:* The requirements of applications that have been widely used and well understood are less likely to undergo substantial modification on installation than those that are still in their infancy. For example, accounts and payroll packages are likely to be subject to fewer requests for changes in requirements than a medical information system. Accounts and payroll packages have been in operation for a long time and their requirements have stabilised. In comparison, the requirements of medical information systems - used for improving the quality of patient care by providing accurate, reliable and comprehensive information - are only now becoming apparent [142, 83, 90, 53, 54, 55, 56]. An aspect that may also affect maintenance is the inherent difficulty of the original problem. For example, programs dealing with simple problems, such as sorting a list of integers, are easier to handle than those used for more complex computations, such as weather forecasting.

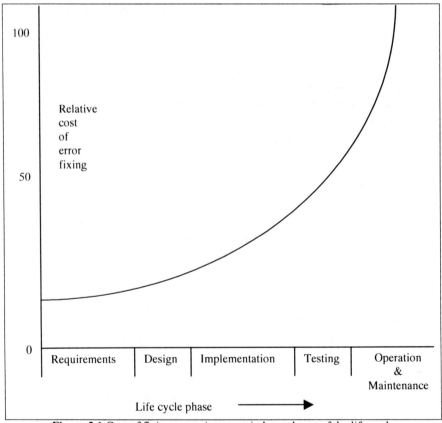

Figure 2.1 Cost of fixing errors increases in later phases of the life cycle

- *Quality of the documentation:* The lack of up-to-date systems' documentation is one of the major problems that software maintainers face [76]. Programs are often modified without a corresponding update of the documents affected. Even in environments where there are automatic documentation support tools, their contents may be inaccurate. Worse still, there may be no documentation at all. Inadequate documentation adversely affects maintenance productivity even for a programmer maintaining his / her own program, and in the vast majority of cases people are maintaining programs written by others.
- *Malleability of the programs:* The malleable or 'soft' nature of software products makes them more vulnerable to undesirable modification than hardware items. With other more orthodox engineering deliverables, there is a well-defined approach to implementing a change.

> ### Mini Case Study – The 'Software Airbag'
>
> Prior to the inclusion of an airbag into a make of car that did not have one, a feasibility study would be carried out to establish how such a component would be designed, and how its addition would affect other parts of the car. On approval of the change, the airbag would be designed. After it had been established that its inclusion adhered to current quality and safety regulations, the design could then be approved and construction of the airbag finally commissioned.
>
> Because of the tendency to treat software change in a less formal way, the software "airbag" will be bolted onto the car with no regard to safety considerations or appropriate design. Issues of safety, correct placing, and how other components are affected are unlikely to be considered until problems with the bolted-on version arise.

Ad hoc software changes may have unknown and even fatal repercussions. This is particularly true of **safety-related** or **safety-critical** systems [144].

- *Inherent quality:* The nature of the evolution of a software product is very closely tied to the nature of its associated programs [168]. Based on the results derived from empirical observations of large industrial software systems, Lehman concluded in his Law of continuing change that:

> *"A program that is used and that as an implementation of its specification reflects some other reality, undergoes continual change or becomes progressively less useful. The change or decay process continues until it is judged more cost effective to replace the system with a recreated version."*
>
> Lehman ([169] p.412)

This tendency for the system to decay as more changes are undertaken implies that preventive maintenance needs to be undertaken to restore order in the programs, thereby changing the product to a better and more sophisticated state.

2.3.1.5 Maintenance Personnel

It should never be forgotten that people are involved at all stages of the maintenance process and as such are components within the maintenance framework. Maintenance personnel include maintenance managers, analysts, designers, programmers and testers. The personnel aspects that affect maintenance activities include the following:

- *Staff turnover:* Due to the high staff turnover within the Information Technology industry, especially with regard to software maintenance [76], most systems end up being maintained by people who are not the original authors. In many cases, there is no comprehensive record of "successful and unsuccessful change attempts previously tried" [272 p.94] or documentation on choice of algorithms and assumptions made. Consequently, anyone other than the author, attempting to understand what the system does in order to identify sections of the code that need to be changed, will spend a substantial proportion of the maintenance effort just understanding the code. Even the original author will have the same problems with his / her own code if documentation is not kept up to date. Comprehension takes up about half of maintenance effort. This is discussed in detail in chapter 6.

- *Domain expertise:* The migration of staff to other projects or departments can mean that they end up working on a system for which they have neither the system domain knowledge nor the application domain knowledge. The lack of such knowledge may mean that the programmers can introduce changes to programs without being aware of their effects on other parts of the system - the ripple effect. This problem will be worsened by the absence of documentation. Even where documentation exists, it may be out of date or inadequate. These problems all translate to a huge maintenance expenditure.

- *Working practices:* Software systems do not change unless they are changed by people [169 ch.19 pp.393-449]. The way the change is carried out is an important factor in how easy the resulting system will be to understand. Various factors that affect the way a change is made have a significant effect on how easy or difficult the next maintenance programmer's job will be. Factors that can make the job more difficult include such things as

  − a maintainer's desire to be creative (or 'clever');
  − the use of undocumented assumption sets [170];
  − undocumented design and implementation decisions. It should always be borne in mind that after time has elapsed, programmers find it difficult to understand their own code.

Exercise 2.1 Discuss the issues that can contribute to high maintenance costs. How would you minimise their effects?

Exercise 2.2 What are the factors that impinge on the evolution of software products?

2.3.2 Relations Between the Maintenance Factors

It is a change in, or interaction between, the factors discussed above that causes software products to evolve and hence causes maintenance problems to arise. Three major types of relation and interaction that can be identified are product/environment, product/user and product/maintenance personnel (Figure 2.2).

- *Relation between product and environment:* A software product does not exist in a vacuum, rather it can be seen as an entity which is hosted by its organisational and operational environments. As such, it inherits changes in the elements of these environments − taxation policies, software innovations, etc., a view captured by Brooks:

  > *"The software is embedded in a cultural matrix of applications, laws and machine vehicles. These all change*

continually, and their changes inexorably force change upon the product."

Brooks [47]

- *Relation between product and user:* One of the objectives of a software product is to serve the needs of its users. The needs of the users change all the time. In order for the system to stay useful and acceptable it has to change to accommodate these changing requirements.

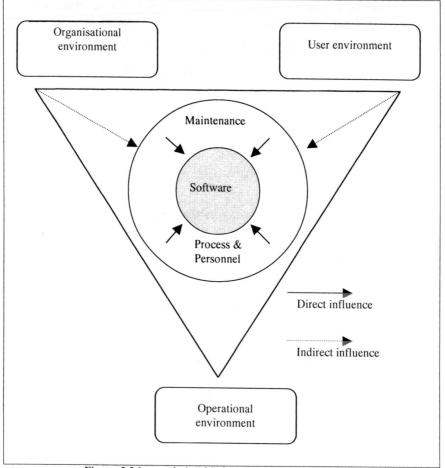

Figure 2.2 Inter-relationship between maintenance factors

- *Interaction between personnel and product:* The maintenance personnel who implement changes are themselves the conduit through which change is implemented. Changes in factors such as user requirements, the maintenance process, or the organisational and operational environments, will bring about the need for a change in the software product. However, the software product will not be affected until the maintenance personnel implement the changes. The type of maintenance process used and the nature of the maintenance personnel themselves, will affect the quality of the change.

The effects of the above relations and interactions are reflected in changes in some fundamental characteristics of the software product, such as its size and complexity; That is, changes in these product attributes are brought about by changes in the environment and user requirements. The size – measured in number of program modules or lines of code – tends to increase with an increase in the functionality being offered by the system. Similarly, the complexity – measured in terms of the difficulty of understanding the program source code – tends to increase as the programs are modified.

2.4 Summary

The key points covered in this chapter are:

- Software maintenance is carried out within, and interacts with, the world around it.
- The software maintenance framework comprises the users, the operational and organisational environments, the maintenance process, the software product and the maintenance personnel.
- Interactions between the components of the software maintenance framework are the driving forces behind the need for software change.
- The major types of interaction are between the product and its environment, the product and its users, the product and the maintenance personnel.
- A good understanding of the context in which software maintenance is carried out is vital in effective implementation of software change.

The maintenance framework gives the context in which maintenance activities are carried out. The next chapter goes on to explore in detail the fundamentals of software change.

3

Fundamentals of Software Change

"The tendency to change is necessary to optimally adjust to environmental requirements"

Damsté [74]

This chapter aims to
1. Discuss different types of software change and give reasons why changes occur.
2. Show how on-going support, as well as software change, can be classified as a maintenance activity.
3. Explain the tendency of software systems to evolve.
4. Introduce important areas of background theory via a discussion of Lehman's Laws.

3.1 Introduction

This chapter like the last, looks at the way software changes and evolves over time, but we now look at the detail of software change – what types of change there are and how to categorise them. Additionally, fundamental theory is discussed and Lehman's Laws are introduced.

3.2 Definitions

Adaptive change – a change made in order to become suited to different conditions.

Change - the act, process, or result of being made different in some particular

Corrective change – a change made in order to remove faults.

E-type system – a system in which the criteria for acceptability is that stakeholders are satisfied with the system in terms of its performance in a real world situation.

On-going support – a service offered to customers to assist their continuing use of a product.

Perfective change – a change made in order to improve.

Post-delivery evolution – software evolution referring explicitly to the period after the product is delivered to the customer.

Preventive change – a change made in order to forestall or reverse deterioration.

Ripple effect – consequences of an action in one place, occurring elsewhere e.g. a stone dropped in a pond resulting in waves / ripples far from the point of impact.

S-type system – a system in which the criteria for acceptability is that it is correct relative to an absolute specification [167].

Software evolution – the tendency of software to change over time.

3.3 Software Change

3.3.1 Classification of Changes

In order to achieve the objectives of maintenance discussed in chapter 1, a wide spectrum of change to the software product may be necessary. Various authors have attempted to classify these changes, resulting in a taxonomy which consists of corrective, adaptive, perfective and preventive changes [4, 12, 176, 191, 209].

We will look in detail at each type of change and then go on to discuss the wider issue of why it is important to make these distinctions.

3.3.1.1 Corrective Change

Corrective change refers to modification initiated by defects in the software. A defect can result from design errors, logic errors and coding errors [209].

- **Design errors** occur when, for example, changes made to the software are incorrect, incomplete, wrongly communicated or the change request is misunderstood.

- **Logic errors** result from invalid tests and conclusions, incorrect implementation of design specifications, faulty logic flow or incomplete testing of data.

- **Coding errors** are caused by incorrect implementation of detailed logic design and incorrect use of the source code logic. Defects are also caused by data processing errors and system performance errors [176].

All these errors, sometimes called 'residual errors' or 'bugs', prevent the software from conforming to its agreed specification.

In the event of a system failure due to an error, actions are taken to restore operation of the software system. Under pressure from management, maintenance personnel sometimes resort to emergency fixes known as 'patching' [26]. The *ad hoc* nature of this approach gives rise to a range of problems that include increased program complexity and unforeseen ripple effects.

Increased program complexity usually stems from degeneration of program structure which makes the program increasingly difficult, if not impossible, to understand. This is sometimes referred to as the 'spaghetti syndrome' or 'software fatigue' (cf. 'metal fatigue'), which implies the resistance of the program to change is at its maximum. As Rushby explains,

"A badly structured program is likened to a plateful of spaghetti: if one strand is pulled, then the ramifications can be seen at the other side of the plate where there is mysterious turbulence and upheaval"

Rushby ([193], p.162).

3.3.1.2 Adaptive Change

Even where residual errors are not causing problems, the software is bound to change as attempts are made to adapt it to its ever-changing environment. Adaptive change is a change driven by the need to accommodate modifications in the environment of the software system. The term environment in this context refers to the totality of all conditions and influences which act from outside upon the system, for example business rules, government policies, work patterns, software and hardware operating platforms. A change to the whole or part of this environment will warrant a corresponding modification of the software [47].

Adaptive maintenance includes any work initiated as a consequence of moving the software to a different hardware or software platform – compiler, operating system or new processor. For example, the acceptance of distributed processing as a solution to the increasing demands for enhanced performance opened up the possibility of the migration of millions of lines of sequential code to parallel environments [124].

Another example is change resulting from modification to a virtual machine that runs the underlying programs. Virtual machines can be hardware (in the case where there are no higher-level programming languages) or other software systems (such as compilers, operating systems and database management systems). Programs can be changed as a result of a new compiler, which performs additional optimisations to generate smaller and faster code. Similarly, programs sometimes need to be modified in order to take full advantage of additional facilities provided by a new version of the operating system or the introduction of a new database management system. Examples would include saving disk space and taking efficient measures to recover from failures.

An example of a government policy having far-reaching effects on software systems was the introduction of the Euro to countries of the European Union. This required significant change to software systems in many areas, for example banking, retail and share trading.

3.3.1.3 Perfective Change

This term is used to describe changes undertaken to expand the existing requirements of a system. A successful piece of software tends to be subjected to a succession of changes resulting in an increase in its

Fundamentals of Software Change

requirements. This is based on the premise that as the software becomes useful, the users experiment with new cases beyond the scope for which it was initially developed [47, 210]. Expansion in requirements can take the form of enhancement of existing system functionality or improvement in computational efficiency, for example providing a Management Information System with a data entry module or a new message handling facility [258].

Consider a system consisting of a simple program that requires three modules to produce two outputs (Figure 3.1). When a request for enhancement is made, a number of questions need to be answered by the maintenance personnel prior to the implementation of the change. One question is: can the new requirement, represented as an output, be satisfied by the programs that already exist in the system, or will more programs, represented as modules, be needed to produce the new output? If programs that already exist in the system can produce the output, then it will be pointless creating a separate program to implement that requirement since this will lead to duplication of effort.

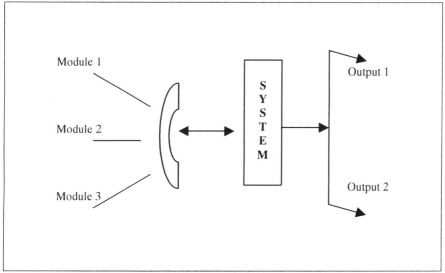

Figure 3.1 Diagram of a basic system, S

Let us now suppose that system S needs to be enhanced in order to accommodate new requirements, but that these new requirements will also need to have access to some of the data of the existing program. In the course of modifying the system, it may be necessary to provide additional modules, which are eventually included. The enhanced version of system S, S', is shown in Figure 3.2. How the new modules interface with existing modules is another significant area to be addressed in connection with this change.

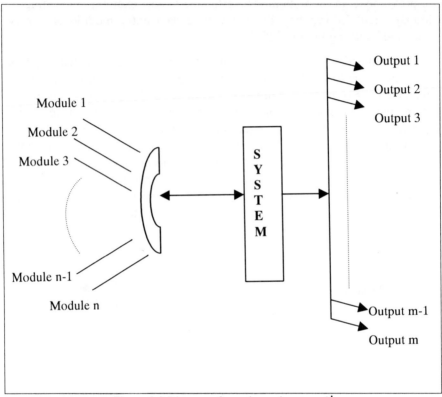

Figure 3.2 Diagram of an enhanced system, S'

The program continues to grow in this fashion with each enhancement, and one can visualise what the program size will be after a number of years of modification. During this process, the system evolves from an average-sized program of average maintainability to a very large program that offers great resistance to change.

Apart from adding new functions or refining those already provided, some system functions can be withdrawn. In the event of some facility becoming redundant or being rejected by users, the programs developed to cater for that function should be removed or modified.

> *Mini case study – redundant functionality*
>
> The ACME Health Clinic, during reorganisation, switched its diabetes education program from a general clinic to a specialist clinic. Thus the diabetes education module was no longer necessary as part of its general clinic's software system and was removed, thus increasing resources, notably disk space and memory.

3.3.1.4 Preventive Change

The long-term effect of corrective, adaptive and perfective changes is expressed in Lehman's law of increasing entropy (see section 3.5). Work done on a software system to address problems of deteriorating structure is known as preventive change.

Preventive change is undertaken to prevent malfunctions or to improve maintainability of the software [26]. The change is usually initiated from within the maintenance organisation with the intention of making programs easier to understand and hence making future maintenance work easier. Preventive change does not usually give rise to a substantial increase in the baseline functionality.

Examples of preventive change include code restructuring, code optimisation and documentation updating. After a series of quick fixes to a software system, the complexity of its source code can increase to an unmanageable level, thus justifying complete restructuring of the code. Code optimisation can be performed to enable the programs to run faster or make more efficient use of storage. Updating user and system documentation, though frequently ignored, is often necessary when any part of the software is changed. The documents affected by the change should be modified to reflect the current state of the system. The issue of documentation is explored further in chapters 6 and 11.

Unforeseen ripple effects imply that a change to one part of a program may affect other sections in an unpredictable fashion, thereby leading to a distortion in the logic of the system. This is often due to the lack of time to carry out a thorough **impact analysis** before effecting a change. Program slicing techniques [285, 106] and concepts such as modularization and information hiding can be used to address these problems (see chapter 13 for a detailed treatment of these techniques and concepts).

3.3.2 The Importance of Categorising Software Changes

In principle, software maintenance activities can be classified individually. In practice, however, they are usually intertwined. For example, in the course of modifying a program due to the introduction of a new operating system (adaptive change), obscure bugs may be introduced. The bugs have to be traced and dealt with (corrective maintenance). Similarly, the introduction of a more efficient sorting algorithm into a data processing package (perfective maintenance) may require that the existing program code be restructured (preventive maintenance). Figure 3.3 shows the potential relationships between the different types of software change.

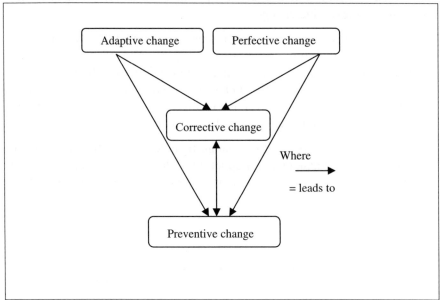

Figure 3.3 Potential relation between software changes

Despite the overlapping nature of these changes, there are good reasons to distinguish between them. Some changes require a faster response than others. Understanding the nature of the changes to be implemented allows more effective prioritisation of change requests.

3.3.3 Case Study – The Need to Support an Obsolete System

At the research institute attached to the ACME Health Clinic, the payroll system was computerised in the 1960's. The maximum salary with which the system could cope was a factor of hardware and memory restrictions. There was no allowance for salaries above this maximum. Should a calculation yield a higher figure, the number would 'flip over' and become a large negative number. After a decade of inflation this maximum salary, which had been considered far above the amount to which the senior director could aspire, was barely above the average starting salary for a technician. A firm of consultants was called in and given two tasks. One was to develop a new up-to-date system and the other was to see that all wages were paid correctly and on time.

This situation demonstrates the different priorities that can face software maintainers. The long-term solution was obviously the development of the new system. The upkeep of the old system was, in a sense, a dead-end task. The system, no matter how much resource was put into it, would be taken out of service at the first possible opportunity. In fact, resource given to the old system was resource taken from the new one and would delay implementation. Despite this, top priority had to be given to keeping the old system running and producing accurate results up to the moment that the new system was up and running and well enough tested to be relied upon.

The balance to be struck was the expenditure of as little as possible resource on the old system while giving adequate resource to the development of the new; too little resource and wages would not be paid; too much and the project would run out of money before the new system was ready.

The consultants did their job, all wages were paid on time and the new system ran relatively smoothly for many years until superseded by new advances in both hardware and software technology.

3.3.4 Incremental Release

The changes made to a software product are not always done all together [136]. The changes take place incrementally, with minor changes usually implemented while a system is in operation. Major enhancements are usually planned and incorporated, together with other minor changes, in a new release or upgrade. The change introduction mechanism also depends on whether the software package is bespoke or off-the-shelf. With bespoke software, change can often be effected as the need for it arises. For off-the-shelf packages, users normally have to wait for the next upgrade. Figure 3.4 shows the stages at which changes can be introduced during the life-cycle of a software product. The detailed process of effecting changes has been discussed in chapter 1.

Exercise 3.1 Describe the different changes that a software product can undergo and indicate the rationale for each.

Exercise 3.2 Explain why it is important to distinguish between the different types of software change.

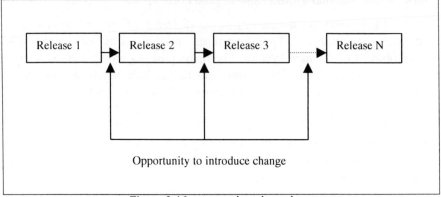

Figure 3.4 Incremental product release

3.4 Ongoing Support

This category of maintenance work refers to the service provided to satisfy non-programming-related work requests. Ongoing support [4], although not a change in itself, is essential for successful communication of desired changes. The objectives of ongoing support include effective communication between maintenance and end-user personnel, training of end-users and providing business information to users and their organisations to aid decision making [1].

- *Effective communication:* This is essential between the parties affected by changes to a software system [4]. Maintenance is the most customer-intensive part of the software life-cycle [58] since a greater proportion of maintenance effort is spent providing enhancements requested by customers than is spent on other types of system change. The time and resources spent need to be justified by customer satisfaction [170]. It is time well spent for the maintenance organisation to establish good customer[5] relations and co-operation, and continually demonstrate that they aim to satisfy the customers' needs [243] so that both parties understand each other.

This rapport is of paramount importance. It can lead to enhanced communication between supplier and user, thus giving less room for misinterpretation of users' change requests. It means that the maintenance organisation will be in a better position to understand users' business needs, and hence can avoid technical decisions that contradict business decisions [243]. Also, there is a potential to increase user involvement in the maintenance process, an essential ingredient for successful maintenance and ultimate user satisfaction. Failure to achieve a successful level of communication between the maintenance organisation and those affected by the software changes can lead to software failure [209].

- *Training of end-users:* Training refers to the process of equipping users with sufficient knowledge and skills to enable them use a system to its full potential. This can be achieved in different ways. Users are traditionally supplied with supposedly comprehensive and easy-to-use manuals, which are designed to facilitate the use of the system. Manuals, however, do not always provide the information needed or do not provide the information in an easily understood way. Users, as a result, resort to other means such as on-line help or telephone queries. If this fails, arrangements can be made for on-site visits. Formal or informal short courses are arranged to train users in the use of the software and how to deal with problems that arise. In either case, the degree of commitment depends on the maintenance agreement between both parties [262].

    Users can also receive peer group training through a 'user group'. This is an association of users with a common interest, for instance those using a particular Computer Aided Design (CAD) system. Ideally, a user group offers a user an opportunity to form a 'symbiotic' relationship with other users – both parties learning from one another's experiences.

---

[5] Throughout this book, the words 'customer' and 'user' will be used interchangeably to refer to any individual who uses the software system in whole or in part. Some authors distinguish between the two [243].

- *Providing business information:* Users need various types of timely and accurate information to enable them take strategic business decisions. For instance, a company planning to make major enhancements to its database management system may first want to find out the cost of such an operation. With such information, the company is in a better position to know whether it is more economical to enhance the existing system or to replace it completely.

> **Exercise 3.3** Ongoing support does not necessarily lead to modification of programs, thus it should not be considered as part of maintenance. What are your opinions on this view?

3.5 Lehman's Laws

When we talk about software evolution and maintenance, we are talking about software that is actively being used to solve problems or address applications in real world domains [169]. To demonstrate concepts and principles, we often use examples that do not fit this definition, but you should always bear in mind that these are examples, being used for purposes of simplifying explanations.

To gain a real understanding of software evolution, we need to tease out the theory that underlies it. Work on formulating and understanding this theory really began in the late 1960's with Lehman's investigation of the software process [166]. This led, over a period of 20 years, to Lehman's eight Laws of Software Evolution.

A brief summary of the laws is as follows:

I. Law of continuing change: formulated in 1974 - systems must be continually adapted or they become progressively less satisfactory to use. This law says that systems evolve in a way comparable with biological organisms. The difference is that it is the variance between the system and its operational context that leads to feedback pressures forcing change in the system.

II. Law of increasing complexity: formulated in 1974 - as a system evolves, its complexity increases unless work is done to maintain or reduce it. If changes are made with no thought to system structure, complexity will increase and make future change harder. On the other hand, if resource is expended on work to combat complexity, less is available for system change. No matter how this balance is reconciled, the rate of system growth inevitably slows.

III. Law of self-regulation: formulated in 1974 - evolutionary aspects of system evolution processes tend to display a degree of statistical regularity. Industrially produced E-type software is implemented within the context of a wider organisation. Thus the objective of getting the system finished is constrained by the wider objectives and constraints of organisational goals at all levels. Positive and negative feedback controls within this wider context ultimately determine the way the system evolves.

IV. Law of conservation of organisational stability: formulated in 1978 - the average work rate in an E-type process tends to remain constant over periods of system evolution. This is counter-intuitive because one tends to assume that management decision-making will determine the effort expended on system change. However, analyses to date suggest that the many inputs to satisfactory system change combine to give an essentially constant work rate.

V. Law of conservation of familiarity: formulated in 1978 - the average incremental growth of systems tends to remain constant or decline. The more changes that are required means it is harder for those involved to get to grips with all that is required of them. This affects the quality and progress of the change.

VI. Law of continuing growth: formulated in 1991 - functional capability must be continually increased over a system's lifetime to maintain user satisfaction. This is closely related to the first law. In any system implementation, requirements have to be constrained. Attributes will be omitted. These will become the irritants that trigger future demand for change. Thus, E-type system growth is driven by feedback from its users.

VII. Law of declining quality: formulated in 1996 - unless rigorously adapted to meet changes in the operational environment, system quality will appear to decline. A system is built on a set of assumptions, and however valid these are at the time, the changing world will tend to invalidate them. Unless steps are taken to identify and rectify this, system quality will appear to decline especially in relation to alternative products that will come onto the market based on more recently formulated assumptions.

VIII. Law of feedback systems: formulated in 1996 (but recognised as early as 1971) - evolution processes are multi-level, multi-loop, multi-agent feedback systems. Feedback plays a role in all the laws. The key role of feedback was recognised in the 1968 study referred to earlier [166]. Studies in the 1970's showed self-stabilising feedback system behaviour. "The process leads to an organisation and a process dominated by feedback," [167].

Since Lehman first used the term law, it has been criticised [62, 162]. Were these laws, or were they observations or hypotheses? Lehman himself admits that "strong intuition played a part in the decision to use the term law." [172] However, that intuition has proven to be sound [268].

3.6 Summary

The key points covered in this chapter are:

- Maintenance activities consist of corrective, adaptive, perfective and preventive changes, and ongoing support. In principle, these can be distinguished but in practice they are intertwined.

- Unrealistically small programs will be used to demonstrate principles, but real maintenance is done on systems that are actively being used to solve problems or address applications in real world domains.

- Lehman's laws describe principles common to all large, live software systems.

In an ideal world, we would build and modify software with no regard to time and cost constraints. Of course, in an ideal world, the system would always be perfect. However, we have to operate in the real world where it is vital to appreciate the realities and costs of software evolution. This is the subject of the next chapter.

4

Limitations and Economic Implications to Software Change

"The most expensive solution is frequently not the best solution"

Edward Guy, information technology consultant [119]

This chapter aims to

1. Discuss the economic implications of modifying software.
2. Explore the nomenclature and image problems of software maintenance.
3. Identify potential solutions to maintenance problems and discuss their strengths and weaknesses.

4.1 Introduction

The cost of modifying software is enormous. With the rapid advances in technology that see new systems outdated in months, most maintenance is done on systems that are obsolete to some degree. Supporting obsolete systems is costly, yet building new can be costlier still and not provide the best solution (see the case study in chapter 1). We have to find the route that provides the best results in terms of cost, reliability and timeliness.

4.2 Definitions

Image – character or attributes as generally perceived.

Maintenance crisis – The current predicament where the demand for high quality sophisticated software systems far outstrips the supply of such systems, but existing systems lack the capacity to evolve appropriately with technological advancement.

Nomenclature – terminology, naming system within a particular context.

4.3 Economic Implications of Modifying Software

As mentioned previously, a substantial proportion of the resources expended within the Information Technology industry goes towards the maintenance of legacy software systems. The following extract emphasises this:

> *"In the '90's, yearly corporate expenditures for software will reach $100 billion dollars. At least $70 billion is spent yearly on maintaining systems, while only $30 billion on new development. Maintenance costs grow at 10% a year, at the same rate as the size of system growth."*

Bernstein ([28], p.94)

A number of studies have been undertaken to investigate the costs of software maintenance [176, 35, 4, 160, 213] and many of their findings are in line with the *development : maintenance* ratio quoted in the above extract. Figure 4.1 gives a comparison of costs for maintenance and new development). In these studies, the maintenance costs range from 49% for a pharmaceutical company [4] to 75% for an automobile company [91].

One might have expected that maintenance costs would have fallen, in line with the widespread use of software engineering methodologies to develop large software systems [137], but according to these figures, there was very little reduction in maintenance costs from the 1970's [91] to the 1990's [160][6].

In their study of 487 data processing organisations, Lientz and Swanson [176] reported on the proportion of maintenance effort

---

[6] In the article [160], the definition of maintenance is slightly different from the one used in this book since it does not include the 'enhancement of existing systems'. But when interpreted in the context of this book, maintenance consumes 56% of the users' resources.

allocated to each category of system change. Corrective maintenance accounted for 20%; adaptive maintenance consumed 25%; 50% was accounted for by perfective maintenance; and the remaining 5% was spent on preventive maintenance-related activities (Figure 4.2).

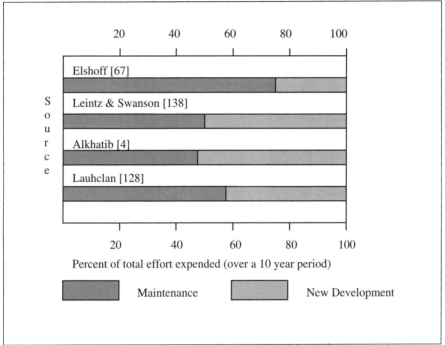

Figure 4.1 Comparison of maintenance and new development costs

Considering that the above figures for maintenance may not necessarily apply to other applications and settings, due to differences in the applications, maintenance personnel expertise and the nature of accompanying documentation and environment, it is not advisable to base maintenance decisions on these figures alone (see chapter 2 for detailed explanations). They are simply a reflection of the scale of the maintenance problem.

There are approaches which can be used to estimate the cost of a proposed maintenance project. This way, the user can decide whether it is worth enhancing an existing system or whether to replace it altogether. Such a feasibility analysis can lead to considerable savings. Examples of cost estimation models include Boehm's COCOMO [35] and COCOMO II [37] models.

50 Software Maintenance: Concepts and Practice

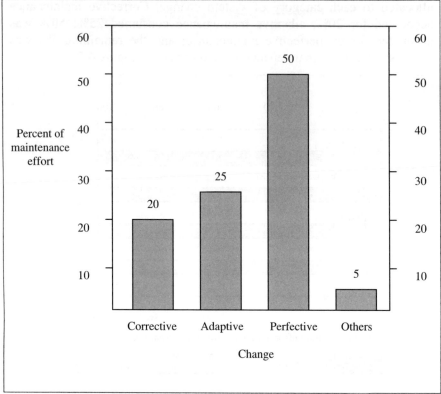

Figure 4.2 Expenditure on the different changes

4.4 Limitations to Software Change

Ideally, the types of changes discussed in the last chapter would be implemented as the need for them arises. In practice, however, that is not always possible for several reasons [36].

4.4.1 Resource Limitations

One of the major impediments to the quality and productivity of maintenance activities is the lack of resources. The lack of skilled and trained maintenance programmers, the lack of suitable tools and environment to support their work, and lack of sufficient budget allocation are issues that hold back change.

4.4.2 Quality of the Existing System

In some 'old' systems, quality can be so poor that any change can lead to unpredictable ripple effects and a potential collapse of the system. Industry spends significant sums of money on maintaining obsolete code, even to the extent of maintaining obsolete hardware, because the risk of unforeseen ripple effects of excising the code is too great.

Quality can become so poor that change is virtually impossible. This means that errors cannot be addressed and the system cannot evolve with progress in technology. This can lead to users tied into old systems (software and hardware), with huge maintenance costs, and with a system that provides less functionality that cheaper competitor systems. They cannot swap because of the data tied into the old system.

There comes a point where maintaining an old system is no longer viable. Unfortunately, this does not mean that developing a new one is viable. A point can be reached where the software developer goes out of business and the users are left high and dry with years' worth of data locked inside an obsolete system. Building software that avoids this sort of problem is explored in chapter 13.

4.4.3 Organisational Strategy

The desire to be on a par with other organisations, especially rivals, can be a great determinant of the size of a maintenance budget. It is often these strategic decisions, far more than objective analysis of the problem being tackled that determines the maintenance budget. This is not the ideal way to ensure the job gets done in the best way.

4.4.4 Inertia

The resistance to change by users may prevent modification to a software product, however important or potentially profitable such change may be. This is not just unthinking stubbornness. For many decades, users have been promised the earth from software enterprises who can see the potential of the technology, but who have been unable to deliver for a variety of reasons. Sometimes the hardware has been inadequate (the days of overheating valves spiked many a budding software engineer's guns). Sometimes the theoretical base has been non-existent, and software developers have been building on quicksand without realising it.

As with any new field, things that look obvious in hindsight, catch people out the first time round. Initial versions of software-controlled missiles are a case in point. When fired from aeroplanes in flight, the essential sequence of instructions is "release-the-missile", "fire-the-missile". But software is fast and literal. The sequence should actually be "release-the-missile", "pause-long-enough-for-the-missile-to-be-released", "fire-the- missile".

4.4.5 Attracting and Retaining Skilled Staff

The high costs of keeping systems operational and ensuring that user needs are satisfied – as implied by the quoted case surveys – are partly due to the problem of attracting and retaining highly skilled and talented software maintenance personnel [76]. The historical reason for the lack of skilled staff and high personnel turnover was largely an image problem. Problems still persist today for a variety of reasons. Attracting and retaining good staff are management issues dealt with in a later chapter.

> **Exercise 4.1** Pick a software package you are familiar with that has evolved through several versions. List some of the modifications that were implemented in the different versions. What barriers might there have been to implementation of certain of these features in earlier versions?

4.5 The Nomenclature and Image Problems

The use of the word "maintenance" to describe activities undertaken on software systems after delivery has been considered a misnomer due to its failure to capture the evolutionary nature of software products. Maintenance has traditionally meant the upkeep of an artefact in response to the gradual deterioration of parts due to extended use [108]. This is simply corrective maintenance and takes no account of adaptive and perfective changes [260, 176]. As is shown in Figure 4.2, corrective change accounts for less than a quarter of the maintenance effort.

The incorporation of adaptive and perfective changes in the software maintenance taxonomy shows that work undertaken on operational systems does not only involve correction of malfunctions, but also entails adapting and enhancing the systems to meet the evolving needs of users [176] and their organisations. Consequently, a number of authors have advanced alternative terms that are considered to be more inclusive and encompass more of the activities undertaken on existing software to keep it operational and acceptable to the users. These include 'software evolution' [12, 108, 169 ch.2], 'post-delivery evolution' [192] and 'support' [100, 163].

Software evolution and **post-delivery evolution** are similar because they both describe the tendency of software to evolve and they are used synonymously by many authors. There is however a difference. The transition from an idea to develop a software system to its detailed specification, then to its design and implementation, are all part of the evolving software. Thus, software evolution can refer to any phase of the evolution, including those preceding delivery of the software. On the other hand, post-delivery evolution is more specific and refers to that part of the evolutionary development of software that occurs after the software is in live use.

The inclusion of the word maintenance in software maintenance has been linked to the negative image associated with software maintenance. Higgins describes the problem:

"...programmers... tend to think of program development as a form of puzzle solving, and it is reassuring to their ego when they manage to successfully complete a difficult section of code. Software maintenance, on the other hand, entails very little new creation and is therefore categorised as dull, unexciting detective work."

Higgins ([129], p.5)

This denial of the creativity inherent in the software maintenance process, arguably far greater than in software development, has caused significant problems by artificially lowering the status of a very skilled task. Schneidewind went further than Higgins in contending that to work in maintenance has been likened to having bad breath [245]. Some authors argue that the general lack of consensus on software maintenance terminology has also contributed to the negative image [211].

It can be argued that there is nothing wrong with using the word "maintenance" provided software engineers are educated to accept its meaning within the software engineering context, regardless of what it means in non-software engineering disciplines. After all, any work that needs to be done to keep a software system at a level considered useful to its users will still have to be carried out regardless of the name it is given.

Although software maintenance was a neglected area, the demands of the software industry are forcing a greater appreciation of maintenance-related issues, and managers are having to address the improvement of maintenance support [78].

Despite the reservations expressed, the term software maintenance is still very widely used. Within the scope of this book, the term software maintenance will be used as a generic term that refers to any modification undertaken after installation of a software product.

So far, we have examined the concept of software maintenance and its constituent activities emphasising the problems that comprise the maintenance challenge. In the next section, we will look at potential solutions.

4.6 Potential Solutions to Maintenance Problems

There are three overall approaches to maintenance problems:

(i) budget and effort reallocation – reassigning maintenance resources to develop more maintainable systems;

(ii) complete replacement of existing systems; and

(iii) enhancement of existing systems.

4.6.1 Budget and Effort Reallocation

Based on the observation that software maintenance costs at least as much as new development, some authors [117] have proposed that rather than allocating less resource to develop unmaintainable or difficult-to-maintain systems, more time and resource should be invested in the development – specification and design – of more maintainable systems.

The use of more advanced requirement specification approaches [147], design techniques and tools [300], quality assurance procedures and standards such as the ISO 9000 series [141] and maintenance standards [272] are aimed at addressing this issue. It is believed that the deployment of these techniques, tools and standards earlier on in the development life-cycle will lead to more maintainable systems.

However, it is only recently that empirical evidence is emerging to support this [50]. See for example the work of the FEAST projects [94].

4.6.2 Complete Replacement of the System

After having examined the problems that the maintenance of legacy systems poses for many medium-size to large organisations, particularly their unwelcome economic impact on the software budgets of these organisations, one might be tempted to suggest that if maintaining an existing system costs as much as developing a new one, why not develop a new system from scratch? This suggestion is understandable, but in practice it is not so simple. The risks and costs associated with complete system replacement are very high [273] and the following must be considered:

- *Economic constraints:* Corrective and preventive maintenance take place periodically at relatively small but incremental costs. With few exceptions, enhancement and adaptive work requests are also undertaken intermittently at a fraction of the cost of developing a new system. In the long term, the total costs incurred in undertaking these activities add up to a considerable sum during the system's lifetime. In the short term, however, the organisation can afford to pay these comparatively small maintenance charges while at the same time supporting more ambitious and financially demanding projects. For example, in a survey carried out by Tamai and Torimitsu, several of the respondents who once considered replacement of their systems abandoned the idea because it was too expensive [263].

- *Residual errors in new systems:* The creation of another system is no guarantee that it will function better than the old one. On installation, errors may be found in functions the old system performed correctly and such residual errors will need to be fixed as they are discovered. As Bernstein points out, 'if there are no problems, there's trouble' [28]. A new system will not be error-free.

- *Database of information:* The old system is a collection of functions, and as such, it embodies a wealth of experience, represents a repository of ideas that could enable the identification of building blocks of future systems [245], and may contain management, operational and financial information about an organisation as well as business rules [211] that have accrued over many years. A collection of assumption sets (sometimes known as the assumption knowledge base system) that underlie the different paradigms and functions used to develop the system, are embedded in these old systems. The availability of such knowledge could prove useful for the development of future systems, thereby reducing the chances of re-inventing the wheel. It will be unrealistic for an organisation to part with such an asset [69].

4.6.3 *Maintenance of the Existing System*

Complete replacement of the system is not usually a viable option. An operational system in itself can be an asset to an organisation in terms of the investment in technical knowledge and the working culture engendered. The 'budget/effort reallocation' approach, though theoretically convincing, is somewhat difficult to pursue. Even if the latter were possible, it would be too late for systems that are already in what is being termed the *maintenance crisis*.

As an alternative, the current system needs to have the potential to evolve to a higher state, providing more sophisticated user-driven functionality, the capability of deploying cutting edge technology, and of allowing the integration of other systems in a cost-effective manner. A number of techniques, methods, tools and management practices are used to meet these goals. These issues provide the underlying framework for much of the remainder of this book.

4.7 Summary

The key points covered in this chapter are:

- The high expenditure on software maintenance is partly due to the evolutionary nature of software products and partly due to other problems such as badly structured code, incomplete or non-existent documentation, staff turnover and changes in the environment of the product.

- Possible solutions to the maintenance problems include: (i) investing more resources during the earlier phases of the software life-cycle so as to develop more maintainable systems. This may be achieved by the use of evolutionary development paradigms, although these are not yet proven to be practical; (ii) complete replacement of the existing system. However the latter, though sometimes necessary, is not usually economically viable.

Having looked at the framework within which maintenance operates, we have now identified that it is not always economically viable to replace a system from scratch and that the budget reallocation approach is yet to be proven. We now need to look at what are the most acceptable ways of keeping software systems at levels considered useful and acceptable. In order to discuss how specific methods are applied, it is important to understand the software maintenance process and how it has been modelled. This is the theme of the next chapter.

5

The Maintenance Process

"Modelling is a tool for coping with problems of largeness"

DeMarco ([79], p 42)

This chapter aims to

1. Discuss the importance of process models.
2. Explain the weaknesses of traditional life-cycle models with respect to maintenance.
3. Identify ways of accommodating the evolutionary tendency of software within traditional software life-cycle models.
4. Study examples of maintenance process models.
5. Compare and contrast different types of maintenance process model.
6. Discuss the strengths and weaknesses of each maintenance process model.
7. Look at the issue of process maturity.

5.1 Introduction

We have looked at different types of change, why and when they might be carried out, and the context in which this will be done. This chapter will look at the change process by looking in detail at different ways in which the process of maintenance has been modelled. In order to study maintenance process models effectively, they need to be seen in the context of traditional life-cycle models. A comparison of traditional and maintenance models helps to highlight the differences between software development and software maintenance and shows why there is a need for a 'maintenance-conscious' process model.

5.2 Definitions

Life-cycle – the cyclic series of changes undergone by an entity from inception to 'death'. In terms of software, the life-cycle is the series of recognised stages through which a software product cycles during its development and use.

Model – the representation of an entity or phenomenon.

Process – the progress or course taken, methods of operation, a series of actions taken to effect a change.

> *"A specific activity or action performed by a human being or machine during a software project"*
>
> Basili & Abd-El-Hafiz ([15], p.3)

Process model – the representation of the progress or course taken – i.e. the model of the process.

Software maintenance process – the series of actions taken to effect change during maintenance.

5.3 The Software Production Process

The software production process encompasses the whole activity from the initial idea to the final withdrawal of the system (Figure 5.1).

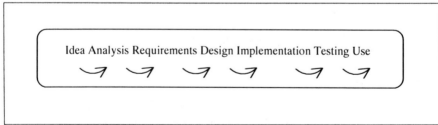

Figure 5.1 Stages in the evolution of a software system

A process, being the series of discrete actions taken to effect a change, is distinct from the life-cycle which defines the order in which these actions are carried out.

The software life-cycle starts with an idea, then goes through the stages of feasibility study, analysis, design, implementation, testing, release, operation and use. The software evolves through changes which lead to, or spring from, new ideas that start the cycle off again. A familiar example is that of the metamorphosis of an insect (Figure 5.2). The adult insect lays the egg from which the pupa emerges which becomes the chrysalis from which the adult emerges which lays the egg... and so on.

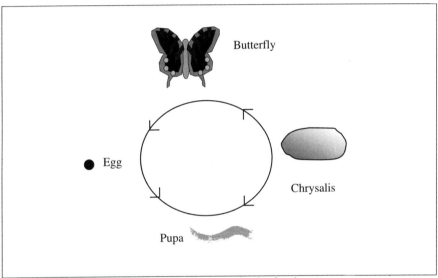

Figure 5.2 The metamorphosis of an insect

Mini Case Study – The Analysis of Patient Questionnaires at the ACME Health Clinic

The person whose job it was to analyse patient questionnaires became disillusioned with the tediousness of sifting through sheets of paper and collating responses. She had the idea of computerising the process and thereby automating it. The objectives were to speed the process up and to allow the computer to deal with the tedium of adding and collating, removing the time-consuming need for double-checking of calculations done by hand, thus making the process more reliable.

The technician had to ask the following:

a) Would it be feasible?
b) Could the job be done with available equipment and resources?

The answers being yes, the 'system' progressed to the next stage - a detailed appraisal of exactly what was needed. Once this was decided, the system was designed and implemented. Once implemented, the system was tested to the point where it was deemed reliable enough to use for real.

In this instance, one person creating a system for her own use progressed from the original idea to the system in use in a few hours. Interestingly, but not surprisingly, as soon as it became known that the system had been computerised, many requests for further data analysis came in. Not a single one of these could be accommodated. The person concerned had automated a specific set of analyses, with no consideration for further expansion.

We are familiar with the life-cycle as a cyclic series of stages (Figure 5.3) but what exactly comprises these stages?

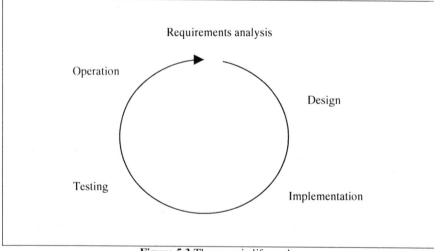

Figure 5.3 The generic life cycle

Design, for example, can be a pile of documents, a set of diagrams, ideas in someone's head, drawings on a blackboard. How do we deal with this plethora of information and make sense of it? We need a means of representing it in a way that hides the confusing detail and allows us to understand the major concepts. We need a model.

A familiar example is a map. A map provides an abstract representation of an area, and a very useful one. Given the real thing, the area, it is very difficult to know where anything is or how to find one's way about. Given an abstract and manageable representation, a map, the task becomes much easier.

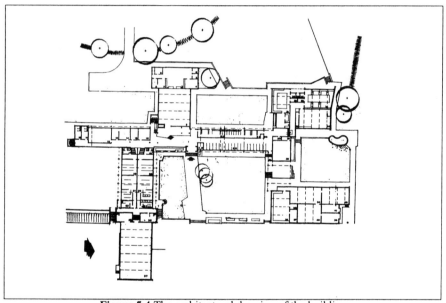

Figure 5.4 The architectural drawing of the building

Similarly, an architect's drawings (Figure 5.4) represent the information needed to construct a building. Such a representation gives more than just the idea of the shape or look of the building (Figure 5.5), it contains the information needed to enable safe construction of the building.

In software terms the model is the abstract representation of the software production process, the series of changes through which a software product evolves from initial idea to the system in use. For software maintenance, it is the representation of those parts of the process specifically pertaining to the evolution of the software.

Figure 5.5 The finished building

A process model gives an abstract representation of a way in which to build software. Many process models have been described and we will look at a number of such models.

The term process implies a single series of phases. Life-cycle implies cycling through this series of phases repeatedly. However, you will find that some texts use the term software process as an alternative to software life-cycle. In this case, the term process as opposed to life-cycle is being used to give a different emphasis rather than implying a series versus a cyclic repetition of a series. The pivotal points of the software life-cycle in this case are the products themselves and software process shifts the emphasis to the processes by which the products are developed.

Exercise 5.1 Define the terms process, life-cycle and model.

Exercise 5.2 Explain the differences between a software life-cycle and a software process.

5.4 Critical Appraisal of Traditional Process Models

The history and evolution of life-cycle models is closely tied to the history and evolution of computing itself. As with other areas (the creation of programming languages, system design and so on) there was an evolutionary path from the *ad hoc* to the structured.

In the days when computer system development was a case of one person developing a system for his or her own use, there were no major problems with *ad hoc* and hit or miss methods. Such methods, in fact, are integral to the learning process in any field. As the general body of knowledge and experience increases, better understanding results and better methods can be developed.

Other factors influence the move from the *ad hoc* to the structured: risk factors, for example; safety considerations and the ramifications of failure when a large customer base has to be considered. Thus need, knowledge and experience lead to better structured and better understood models.

However, there is a specific aspect to be considered when looking at the historical development of models for maintenance. The evolution of models went in parallel with the evolution of software engineering and computer science in general. It must be remembered that the level of awareness of software maintenance-related issues was low until relatively recently. Software maintenance itself as a field of study is new compared to software development. The process and life-cycle models have evolved in an environment of high awareness of software development issues as opposed to maintenance issues and, as such, are development models.

There are very many software process and life-cycle models and, of these, many have a variety of permutations. In this section we will look at three which are representative of the area of process models in general: code-and-fix, waterfall and spiral, representing respectively the old, the well established and the new. An outline of these is given below to provide a framework for subsequent discussion of maintenance process models. The details of the traditional models are extensively covered in other texts [255, 274].

5.4.1 Code-and-Fix Model

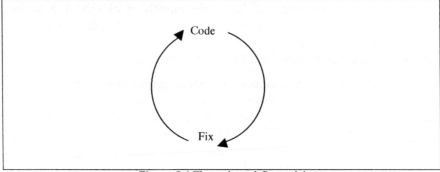

Figure 5.6 The code-and-fix model

This is *ad hoc* and not well defined. It is a simple two-phase model (Figure 5.6). The first phase is to write code. The next phase is to 'fix' it. Fixing in this context may be error correction or addition of further functionality. Using this model, code soon becomes unfixable and unenhanceable. There is no room in this model for analysis, design or any aspect of the development process to be carried out in a structured or detailed way. There is no room to think through a fix or to think of the future ramifications, and thus errors increase and the code becomes less maintainable and harder to enhance. On the face of it, this model has nothing to recommend it. Why then consider it at all? The reason is that despite the problems, the model is still used, the reason being that the world of software development often dictates the use of the code-and-fix model. If a correction or an enhancement must be done very quickly, in a couple of hours say, there is no time for detailed analysis, feasibility studies or redesign. The code must be fixed. The major problems of this scenario are usually overcome by subsuming code-and-fix within a larger, more detailed model. This idea is explored further in the discussion of other models.

The major problem with the code-and-fix model is its rigidity. In a sense, it makes no allowance for change. Although it perhaps does not assume the software to be correct from the off - it does have a fix stage as well as a code stage - it makes no provision for alteration and repair. The first stage is to code. All the other stages through which a software system must go (analysis, specification, design, testing) are all bundled together either into the fix stage or mixed up with the coding. This lack of properly defined stages leads to a lack of anticipation of problems.

Ripple effects, for example, will go unnoticed until they cause problems, at which stage further fixes may have become unviable or impossible. There is no acknowledgement in the model that one route may be better or less costly than another. In other, more structured models, explicit provision is made for the following of a particular route, for example a lesser risk route or a less expensive route. Because there is no such provision in the code-and-fix model, code structure and maintainability will inevitably deteriorate. Recognition of the problems of *ad hoc* software development and maintenance led to the creation of better structured models.

5.4.2 *Waterfall Model*
The traditional waterfall model gives a high-level view of the software life-cycle. At its most basic it is effectively the tried and tested problem-solving paradigm:

- Decide what to do
- Decide how to do it
- Do it
- Test it
- Use it.

The phases in the waterfall model are represented as a cascade. The outputs from one phase become the inputs to the next. The processes comprising each phase are also defined and may be carried out in parallel (Figure 5.7).

Many variations on this model are used in different situations but the underlying philosophy in each is the same. It is a series of stages where the work of each stage is 'signed off' and development then proceeds to the following phase. The overall process is document driven. The outputs from each stage that are required to keep the process moving are largely in the form of documents.

The main problem with the original waterfall model lay in its sequential nature, highlighted by later refinements which adapted it to contain feedback loops. There was recognition in this of the ever-increasing cost of correcting errors. An error in the requirements stage, for example, is far more costly to correct at a late stage in the cycle and more costly than a design error.

Nonetheless, the model still fails to capture the evolutionary nature of the software. The model allows for errors in the specification stage, for example, to be corrected at later stages via feedback loops, the aim being to catch and correct errors at as early a stage as possible. However, this still assumes that at some point a stage can be considered complete and correct, which is unrealistic. Changes - in specification for example - will occur at later stages in the life-cycle, not through errors necessarily but because the software itself is evolutionary.

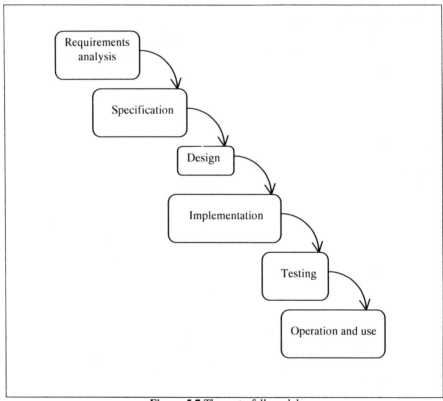

Figure 5.7 The waterfall model

A specification may be correct at a particular point in time but the system being specified is a model of some part of the world - complex air traffic control perhaps, or simple analysis of questionnaire answers. A system models an aspect of reality which is subject to change. Systems become incorrect not always through error or oversight but because we live in an ever-changing world and it is this evolutionary aspect of software systems that the waterfall model fails to capture.

More recently developed models take a less simplistic view of the life-cycle and try to do more to accommodate the complexities.

5.4.3 Spiral Model

The phases in this model are defined cyclically. The basis of the spiral model is a four-stage representation through which the development process spirals. At each level

- objectives, constraints and alternatives are identified,
- alternatives are evaluated, risks are identified and resolved,
- the next level of product is developed and verified,
- the next phases are planned.

The focus is the identification of problems and the classification of these into different levels of risk, the aim being to eliminate high-risk problems before they threaten the software operation or cost.

A basic difference between this and the waterfall model is that it is risk driven. It is the level of risk attached to a particular stage which drives the development process. The four stages are represented as quadrants on a Cartesian diagram with the spiral line indicating the production process (Figure 5.8).

One of the advantages of this model is that it can be used as a framework to accommodate other models. The spiral model offers great advantage in its flexibility, particularly its ability to accommodate other life-cycle models in such a way as to maximise their good features and minimise their bad ones. It can accommodate, in a structured way, a mix of models where this is appropriate to a particular situation. For example, where a modification is called for quickly, the risks of using the code-and-fix scenario can be evaluated and, if code-and-fix is used, the potential problems can be addressed immediately by the appropriate procedures being built into the next phase.

A problem with the spiral model is a difficulty in matching it to the requirements for audit and accountability which are sometimes imposed upon a maintenance or development team. The constraints of

70 Software Maintenance: Concepts and Practice

audit may be incompatible with following the model; for example, a very tight deadline may not allow sufficient time for full risk evaluation. This may well be an indication that the constraints imposed in terms of audit and accountability are less than optimal.

The fact that the model is risk driven and relies heavily on risk assessment is also a problem area. In breaking down a problem and specifying it in detail, there is always a temptation to 'do the easy bits first' and leave the difficult bits until last. The spiral model requires that the high-risk areas are tackled first and in detail. Although 'difficult' does not always equate to 'high risk' it often does. A team inexperienced in risk assessment may run into problems.

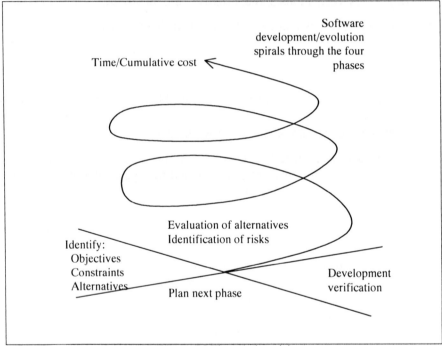

Figure 5.8 The spiral model

Exercise 5.3 Investigate the ways in which the basic waterfall model has been enhanced and modified. Describe these modifications and explain why they were made.

5.5 Maintenance Process Models

The need for maintenance-conscious models has been recognised for some time but the current situation is that maintenance models are neither so well developed nor so well understood as models for software development.

In the early days, problems with system development were overwhelming and it is not surprising that the evolutionary nature of software that is at the heart of maintenance was to an extent ignored [26]. To attempt to take account of future changes in systems, prior to good understanding of the development process, was akin to asking for the incorporation of a crystal ball into the model. However, our understanding of the maintenance process, just like our understanding of the development process, moved on and maintenance process and life-cycle models emerged.

Expanding on the example given in chapter 1, let us consider the addition of a room to a building. When the house was built to its original design, rooms A and B were built side by side. Some years later, a third room is needed. Had this need been perceived originally, three smaller rooms would have been built (Figure 5.9).

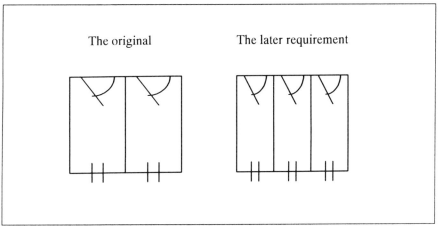

Figure 5.9 We need an extra room!

At the time of the original building, there was no need for a third room. But, after the building had been in use for some time, a need for a third room emerged. The addition of the third room to the existing building is a very different proposition from constructing the third room in the first place.

This is directly analogous to the addition of new requirements to a software system. Planning to build three rooms from the start is relatively easy, as is initial development of a particular functionality. Deciding to add the third room prior to commencement of building work is a little harder and requires alteration of plans. This equates to the case where there is a change in requirements subsequent to designing a piece of software but prior to implementing it. The addition of the extra room after the building has been completed and is in use is a very different matter, as is modification to software which is in use.

- The wall between rooms A and B must be knocked down.

    Software interfaces between different components may have to be altered.

- This is a building in use - the problem of creating and removing a pile of rubble must be addressed. The resultant dust with which the original building site could have coped may now pose a major threat to sensitive equipment. At the time of original building, rubbish chutes and skips would have been on site.

    There is far less leeway to allow for the introduction of errors and ripple effects in a piece of software which must be released quickly to a large customer base. During initial development, there was a specific and resourced testing phase. Reintroduction of modified software may be subject to tight time deadlines and resource constraints.

- Adding the third room may well require people and materials to travel through, and thus affect, parts of the building they would not have had to access originally. The work will impact differently upon the environment upon which it is carried out. The effects of adding the third room as opposed to building it in the first place will cause disruption at a different level, to a different group of people and in different places. All this needs to be assessed and addressed.

    Similarly, a modification to a large and complex software system has the potential to affect parts of the software from which it could have been kept completely separate had it been added originally.

- The physical effect on the building itself will be different. Is the wall between A and B a load-bearing wall? If so, there will be a need for a supporting joist. Had the original plans catered for a third room, there would have been no supporting joist across the middle of a room in this way. It would have been unnecessary, a design flaw in fact, had it appeared in the original, and yet in the conversion it is an absolute necessity

  The software will have to be modified to cater for the addition of the new functionality. Suppose that the new functionality calls for data to be held in memory in a large table. It may be that the existing system does not allow the creation of such a structure because of memory constraints. Data structures in other parts of the system may not have left enough room for a large table. If it is not feasible to make extensive alteration to the rest of the data structures, then something other than a large table must be used. This something else, a linked list perhaps, may seem wholly inappropriate. And yet, the demands of the maintenance environment insist upon it.

- Does the wall contain central heating pipes, wiring ducts, network cables or anything else which may have to be taken into account prior to its being demolished?

  Likewise, are there hidden dependencies within the software modules which are to be modified? In theory, these will all be documented. In practice, buildings tend to be better documented than software systems.

It is all too easy to assume that an enhancement to an existing software system can be tackled in exactly the same way as adding that feature from the start. This misconception may be due to the malleable nature of software. It is not as obvious with software, as it is with a building, that adding something later is a very different case from adding it in the first place.

It is this concept, that maintenance is a very different matter from initial development, that a maintenance-conscious model must encompass.

One can go only so far along the road towards predicting a future need for an extra room. And yet traditional engineering methods allow us to add new rooms to buildings without having to demolish the building or make it unsafe. In software engineering, there is a great deal of demolition work going on simply because we cannot add the 'extra room' safely. Predicting every future need is not possible and attempting to do so is very costly. We can, however, do more to encompass the genuine needs of maintenance within the models with which we work.

An obvious example is documentation. Engineers in other fields would not dream of neglecting, or working without, documentation. If proper documentation did not exist, road workers would cut off mains services almost every time they dug a hole in a city street. Yet software engineers often have to rely on their own investigations to discover dependencies between software modules or to discover potential ripple effects because the original system and subsequent changes are not documented.

It is important to recognise the differences between new development and maintenance but it is also important to recognise the similarities. In the building analogy; it is the same skills and expertise that are required to build the new wall whether constructing it in the new building or adding it later. What will make the difference is whether the work is being done on a building site or in a building in use.

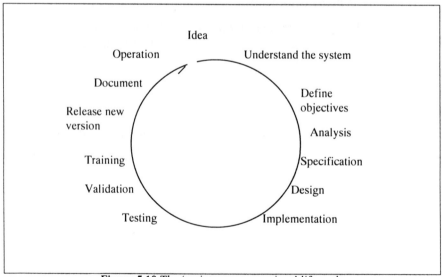

Figure 5.10 The 'maintenance conscious' life cycle

The generic stages in a maintenance-conscious model (Figure 5.10) compared with the traditional development model appear similar on the surface but within the stages there are great differences in emphasis and procedure. There is more effort required and very different emphases on the early stages, and conversely less effort required in the later stages, of the maintenance model as opposed to the development model (Figure 5.11).

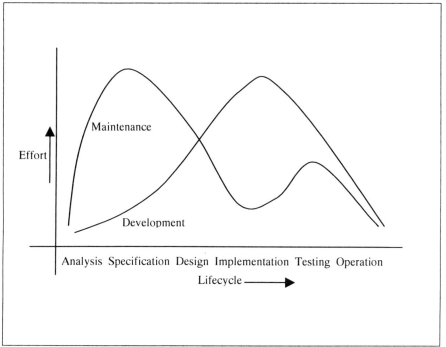

Figure 5.11 Effort needed in the different stages

Consider the building example again. Buildings are built for a particular purpose but often change use during their lifetime. A private house is converted to a shop. A stately home is converted to offices. The fact that the private house was not originally built with provision for a shop window or a counter does not mean that the house must be entirely demolished. Appropriate skills are brought to bear and the required conversions carried out. If the hopeful shopkeepers were to say to the builder 'If you were building this window into a new building whose design had allowed for it, it would take you x person-hours and you would use these specific materials and spend z pounds. Here are z pounds, build it this way,' the builder would turn down the job and wonder why these people wanted to insist on dictating details of something they appeared to know nothing about. And yet, much software maintenance is carried out this way. Had an original specification allowed for a particular functionality, it might have taken as little as five minutes to implement. 'Please deliver the modified software in five minutes!' Is it any surprise that software collapses under conversion to a greater extent than buildings do?

The essence of the problems at the heart of all the traditional models is in their failure to capture the evolutionary nature of software. A model is needed which recognises the requirement to build maintainability into the system. Once again, there are many different models and we will look only at a representative sample of four of them.

5.5.1 Quick-Fix Model

This is basically an *ad hoc* approach to maintaining software (Figure 5.12). It is a 'firefighting' approach, waiting for the problem to occur and then trying to fix it as quickly as possible, hence the name.

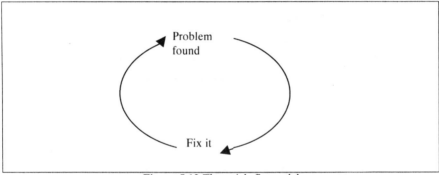

Figure 5.12 The quick-fix model

In this model, fixes would be done without detailed analysis of the long-term effects, for example ripple effects through the software or effects on code structure. There would be little if any documentation. It is easy to see how the model emerged historically, but it cannot be dismissed as a purely historical curiosity because, like the code-and-fix model, it is still used.

What are the advantages of such a model and why is it still used? In the appropriate environment it can work perfectly well. If for example a system is developed and maintained by a single person, he or she can come to learn the system well enough to be able to manage without detailed documentation, to be able to make instinctive judgements about how and how not to implement change. The job gets done quickly and cheaply.

However, such an environment is not the norm and we must consider the use of this model in the more usual setting of a commercial operation with a large customer base. Why does anyone in such a setting still allow the use of an unreliable model like the quick-fix? It is largely through the pressure of deadlines and resources. If customers are demanding the correction of an error, for example, they may not be willing to wait for the organisation to go through detailed and time-consuming stages of risk analysis. The organisation may run a higher risk in keeping its customers waiting than it runs in going for the quickest fix. But what of the long-term problems? If an organisation relies on quick-fix alone, it will run into difficult and very expensive problems, thus losing any advantage it gained from using the quick-fix model in the first place.

The strategy to adopt is to incorporate the techniques of quick-fix into another, more sophisticated model. In this way any change hurried through because of outside pressures will generate a recognised need for preventive maintenance which will repair any damage done.

By and large, people are well aware of the limitations of this model. Nonetheless, it often reflects only too well the real world business environment in which they work. Distinction must be made between short-term and long-term upgrades. If a user finds a bug in a commercial word processor, for example, it would be unrealistic to expect a whole new upgrade immediately Often, a company will release a quick fix as a temporary measure. The real solution will be implemented, along with other corrections and enhancements, as a major upgrade at a later date.

5.5.1.1 Case Study – Storage of Chronological Clinical Data

When the ACME Health Clinic system was originally developed, it catered only for a single recording per patient for things such as blood pressure, weight, medication and so on. This was because of a misunderstanding during requirements analysis which did not come to light until the system was in use. In fact, the system needed to store chronological series of recordings. At that stage, the need for storage of chronological data was immediate. The maintenance programmer assigned to the task drew up a mental model of data held in small arrays to allow speedy retrieval and proceeded to implement the change. This quick-fix method identified the need

- for the arrays,
- to amend the data structures to allow for linking of the chronological data,
- for a small restructuring program to modify the existing data.

There was no update of documentation, no documentation of the changes other than a few in-code comments and no in-depth analysis.

Because this was done speedily as a quick fix, problems such as array overflow were not considered. In fact, once enough information was stored, data was going to 'drop off the end' of the arrays and disappear. This would lead to data corruption in that the chronological links would be broken and missing links would appear in the middle of the data chains (Figure 5.13).

This was noticed while another enhancement was being tested, the potential seriousness of the problem was recognised and the race was on to solve it before the clinic stored sufficient data to cause the problem. This imposed yet another tight deadline and the fastest fix had to be found. The 'best' solution, a radical restructuring of the data and procedures for data retrieval and storage, was recognised, but could not be implemented because of the time restriction. Another quick fix had to be found. The only solution was to 'catch' data overflowing the temporary array and store it in the patient file. This meant that chronological links were maintained, but the data was being stored in the patient's file without being explicitly saved by the clinician. This not only led to less well-structured code, documentation further out of date and a situation even harder to retrieve, but was also in contravention of an original requirement regarding permanent saving of data.

This ACME Health Clinic case study highlights the difficulties of the quick-fix model. Ripple effects that should have been obvious were missed. These forced the adoption of a further fix which was known to be wrong. The resources that had to be diverted into this emergency repair lessened the likelihood of time being devoted to documentation update, thus decreasing the chances of the error being successfully retrieved.

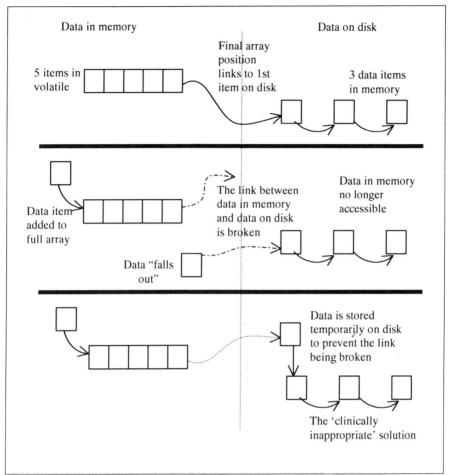

Figure 5.13 Enhancing the system to deal with chronological data

The underlying basis of the problem is that the quick-fix model does not 'understand' the maintenance process. The problems experienced were not hard to predict and the 'advantage' gained by the original quick fix was soon lost.

Many models have subsequently been developed which look at, and try to understand, the maintenance process from many different viewpoints. A representative selection of these is given below.

5.5.2 Boehm's Model

In 1983 Boehm [36] proposed a model for the maintenance process based upon economic models and principles. Economic models are nothing new. Economic decisions are a major driving force behind many processes and Boehm's thesis was that economic models and principles could not only improve productivity in maintenance but also help understanding of the process.

Boehm represents the maintenance process as a closed loop cycle (Figure 5.14). He theorises that it is the stage where management decisions are made that drives the process. In this stage, a set of approved changes is determined by applying particular strategies and cost-benefit evaluations to a set of proposed changes. The approved changes are accompanied by their own budgets which will largely determine the extent and type of resource expended.

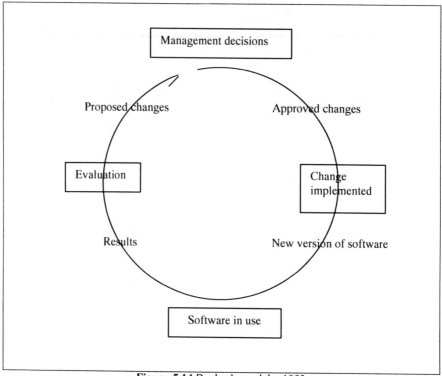

Figure 5.14 Boehm's model – 1983

The survey by Leintz and Swanson [176] (Figure 5.15) showed that almost half maintenance effort was devoted to non-discretionary maintenance activities.

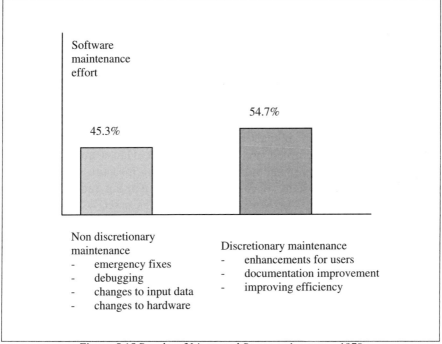

Figure 5.15 Results of Lientz and Swansons' survey – 1978

In terms of the production function – the economic relationship between the inputs to a process and its benefits – this reflects the typical three-segment graph of:

- *Investment:* This is a phase of low input of resource and low benefit. This correlates to a newly released software product which has a high requirement for emergency fixes and mandatory enhancements.
- *High payoff:* An organisation sees increasing benefit from the software product and the initial problems are ironed out. This is a phase during which resource is put into user enhancements and improvements in documentation and efficiency. Cumulative benefit to the organisation increases quickly during this phase.
- *Diminishing returns:* Beyond a certain point, the rate of increase of cumulative benefit slows. The product has reached its peak of

usefulness. The product has reached the stage where radical change becomes less and less cost effective.

Boehm [36] sees the maintenance manager's task as one of balancing the pursuit of the objectives of maintenance against the constraints imposed by the environment in which maintenance work is carried out.

Thus, the maintenance process is driven by the maintenance manager's decisions which are based on the balancing of objectives against constraints.

In the example of the problems with the ACME Health Clinic system, this approach to maintenance would have recognised that the quick-fix approach adopted was not appropriate. Had a quick fix been essential, it would have been a temporary holding measure which would have allowed the system to continue running without radical and ill-thought-out changes. These would have been assessed as part of the overall strategy and would have allowed a progression towards the real solution instead of the inevitable path away from it.

5.5.3   *Osborne's Model*

Another approach is that proposed by Osborne [210]. The difference between this model and the others described here is that it deals directly with the reality of the maintenance environment. Other models tend to assume some facet of an ideal situation - the existence of full documentation, for example. Osborne's model makes allowance for how things are rather than how we would like them to be.

The maintenance model is treated as continuous iterations of the software life-cycle with, at each stage, provision made for maintainability to be built in. If good maintenance features already exist, for example full and formal specification or complete documentation, all well and good, but if not, allowance is made for them to be built in.

The stages in the maintenance life-cycle are shown in Figure 5.16 and include recognition of the steps where iterative loops will often occur.

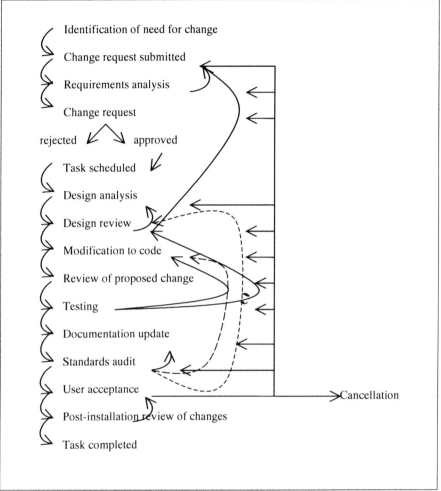

Figure 5.16 Osborne's model of the software maintenance process

Osborne hypothesises that many technical problems which arise during maintenance are due to inadequate management communications and control, and recommends a strategy that includes:

- the inclusion of maintenance requirements in the change specification;
- a software quality assurance program which establishes quality assurance requirements;

- a means of verifying that maintenance goals have been met;
- performance review to provide feedback to managers.

5.5.4 Iterative Enhancement Model

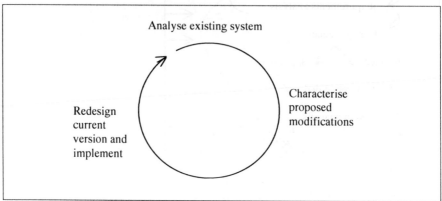

Figure 5.17 The three stages of iterative enhancement

This model has been proposed based on the tenet that the implementation of changes to a software system throughout its lifetime is an iterative process and involves enhancing such a system in an iterative way. It is similar to the evolutionary development paradigm during pre-installation.

Originally proposed as a development model but well suited to maintenance, the motivation for this was the environment where requirements were not fully understood and a full system could not be built.

Adapted for maintenance, the model assumes complete documentation as it relies on modification of this as the starting point for each iteration. The model is effectively a three-stage cycle (Figure 5.17):

- Analysis.
- Characterisation of proposed modifications.
- Redesign and implementation.

The existing documentation for each stage (requirements, design, coding, testing and analysis) is modified starting with the highest-level document affected by the proposed changes. These modifications are propagated through the set of documents and the system redesigned.

The model explicitly supports reuse (see chapter 8) and also accommodates other models, for example the quick-fix model.

The pressures of the maintenance environment often dictate that a quick solution is found but, as we have seen, the use of the 'quickest' solution can lead to more problems than it solves. As with the previous model, iterative enhancement lends itself to the assimilation of other models within it and can thus incorporate a quick fix in its own more structured environment. A quick fix may be carried out, problem areas identified, and the next iteration would specifically address them.

The problems with the iterative enhancement model stem from assumptions made about the existence of full documentation and the ability of the maintenance team to analyse the existing product in full. Whereas wider use of structured maintenance models will lead to a culture where documentation tends to be kept up to date and complete, the current situation is that this is not often the case.

5.5.5 *Reuse-Oriented Model*

This model is based on the principle that maintenance could be viewed as an activity involving the reuse of existing program components. The concept of reuse is considered in more detail in chapter 8. The reuse model described by Basili [16] has four main steps:

- Identification of the parts of the old system that are candidates for reuse,
- Understanding these system parts,
- Modification of the old system parts appropriate to the new requirements,
- Integration of the modified parts into the new system.

A detailed framework is required for the classification of components and the possible modifications. With the full reuse model (Figure 5.18) the starting point may be any phase of the life-cycle – the requirements, the design, the code or the test data – unlike other models. For example, in the quick-fix model, the starting point is always the code.

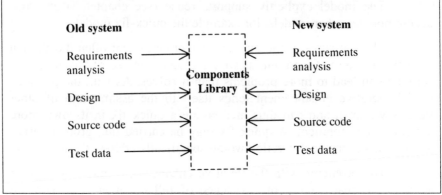

Figure 5.18 The reuse model

Exercise 5.4 Compare and contrast Osborne's maintenance process model with the other maintenance process models dealt with in this chapter.

Exercise 5.5 Describe how the ACME Health Clinic system might have been more effectively modified. Assume the same tight deadlines but investigate the incorporation of the quick-fix model into another, more structured model.

5.6 When to Make a Change

So far discussion has been about the introduction of change into a system without considering whether or not that change should be made at all. In other words, the ways in which different models approach the implementation of change has been considered but without addressing the important question of how to decide when a change should be made. It cannot simply be assumed that everyone involved with a system, from the developers to the users, can throw their ideas into the arena and automatically have them implemented. That would lead to chaos.

Not all changes are feasible. A change may be desirable but too expensive. There has to be a means of deciding when to implement a change. Ways of doing this, e.g. via a Change Control Board, are explored in detail in chapter 11.

Exercise 5.6 What was the last software project you worked on? Was it a commercial project, an undergraduate project or a personal project? Write a critical appraisal of the life-cycle model to which you worked. Was it well structured or *ad hoc?* Would you work to a different model if you were to start this project again?

Exercise 5.7 You are the IT manager in charge of a large library software system which fails unexpectedly one Monday morning. How would you go about the process of solving this problem

1. if it is imperative that it is up and running within two hours?
2. if the library is able to function adequately for several days without its software system?

5.7 Process Maturity

We have looked at how processes are modelled, but a vital issue is of course, how they are used.

Knowledge of the theory does not lead automatically to effective use in practice. Many undergraduate software engineering programmes include a group project where students work together on a large software project, to mimic the commercial environment. Processes will have been learnt in other parts of the course. If the application of these to the group work is *ad hoc* and not controlled, the results of such projects will be unpredictable. Outcomes will depend upon chance, individual flair of team members and will by and large be random. Well-organised projects, in contrast, should allow all groups to use effectively the processes they have learnt in their theoretical courses.

A similar situation holds in a commercial software house. Some companies carry on successful operations for a long time reliant on a few very good programmers. If they do not put resources into building the maturity of the processes themselves, there will come a point where the operation cannot continue. The burden will become far too great for the few people carrying it. They will leave and the whole operation will collapse.

Organisations need a means by which to assess the maturity and effectiveness of their processes.

5.7.1 Capability Maturity Model® for Software

The Software Engineering Institute (SEI) developed a capability maturity model for software [217]. Using this, the maturity of processes can be assessed. Five levels are defined:

1) Initial. The software process is *ad hoc*. Few processes are defined. Success depends on individual flair of team members.

2) Repeatable. Basic processes are established, tracking cost, scheduling, and functionality. Successes can be repeated on projects with similar applications.

3) Defined. Processes are documented and standardised. There exists within the organisation standard processes for developing and maintaining software. All projects use a tailored and approved version of the standard process.

4) Managed. Detailed measures are collected, both of the process and the quality of the product. Quantitative understanding and control is achieved.

5) Optimising. Quantitative feedback is evaluated and used from the processes and from the piloting of innovative ideas and technologies. This enables continuous process improvement.

The SEI's model is not the only one in use, but is widely referenced and other models [63] tend to be closely cross-referenced with it. The benefits accruing from software process improvement based upon the SEI's model have been studied and documented [128, 161].

5.7.2 Software Experience Bases

The idea of an organisation continually improving through sharing experience is a concept that can counter the vulnerability inherent in having experience concentrated in a few skilled employees.

Knowledge can be formalised into guidelines and models, or may be embodied in the skills of the personnel involved. The latter is as much an asset as a company's software systems, built using such knowledge, but harder to turn into an asset that can effectively be shared and retained.

Organisations have created systems to support knowledge and experience sharing e.g. knowledge and experience databases, with varying degrees of success. Conradi *et al* [67] suggest that software experience base is a more useful term than database, to avoid inappropriate comparison with the traditional database management systems. They propose four factors required for successful implementation of a software experience base:

1. Cultural change – people must become comfortable with sharing knowledge and using others' knowledge and experience, in order that the software experience base is active and used.
2. Stability – an unstable business environment will not be conducive to the development of a culture or a system for knowledge and experience sharing.
3. Business value – in order for any system to be used and useful in today's business world, it must provide a demonstrable payback.
4. Incremental implementation – implementing a software experience base in small increments is of use in keeping the process close to the users and, with effective feedback, prevents the software experience base becoming a remote and irrelevant entity.

5.8 Summary

The key points that have been covered in this chapter are:

- The software life cycle is the cyclic series of phases through which a software system goes during its development and use. A process is a single series of such phases.
- A process model abstracts the confusing plethora of detail from the process of software evolution and allows us to understand it.
- Traditional life-cycle models fail to take account of the evolutionary nature of software systems.
- There are major differences between new development and maintenance although they have many specific phases in common. Maintenance-conscious models can be built from traditional models by catering for the evolutionary tendency of the software.
- There are many different maintenance models. Three representative ones are quick-fix which is an *ad hoc,* fire-fighting approach; iterative enhancement which is based on the iterative nature of

change to a system; and reuse-oriented which sees maintenance as an activity involving the reuse of program components. The most pragmatic approach is given by Osborne's model.

- Models differ in bias: some are oriented towards economic aspects, some towards products and some towards processes.

- All models have strengths and weaknesses. No one model is appropriate in all situations and often a combination of models is the best solution.

- By improving the maturity of their software processes, software developers and maintainers move from as-hoc, ill-defined processes where success is largely a matter of chance, to a situation of predictable and repeatable project outcomes and continual improvement.

This part of the book has put maintenance activities into context and looked at how the maintenance process is modelled. The next stage is to look at what actually happens during maintenance.

PART II: What Takes Place During Maintenance

Overview

This section of the book aims to overview the means by which software is changed in practice.

The actual process of making a change is a complex business and even the simplest changes go through defined stages as they are brought about. Essentially, the following steps will be carried out:

- The maintenance programmer gains an understanding of the current system and the context within which it operates.
- The change is carried out
- The new version is tested and then goes live.

The above steps involve significant software engineering and programming skills, but one very important stage has been omitted – that of initially identifying and agreeing the need for change. This, though requiring an appreciation of software engineering, is a managerial decision, based on knowledge of the overall context within which the proposed change is to be made. The first stage above, that of understanding the current system, affects management decisions on software change and the means by which that change is carried out. Thus,

- the identification of the need for change and agreement to its being carried out is also a stage in the process.

Each of the above steps covers significant effort within the maintenance lifecycle. This section of the book looks in detail at these stages.

- **Understanding the Current System**

Understanding is a vital precursor to implementing change. Without an understanding of what the current system does, it is impossible to safeguard against undesirable ripple effects and unintended modifications. Programme comprehension, in essence breaks down into what, where and how.

- What does the software system actually do?
- Where does the change need to be made?
- How do the relevant parts of the software work?

There are many different aspects to be understood, and in order to be successful in carrying out a change, it is necessary to appreciate different people's comprehension needs. In large complex systems, it would be neither feasible nor desirable to understand every aspect. The skill is to recognise which aspects must be understood.

The process of understanding can itself be modelled, and there are strategies to aid the maintenance programmer. Many factors relevant to software, to the environment or to the maintenance personnel, affect understanding.

- **Carrying Out the Change**

Changing the software itself can be done in many ways. We saw in the chapter on process models, that the way change is effected can be fairly simplistic (cf. Quick-fix model) or very sophisticated (cf. Osborne's model). The simplistic methods have a "feel" of being faster – the programmer can "get down to coding" more quickly. However, the price for this is almost always a more expensive, less effective end result that takes as long, if not longer, to implement.

A common precursor to carrying out a modification is reverse engineering. This essentially is taking the programme apart to see how it works, and has the feel of a backward step. However, the advantages gained in programme understanding allow for far more effective implementation of the steps that build the system back up again e.g. forward engineering, restructuring and re-engineering. An advantage of sound understanding is the potential for reuse of components.

Forward engineering refers to the traditional software development approach, building a system starting with requirements analysis going on to design and then implementation. Forward engineering a modification into an existing system is a very different matter from forward engineering on a green field site. An added stage e.g. of reverse engineering is often a vital precursor.

Restructuring is often required in maintenance. Systems lose structure (as stated in Lehman's second law). Restructuring is a means of restoring order and creating a more maintainable system. It involves changing the abstract representation of the system from one form to another without changing the functionality.

Reengineering is the means by which a system is enhanced using first reverse engineering to aid comprehension and allows an element of restructuring, then forward engineering to produce the new enhanced system.

Vast resources in many industries are wasted on reinventing the wheel. This is more of a problem the less mature a discipline is. The software industry is young compared with many other engineering disciplines, and the nature of software is such that it does not necessarily lend itself to the reuse of components. Nonetheless, reuse is an obvious route to increased effectiveness and is now a major factor at the leading edge of software development and maintenance.

- **Testing**

Systems are tested before they are released in order to ease the process of live implementation as much as possible. Testing can be *ad hoc* or very sophisticated. Issues such as how catastrophic a software failure would be, or where and when a failure might occur, drive the testing process. For example, in a games programme, a software error could become a feature. Those who discover it, exploit the bug to gain advantage in the game. It becomes talked about in games literature. It becomes an integral part of the software. In a railway signalling system however, or an air traffic control system, a software error could be life threatening.

- **Identifying the Need for Change**

Identifying the need for a change can be a trivial task e.g. "when I click on the button labelled *blue background* the background becomes red, and when I click on the button labelled *red background* the background becomes blue." It is easy to identify here that a change is needed. Indeed, one can predict with reasonable certainty what the problem is and how to solve it.

However, this is a different matter from actually agreeing that the change should be made. What if we are dealing with very old source code in the current system? The link between 'red source' and the 'blue button' may not be the straightforward link it might be in modern code. Maybe 'blue' and 'red' within the source code are hard to identify (a likely cause of the original error). The relevant code may not be self-contained in modules or procedures. There may be far-reaching ripple effects. Maybe we have a programmer who has spent some time studying the problem, and can say, 'No, it isn't a trivial matter but yes, it can now be solved.'

Does this mean the change can go ahead? Not necessarily. This is old software that has been in use a long time. There is a big user base out there that is accustomed to this peculiarity. Suppose there are no plans to extend the user base until a fully updated version is available in a few months' time. Correcting the error may serve only to confuse the current users. It may be deemed more effective to distribute an addendum to the user guide to explain this quirk.

This is a simple example, but illustrates the point that agreeing a change is not a decision to be taken lightly.

Discussion Points

These points are intended to stimulate thinking and discussion on fundamental issues in software maintenance. The issues raised are explored in the chapters of this section, but it is a beneficial to think around these areas and try to draw conclusions yourself, before looking for answers in the text.

- **Program Understanding**

At the start of the year, Programmer A has a small software system that he has developed himself. He understands what it does, how it does it and why it operates the way it does. Two years later, the system is a large one with far more functionality. Programmer A no longer has as in-depth understanding of what it does, why or how.

Chart the specific milestones in Programmer A's loss of understanding. What happens to make him lose touch with his software? What are the significant factors that have led from almost perfect understanding to very poor understanding?

- **Effecting Change**

Programmer A is an experienced programmer who has been working on a particular system for a long time. Programmer B has the same skills and level of experience but is new to this system. Would use of the Quick-Fix model to address a software problem be any safer, more effective or less prone to long-term problems if done by Programmer A rather than Programmer B?

- **Testing**

Question: Why do we test software?

Answer: To see if it works.

Discuss why this answer is deficient in terms of why it misses the point of the question. In thinking about this, consider the following exchange and look for points of comparison:

Question: Why did you drive across town today?

Answer: To look at the *opening hours* notice on the shop, to see if it will be open on the 3rd Saturday in June next year.

- **Management**

You are the managing director of a software firm. One of the systems you support needs a major upgrade. You intend to put Team A on this as they are an experienced group already familiar with the system. You have another contract on a system that is new to your firm. The deadlines on this are less critical and it is a less complex piece of software. You intend employing a new team to deal with this, intending to train them up as they carry out the work.

Team A now puts a spanner in the works. They say they do not want to work on the major upgrade. They are bored with the system. They want to widen their experience. They are prepared to take on the new system, but want no responsibility for the old. If assigned to the major upgrade as originally planned, they will leave and work elsewhere.

Team A on the new system will be more expensive than the less experienced team. If Team A is switched to this project, you will have to employ a new team to work on the major upgrade, but because of the complexity and deadlines, you will not be able to employ an inexperienced team to train up. Your options are:-

- Team A on the new project, a new experienced team on the major upgrade,
- A new trainee team on the new project, a new experienced team on the major upgrade.

Discuss the pros and cons of these options.

6

Program Understanding

"Programmers have become part historian, part detective and part clairvoyant"

Corbi ([69], p. 295)

This chapter aims to
1. Explain the role of program understanding in maintenance activities.
2. Discuss the aims of program understanding.
3. Explain the comprehension needs of members of a maintenance project.
4. Discuss comprehension process models and their application to maintenance tasks.
5. Discuss the role of the mental model in understanding programs.
6. Discuss the different comprehension strategies and explain the differences.
7. Discuss the effect of each strategy on various aspects of maintenance activities.
8. Discuss the factors that impact on source code understanding.
9. Give a foundation for the selection of suitable tools, techniques and methods.

6.1 Introduction

Part I discussed the types of change to which a software system can be subjected: corrective (due to defects); adaptive (due to changes in its environment); perfective (to accommodate new requirements); and preventive (to facilitate future maintenance work). It also looked at the framework within which change may be implemented effectively. However, an area not yet touched upon, but which is fundamental to an effective change process, is understanding. Prior to implementing any change, it is essential to understand the software product as a whole and the programs affected by the change in particular [49, 69, 276, 220]. During maintenance, this involves:

- having a general knowledge of **what** the software system does and how it relates to its environment;
- identifying **where** in the system changes are to be effected; and
- having an in-depth knowledge of **how** the parts to be corrected or modified work.

Program understanding consumes a significant proportion of maintenance effort and resources. At Hewlett Packard it was estimated that reading code (a fundamental element in comprehension) costs $200 million a year [212]. Data from industry and other sources also indicates that about half of the total effort expended on effecting change is used up in understanding programs [69, 214]. This expenditure tends to increase in the event of a programmer maintaining programs written by someone else, of inaccurate, out-of-date or even non-existent system documentation, or of deterioration in program structure due to several years of *ad hoc* quick fixes. Unfortunately, these problems are all too familiar to maintenance personnel [76, 212].

This chapter considers the issues that underpin program understanding during maintenance.

6.2 Definitions

Bottom-up – working from the detail to the general overview – starting with small detailed constituents and building them up into larger aspects.

Cause-effect relation – This is the causal relation between a consequence and those parts of the program that brought it about [246].

Chunking – The process of putting together small units of information (such as program statements) into larger units (such as procedures) [194]. Each of these information units is known as a chunk.

Cognitive process – how the knowledge is manipulated in human memory during the formation and use of mental models.

Cognitive structure – the way in which knowledge is stored in human memory.

Comprehension – understanding, the capacity to understand general relations of particulars.

Decision-support feature – An attribute of a software product that can guide maintenance personnel in technical and management decision making processes.

Execution effect – The behaviour of the system when it is run.

Functional requirements – statements of the services that a system should provide.

Mental model – an abstract representation of an entity.

Non-functional requirements – constraints on the services and functions offered by a system.

Opportunistic – taking advantage of favourable circumstances as they arise.

Problem domain – The problem is the task being performed by the software and the problem domain is the area to which the task belongs.

Product-environment relation – This is the connection between the whole system and elements of the sphere within which it operates.

Top-down – working from the general to the specific – starting with large general aspects and breaking them down into smaller more detailed constituents.

Vocabulary problem – The difficulties that arise from the use of identifier names that fail to convey the intended meaning [103].

6.3 Aims of Program Comprehension

The ultimate purpose of reading and comprehending programs is to be able successfully to implement requested changes. This entails acquiring information about certain aspects of the software system such as the problem domain, execution effect, cause-effect relation, product-environment relation and decision-support features of the software (Table 6.1).

Table 6.1 Features of a software product and their importance to understanding

Knowledge	Importance
1. Problem domain	<ul><li>To assist in the estimation of resources</li><li>To guide the choice of suitable algorithms, methodologies, tools and personnel</li></ul>
2. Execution effect	<ul><li>To determine whether or not a change did achieve the desired effect</li></ul>
3. Cause-effect relation	<ul><li>To establish the scope of a change, to predict potential ripple effects and to trace data flow and control flow</li></ul>
4. Product-environment relation	<ul><li>To ascertain how changes in the product's environment affect the product and its underlying programs</li></ul>
5. Decision-support features	<ul><li>To support technical and management decision-making processes</li></ul>

6.3.1 Problem Domain

Being able to capture domain knowledge is now considered a far more important area than it used to be [27]. This is partly because of the proliferation of computers in a wider spectrum of specialist problem areas - for example, specialist clinical environments.

In large software systems, for example in domains such as health care, telecommunications and finance, problems are usually broken down into manageable sub-problems or smaller elements, each of which is handled by a different program unit such as a module, procedure or function. A compiler, for example, consists of elements such as a parser; lexical analyser and code generator, each of which can be decomposed into even smaller components. In order to effect change or simply to estimate the resource required for a maintenance task, knowledge of the problem domain in general and the sub-problems in particular is essential so as to direct maintenance personnel in the choice of suitable algorithms, methodologies and tools. The selection of personnel with the appropriate level of expertise and skills is another aspect. Information can be obtained from various sources - the system documentation, end-users, or the program source code.

6.3.2 Execution Effect

At a high level of abstraction, the maintenance personnel need to know (or be able to predict) what results the program will produce for a given input without necessarily knowing which program units contributed to the overall result or how the result was accomplished. At a low level of abstraction, they need to know the results that individual program units will produce on execution. Knowledge of data flow, control flow and algorithmic patterns can facilitate the accomplishment of these goals. For example, a specialist compiler programmer may want to know, at a higher level of abstraction, the output from a complete compilation process, and at a lower level, the output from the parser. During maintenance, this information can assist the maintenance personnel to determine whether an implemented change achieved the desired effect.

6.3.3 Cause-Effect Relation

In large and complex programs, knowledge of this relation is important in a number of ways.

- It allows the maintenance personnel to reason about how components of a software product interact during execution.
- It enables a programmer to predict the scope of a change and any knock-on effect that may arise from the change.
- The cause-effect relation can be used to trace the flow of information through the program. The point in the program where there is an unusual interruption of this flow may signal the source of a bug.

For example, in Figure 6.1[7] it is important for the programmer to know that Segment A accepts input characters and stacks them, and that Segment B unstacks these characters. As such, if the data structure is

---

[7] This simple example is used only to illustrate the underlying principles and is by no means representative of typical maintenance problems.

changed from Stack to Queue, the cause-effect relation will be used to identify the areas of StringReversing affected by this change.

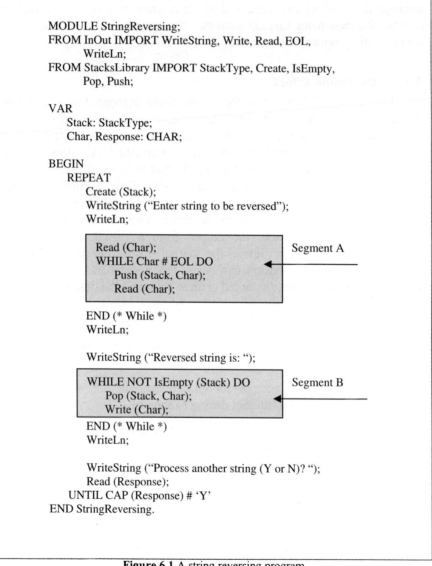

Figure 6.1 A string reversing program

6.3.4 Product-Environment Relation

A product is a software system. An environment is the totality of all conditions and influences which act from outside upon the product, for example business rules, government regulations, work patterns, software and hardware operating platforms. It is essential for the maintenance personnel to know not only the nature but the extent of the relation. This knowledge can be used to predict how changes in these elements will affect the product in general and the underlying programs in particular.

6.3.5 Decision-Support Features

Software product attributes such as complexity and maintainability are examples that can guide maintenance personnel in technical and management decision-making processes like option analysis, decision-making, budgeting and resource allocation. Measures of the complexity of the system (measured by using, say, McCabe's metric [190]) can be used to determine which components of the system require more resource for testing. The maintainability of the system (measured by using, say, Gilb's approach [109]) may be used as an indicator of its quality.

Reverse engineering can be used to study the system to be understood in order to extract these kinds of information. Chikofsky and Cross define reverse engineering as the 'process of analysing a subject system to identify the system's components and their interrelationships and create representations of the system in another form or a higher level of abstraction' [60 p.15]. A detailed discussion of the issues of reverse engineering will be presented in the next chapter.

There are many factors that affect the extent to which maintenance personnel can acquire the above categories of knowledge about a system. These include comprehension strategies, domain expertise, quality of documentation, presentation and organisation, programming practice and implementation issues, and support tools, all of which are discussed later in this chapter.

6.4 Maintainers and Their Information Needs

It is not essential that every member of a maintenance project team understands every aspect of the system being maintained. The process of understanding is driven by the need to know. Members of the maintenance team - managers, analysts, designers and programmers - all have different comprehension or information needs depending on the level at which they function [277].

6.4.1 Managers

Considering that one of the responsibilities of management is making decisions, managers need to have decision-support knowledge in order to make informed decisions. The level of understanding required will depend on the decision to be taken. For example, to be able to estimate the cost and duration of a major enhancement, knowledge of the size of the programs (in terms of lines of code or function points) is required. This estimate can then be used to determine whether or not it is more economical to replace the system with a vendor system. Managers do not necessarily have to know the architectural design of the system or the low-level program implementation details in order to carry out their duties. As Weinberg puts it,

> *"Nobody can seriously have believed that executives could read programs"*
>
> Weinberg ([284], p.5).

6.4.2 Analysts

During software development the analyst requires an understanding of the problem domain (for example, finance or health care) [220] in order to undertake tasks such as determining the functional and non-functional requirements, and to establish the relationship between the system and the elements of its environment. During maintenance, the analysts would be concerned with knowing how changes in this environment (for example, new government regulations or a new operating system) would affect the system. Thus, prior to implementing the change, the analyst needs to have a global view of the system, that is, a general picture of the interaction between the major functional units. The analyst is also required to determine the implications of change on the performance of a system.

Like managers, analysts do not need the local view - a picture of localised parts of the system and how they are implemented. The use of physical models such as context diagrams can be employed to represent the main components of the system and how they relate to the system's environment, thereby assisting the analyst to gain a good understanding of the system without being distracted by low-level design or coding details.

6.4.3 Designers

The design process of a software system can take place at two levels: architectural and detailed design [93]. **Architectural design** results in the production of functional components, conceptual data structures and the interconnection between various components. **Detailed design** results in the detailed algorithms, data representations, data structures and interfaces between procedures or routines. During maintenance, the designer's job is to:

- extract this information and determine how enhancements could be accommodated by the architecture, data structures, data flow and control flow of the existing system;
- go through the existing source code to get a rough idea of the size of the job, the areas of the system that will be affected, and the knowledge and skills that will be needed by the programming team that does the job [69].

The use of concepts such as information hiding, modular program decomposition, data abstraction, object orientation, and good design notations such as data flow diagrams, control flow diagrams, structure charts and hierarchy process input/output (HIPO) charts can help the designer obtain a good understanding of the system before designing changes.

6.4.4 Programmers

Maintenance programmers are required to know the execution effect of the system at different levels of abstraction, the causal knowledge and knowledge of the product-environment relation. At a higher level of abstraction (for instance, at the systems level), the programmer needs to know the function of individual components of the system and their causal relation. At a lower level of abstraction (for example, individual procedures or modules), the programmer needs to understand 'what each program statement does, the execution sequence (control flow), the transformational effects on the data objects (data flow), and the purpose of a set of program statements (functions)' [220 p.54].

This information will assist the programmer in a number of ways:

1. To decide on whether to restructure or rewrite specific code segments;
2. To predict more easily any knock-on effect when making changes that are likely to affect other parts of the system;
3. To hypothesise the location and causes of error;
4. To determine the feasibility of proposed changes and notify management of any anticipated problems.

The use of tools such as static analysers, ripple effect analysers, cross-referencers and program slicers can facilitate the programmer's task. In addition to the use of these tools, experience within the given problem area, the programming task [111] and the programming language used will determine the speed and efficiency with which the program can be understood.

Although in principle, it is possible to categorise the roles of maintenance personnel, in practice the divisions are not clear cut. The responsibilities will depend on factors such as the organisation of maintenance work (see chapter 10) and on the size of the maintenance team. In situations where a few individuals are assigned to maintenance tasks, they tend to perform the duties of the analyst, designer and programmer although not necessarily simultaneously. As such, they would need to understand not just low-level implementation issues such as the control flow, data flow, data structures and algorithmic aspects of the system but would be expected also to understand the architectural design of the system and be aware of any other issues that may be required for successful maintenance and evolution.

In larger companies, which can have 500 to 1000 maintenance personnel (sometimes in different geographical locations), there tend to be well-defined roles for maintainers depending on the organisational mode being used (see Chapter 10). Whatever approach is chosen to organise personnel and maintenance tasks, it is essential to have in place a mechanism that enables them to communicate.

Exercise 6.1 What do you aim to achieve when attempting to understand a program?

Exercise 6.2 Why is it important to understand programs?

Exercise 6.3 Suppose that as a programmer, you are asked to: (i) provide a message handling facility for an operational Management Information System (MIS); and (ii) integrate the MIS into other office automation packages. What information about the MIS would you need, to be able to effect these changes? Indicate your reasoning.

6.5 Comprehension Process Models

Programmers vary in their ways of thinking, solving problems and choosing techniques and tools. Generally, however, the three actions involved in the understanding of a program are: reading about the program, reading its source code, and running it [69]. Figure 6.2 overviews these actions with examples.

- Step 1 - *Read about the program:* At this stage of the process, the 'understander' browses, peruses different sources of information such as the system documentation - specification and design documents - to develop an overview or overall understanding of the system. Documentation aids such as structure charts and data and control flow diagrams can be used. In many large, complex and old systems (developed prior to the advent of good documentation tools, techniques and practice), this phase may be omitted if the system documentation is inaccurate, out of date or non-existent.

- Step 2 - *Read the source code:* During this stage, the global and local views of the program can be obtained. The global view is used to gain a top-level understanding of the system and also to determine the scope of any knock-on effect a change might have on other parts of the system. The local view allows programmers to focus their attention on a specific part of the system. With this view, information about the system's structure, data types and algorithmic patterns is obtained. Tools such as static analysers - used to examine source code - are employed during this phase. They produce cross-reference lists, which indicate where different identifiers - functions, procedures, variables and constants - have been used (or called) in the program. That way, they can highlight abnormalities in the program and hence enable the programmer to detect errors. Bearing in mind that the system documentation may not be reliable, reading program source code is usually the principal way of obtaining information about a software product.

- Step *3-Run the program:* The aim of this step is to study the dynamic behaviour of the program in action, including for example, executing the program and obtaining trace data. The benefit of running the program is that it can reveal some characteristics of the system which are difficult to obtain by just reading the source code.

The details of techniques and tools to support the various phases of the comprehension process are considered in section 6.7. In practice, the process of understanding a program does not usually take place in such an organised manner. There tend to be iterations of the actions and backtracking (indicated by broken lines in Figure 6.2) to clarify doubts and to obtain more information.

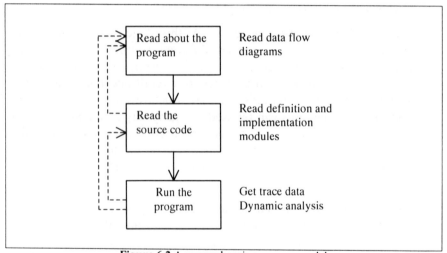

Figure 6.2 A comprehension process model

It is generally assumed that as maintainers go through the steps outlined above (regardless of the order) in an attempt to understand the program[8] they form a mental model - internal representation - of the program [145].

---

[8] Comprehension in a software maintenance sense involves acquisition of knowledge about programs, as well as accompanying documentation and operating procedures, but we shall

Exercise 6.4 How is the comprehension process model in Figure 6.2 different from, or similar to, the one that you tend to use? Indicate your reasons.

6.6 Mental Models

Our understanding of a phenomenon depends to some extent on our ability to form a mental representation, which serves as a working model of the phenomenon to be understood [145].

The phenomenon (how a television set works, the behaviour of liquids, an algorithm) is known as the target system, and its mental representation is called a mental model. For example, if you understand how a television works, then you have a mental model which represents this and, based on that model, you can predict behaviour such as what will happen when the television set is turned on or when a different channel is selected. Using the model you can also explain certain observations such as the occurrence of a distorted image. The completeness and accuracy of the model depends to a large extent on its users' information needs. In the case of the television set, an ordinary user - who uses it solely for entertainment - does not have to understand the internal composition of the cathode ray tube and circuits and how they work, in order to be able to use it. A technician, however, who services the set in the event of breakdown needs a deeper understanding of how the set works and thus requires a more elaborate and accurate mental model.

The content and formation of mental models hinges on cognitive structures and cognitive processes. The mental model is formed after observation, inference or interaction with the target system. It changes continuously as more information about the target system is acquired. Its completeness and correctness can be influenced by factors such as the user's previous experience with similar systems and technical background [145, 177]. The mental model may contain insufficient, contradictory or unnecessary information about the target system. Although it is not necessary for this model to be complete, it has to convey key information about the target system. For example, if it

---

concentrate here on the issues of understanding programs. The underlying principles, however, can also be applied to documentation.

models a piece of software, it should at least embody the functionality of the software.

Research in the area of programmers' cognitive behaviour during maintenance suggests that there are variations in the strategies that programmers use to understand (or form mental models of) programs. That is, the cognitive structures and cognitive processes differ.

6.7 Program Comprehension Strategies

Table 6.2 Program comprehension strategies and their differences

Model	Features		
	Tenet of the model	*Cognitive process*	*Cognitive structure*
Top-down	Program understanding is mapping from how the program works (programming domain) to what is to be done (problem domain)	Top-down reconstruction of knowledge domains and their mappings Reconstruction based on hypotheses creation, confirmation and refinement cycle	Problem and programming domain knowledge Potential intermediate domain knowledge Multiple layers of domain knowledge
Bottom-up	Recognition of recurring patterns in program code	Bottom-up chunking of recognised patterns to produce high-level semantic structures	Mapping between knowledge domains Hierarchical multi-layered arrangement of patterns
Opportunistic	Combination of both top-down and bottom-up strategies	Top-down and bottom-up cues are exploited as they become available An assimilation process is used to obtain information from source code and system documentation	Similar to top-down and bottom-up representations depending on the level of abstraction

A program comprehension strategy is a technique used to form a mental model of the target program. The mental model is constructed by combining information contained in the source code and documentation with the assistance of the expertise and domain knowledge that the programmer brings to the task. A number of descriptive models of how programmers go about understanding programs have been proposed based on the results of empirical studies of programmers. Examples of these models include top-down [48, 130], bottom-up [251, 250] and opportunistic models [130, 220] (Table 6.2).

6.7.1 Top-Down Model

The tenet of this model is that an understander starts by comprehending the top-level details of a program, such as what it does when it executes, and gradually works towards understanding the low-level details such as data types, control and data flows and algorithmic patterns in a top-down fashion. An example of a top-down comprehension model is that proposed by Brooks [48]. The key features of Brooks' model are:

- It views the structure of the knowledge being understood as organised into distinct domains linking the problem domain (represented by the functionality of the system) and the programming domain (represented by the program);

- Program comprehension involves reconstructing knowledge about these domains and the relationship between them. The reconstruction process is top-down, involving creation, confirmation and refinement of hypotheses on what a program does and how it works.

The cognitive structure and cognitive process of a mental model resulting from a top-down strategy can be explained in terms of a design metaphor. Software development in its entirety can be considered to be a design task which consists of two fundamental processes - composition and comprehension [220]. **Composition** represents production of a design and **comprehension** is understanding that design. Composition entails mapping what the program does in the problem domain, into a collection of computer instructions of how it works in the programming domain, using a programming language. Figure 6.3 shows examples of knowledge domains that can be encountered during this process and how they are linked.

Comprehension is the reverse of composition. It is a transformation from the programming domain to the problem domain involving the reconstruction of knowledge about these domains (including any intermediate domains) and the relationship between them. The reconstruction process is concerned with the creation, confirmation and successive refinement of hypotheses. It commences with the inception of a vague and general hypothesis, known as the **primary**

hypothesis. This is then confirmed[9] and further refined on acquisition of more information about the system from the program text and other sources such as the system documentation.

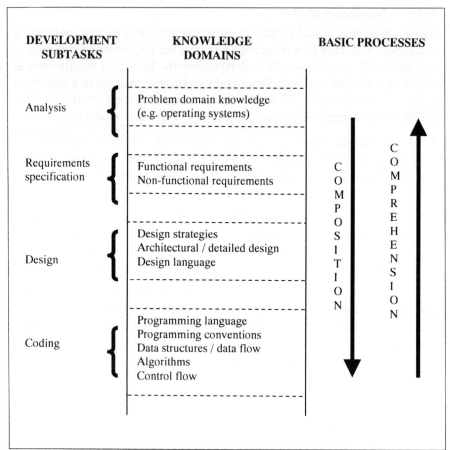

Figure 6.3 Knowledge domains encountered during comprehension

The primary hypothesis is usually generated as soon as the programmer encounters information concerning any aspect of the program, for instance a module name. Thus, the mental model of the program begins to be constructed at the outset, even before the programmer becomes aware of low-level semantic and syntactic details of the program.

---

[9] If the hypothesis is wrong it will be rejected.

The information required for hypothesis generation and refinement is manifested in key features - internal and external to the program - known as **beacons** which serve as typical indicators of the presence of a particular structure or operation [48]. Some examples of beacons are given in Table 6.3. The use of this approach to understand a program is reminiscent of skimming a piece of text to obtain a general, high-level understanding [288], and then rereading the text in detail to gain a deeper understanding.

Table 6.3 Program beacons (adapted from [48], p55)

No	Indicator
	Internal to the program text
1.	Prologue comments, including data and variable dictionaries
2.	Variable, structure, procedure and label names
3.	Declarations or data divisions
4.	Interline comments
5.	Indentation or pretty-printing
6.	Subroutine or module structure
7.	I/O formats, headers, and device or channel assignments
	External to the program
1.	Users' manuals
2.	Program logic manuals
3.	Flowcharts
4.	Cross-reference listings
5.	Published descriptions of algorithms or techniques

6.7.2 Bottom-Up / Chunking Model

Using this strategy, the programmer successively recognises patterns in the program. These are iteratively grouped into high-level, semantically more meaningful structures [18, 219, 250]. The high-level structures are then chunked together into even bigger structures in a repetitive bottom-up fashion until the program is understood. See Figure 6.4 for a diagrammatic representation of the bottom-up model.

The chunking process tends to be faster for more experienced programmers than novices because they recognise patterns more quickly. For example, the following program statements:

```
MaxValue := Table[1];
FOR Index := 2 TO 100 DO
    IF Table [Index] > MaxValue THEN
        MaxValue := Table[Index];
    END;
END;
```

would be grouped by an experienced programmer into a chunk 'find maximum element in array'.

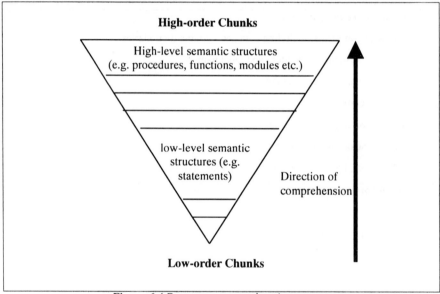

Figure 6.4 Bottom-up comprehension process

The main weaknesses of both the top-down and bottom-up comprehension strategies are:

- failure to take into consideration the contribution that other factors such as the available support tools make to understanding; and
- the fact that the process of understanding a program rarely takes place in such a well-defined fashion as these models portray. On the contrary, programmers tend to take advantage of any clues they come across in an **opportunistic way**.

6.7.3 Opportunistic Model

When using this model the understander makes use of both bottom-up and top-down strategies, although not simultaneously.

> "... the human understander is best viewed as an **opportunistic** processor capable of exploiting both bottom-up and top-down cues as they become available"
>
> Letovsky ([175], pp.69-70) [our emphasis]

According to this model, comprehension hinges on three key and complementary features - a knowledge base, a mental model and an assimilation process:

- *A knowledge base:* This represents the expertise and background knowledge that the maintainer brings to the understanding task.

- *A mental model:* This expresses the programmer's current understanding of the target program.

- *An assimilation process:* This describes the procedure used to obtain information from various sources such as source code and system documentation.

When maintainers need to understand a piece of program, the assimilation process enables them to obtain information about the system. This information then triggers the invocation of appropriate plans[10] from the knowledge base to enable them to form a mental model of the program to be understood. As discussed earlier, the mental model changes continuously as more information is obtained.

6.8 Reading Techniques

Reading techniques are instructions given to the software maintainer on how to read and what to look for in a software product.

Reading is key in both understanding and constructing software. Basili [21] has conducted experiments aimed specifically at increasing our understanding of how to aid the reading process.

---

[10] Plans (or schemas) are knowledge structures representing generic concepts stored in memory [80] and there exist schemas for different problem and programming domains. They have 'slot-types' (equivalent to variables) that can be instantiated with 'slot-fillers' (equivalent to values). An example of a slot-type is a data structure such as a stack, and the slot-filler is any feature in a program which indicates the use of a stack, for instance an operation to 'push' or 'pop' an item.

An issue in developing effective reading techniques, is focussing on the specific context. What is the purpose of this reading exercise? Is it to find errors, or to analyse for specific characteristics? Or is it to allow sufficient understanding to be able to use one element of a system in a different system? Experiments have shown that if the reading technique is focussed on the goal, it is more effective in achieving that goal. On the other hand, the focussed approach needs to be taught and learnt, which implies an overhead, and it also may be slower. Later studies [252] confirm what one would intuitively expect – greater effectiveness comes from suiting the specific method to the particular context.

The motivation to study and understand reading techniques is to develop defined and effective processes that can be taught, rather than relying upon the traditional, *ad hoc* approaches, where effectiveness relies upon the experience of the software maintainer and the *ad hoc*, personalised techniques he or she develops over the years.

Exercise 6.5 List the different types of program understanding strategies and distinguish between them.

Exercise 6.6 Which of these strategies do you use and under what circumstances?

6.9 Factors that Affect Understanding

A number of factors can affect not only the formation of mental models of a program, but also their accuracy, correctness and completeness and hence the ease with which a program can be understood. These factors include: expertise; programming practice and implementation issues; documentation; program organisation and presentation; support tools and evolving requirements. A summary of these factors is given in Figure 6.5.

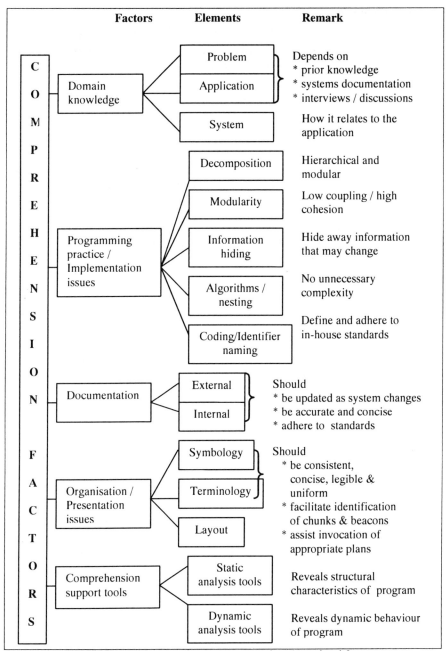

Figure 6.5 Taxonomy of program comprehension-related factors

6.9.1 Expertise

Programmers become experts in a particular application domain or with a particular programming language by virtue of the repertoire of knowledge and skills they acquire from working in the domain or with the language. There is a psychological argument that this expertise has a significant impact on comprehension [99]. Several studies have been undertaken to investigate the effect of expertise on programmers' comprehension and performance in programming tasks [5, 244]. In many of these studies the performance of experts is compared with that of non-experts (or novices). The expert tends to perform better than the novice. A number of explanations for this have been offered. For example, Petre explains that:

> *"Experts differ from novices in both their breadth and their organisation of knowledge: experts store information in larger chunks organised in terms of underlying abstractions. This organisation apparently facilitates quick recognition of problem types and recall of associated solution strategies."*
>
> Petre ([222], p. 107)

In effect, the more experienced a programmer is with an application domain or with a programming language, the easier and quicker it is to understand a program and indeed, the whole software system.

6.9.2 Implementation Issues

There are several implementation issues that can affect the ease and extent to which a maintainer understands a program. The inherent complexity of the original problem being solved by the program is a factor. At the program level, the naming style, comments, level of nesting, clarity, readability, simplicity, decomposition mechanism, information hiding and coding standards can affect comprehension. These have been widely covered elsewhere (for example, [188, 250]). Here, we provide a survey of a few of them – naming style, comments, and decomposition mechanism.

6.9.2.1 Naming Style

Identifiers are symbols that are used in a program to denote the names of entities such as modules, procedures, functions, types, constants and variables. There is a psychological argument that because identifier names indicate the presence of a particular structure or operation, they serve as beacons for comprehension [29]. That is, meaningful identifier names can provide clues that assist programmers to invoke appropriate plans during understanding.

Empirical evidence for the effect of identifier names on understanding, however, seems to be sparse and in some cases results from studies have been inconclusive [247, 250]. For example, in an experimental study carried out to investigate the effect of naming style on comprehension for novices and experts, identifier names were found to affect the comprehension of high-level procedural language programs by novices but not experts [265]. In another study undertaken to investigate the presence of beacons in a sort program, only expert programmers were observed to recall the beacon lines better than the non-beacon lines [289].

There are a number of possible reasons for this. Firstly, some of the variables being tested for significance only affect certain activity components - debugging, enhancement, testing, etc. - and their impact on understanding will be significant only in those situations where these components are important [130]. Secondly, their effect may be neutralised by the 'vocabulary problem' [103].

```
A := FALSE;
WHILE NOT A DO
   IF B.C=B.J THEN
      B.E := B.E+D.F;
      IF G.EOF THEN
         A := TRUE
      ELSE
         ReadBlock (G,D)
      END;
   ELSE
      WriteBlock (H,B);
      ReadBlock (I, B)
   END;
END;
```

Figure 6.6 Non-meaningful identifier names can hinder comprehension

Despite the lack of concrete empirical evidence to support the impact of identifier names on understanding, we can simply by intuition, appreciate the benefits of using meaningful identifier names. For example, the code segment in Figure 6.6 (adapted from [165]) is almost impossible to understand.

When the same program is written using more meaningful identifier names (Figure 6.7), it is easier to see that the program is performing a 'file update'. To minimise the impact of the vocabulary problem, the identifier names should be as informative, concise and unambiguous as possible.

```
EndOfUpdate := FALSE;
WHILE NOT EndOfUpdate DO
   IF UserRec.Id=UserRec.UpdateNumber THEN
      UserRec.Used := UserRec.Used + UpdateRec.ResourcesUsed;
      IF UpdateFile.EOF THEN
         EndOfUpdate := TRUE
      ELSE
         ReadBlock (UpdateFile,UpdateRec)
      END;
   ELSE
      WriteBlock (NewUsersFile,UserRec);
      ReadBlock (UserFile, UserRec)
   END;
END;
```

Figure 6.7 Facilitating comprehension with meaningful identifier names

6.9.2.2 Comments

Program comments within and between modules and procedures usually convey information about the program, such as the functionality, design decisions, assumptions, declarations, algorithms, nature of input and output data, and reminder notes. Considering that the program source code may be the only way of obtaining information about a program, it is important that programmers should accurately record useful information about these facets of the program and update them as the system changes. Common types of comments used are prologue comments and in-line comments. Prologue comments precede a program or module and describe goals. In-line comments, within the program code, describe how these goals are achieved.

The comments provide information that the understander can use to build a mental representation of the target program. For example, in Brooks' top-down model (section 6.7.1), comments - which act as beacons - help the programmer not only to form hypotheses, but to refine them to closer representations of the program. Thus, theoretically there is a strong case for commenting programs. The importance of comments is further strengthened by evidence that the lack of 'good' comments in programs constitutes one of the main problems that programmers encounter when maintaining programs [76].

Although from a theoretical standpoint comments impact upon comprehension, results from empirical studies carried out to investigate the effect of comments on comprehension remain equivocal [261]. Shneiderman [249] carried out a study to investigate the effect of high-level (overall description of program) and low-level (description of individual statements) comments on recall and modification of Fortran programs. The programs with high-level comments were easier to modify. Sheppard *et al* [195] found no such effect on modification of small programs by professional programmers. As with identifier naming, the issue is not that comments do not assist comprehension, but as Sheil explains; these equivocal results may be due to '... both unsophisticated experimental techniques and a shallow view of the nature of programming' [247 p.165]. It has to be pointed out that comments in programs can be useful only if they provide additional information. In other words, it is the quality of the comment that is important, not its presence or absence.

6.9.2.3 Decomposition Mechanism

One of the key factors that affect comprehension of programs is their complexity [73]. One way to deal with this complexity and hence improve comprehensibility depends to some extent on how the entire software system has been decomposed: the strategy used to reduce the system into levels that can be easily handled by the human brain. Modular decomposition and structured programming can be used.

Modular decomposition is a technique for dividing large software systems into manageable components - called modules - that can be easily understood. This is especially important during the design of the system. Modularization should be done around the sources of change: those areas that tend to change during the lifetime of the system. That way, when the change takes place, it is localised to a specific module, thus reducing or eliminating the ripple effect. Psychologists believe that a modular version of a program is a lot easier to comprehend using the 'chunking' process than a non-modular program. There is also empirical evidence to suggest that modularity reduces the time required to effect a change [155].

Structured programming is the approach of using high-level programming languages which aim to reduce the size and complexity of programs to manageable proportions, hence making them more readable and more easily understood.

6.9.3 Documentation

As discussed in the preceding sections, before undertaking any software maintenance work, the maintainer must be able to have access to as much information about the whole system as possible. The system documentation can be very useful in this respect [255, 284], more importantly because it is not always possible to contact the original authors of the system for information about it [26]. This is partly due to the high turnover of staff within the software industry: they may move to other projects or departments, or to a different company altogether. As such, maintainers need to have access to the system documentation to enable them to understand the functionality, design, implementation and other issues that may be relevant for successful maintenance. Sometimes, however, the system documentation is inaccurate, out of date or non-existent. In such cases the maintainers have to resort to documentation internal to the program source code itself - program comments. The subject of documentation is explored in detail in chapter 11.

6.9.4 Organisation and Presentation of Programs

The reading of program source code is increasingly being recognised as an important aspect of maintenance [13, 212], even more so in situations where the program text is the only source of information about a software product. In the light of this, programs should be organised and presented in a manner that will facilitate perusal, browsing, visualisation and ultimately understanding.

Enhanced program presentation can improve understanding by:

- facilitating a clear and correct expression of the mental model of the program and the communication of this model to a reader of the program [13];

- emphasising the control flow the program's hierarchic structure and the programmer's - logical and syntactic - intent underlying the structure; and
- visually enhancing the source code through the use of indentation, spacing, boxing and shading (see Figure 6.8).

A: <u>No blank lines</u>

```
FOR i:=1 TO NumEmployees DO
LowPos:=i
Smallest:=Employees[LowPos].EmployeeAge;
FOR j:=i+1 TO NumEmployees DO
IF Employee[j].EmployeeAge < Smallest THEN
LowPos:=j;
Smallest:=Employee[j].Employee.Age
END (*IF*)
END (* FOR j *)
TempRec:=Employee[LowPos];
Employee[SmallPos]:-Employee[i];
Employee[i]:=TempRec
END (* FOR i *)
```

B: <u>Blank lines / indentation / boxes / shading</u>

```
FOR i:=1 TO NumEmployees DO
LowPos:=i
Smallest:=Employees[LowPos].EmployeeAge;

    FOR j:=i+1 TO NumEmployees DO

        IF Employee[j].EmployeeAge<Smallest THEN
           LowPos:=j;
           Smallest:=Employee[j].Employee.Age
        END (*IF*)

    END (* FOR j *)

    TempRec:=Employee[LowPos];
    Employee[SmallPos]:-Employee[i];
    Employee[i]:=TempRec

END (* FOR i *)
```

Figure 6.8 Blank lines, indentation, boxes and shading to improve program layout

Indentation is used to emphasise the logical or syntactic relation between statements (or groups of statements) in a program, for example the use of indentation to group together statements belonging to a given control structure. There is some experimental evidence that the use of two to four spaces to indent program statements is optimal in enhancing understanding [201].

Spacing, using blank lines and white spaces to separate program segments or comments, can be done manually or automatically. If done manually, it is important that standard in-house procedures for program layout should be drawn up, agreed upon and adhered to by all members of a project team or organisation. **Boxing** and **shading** are employed to highlight the most salient aspects of a program and to indicate relationships between semantic and syntactic components of the program.

In order to reap the benefits of the above layout techniques, there must be consistency in the conventions and rules used. The use of grey scale to shade the program should not affect the legibility of the source text. Automatic program layout tools such as pretty-printers can be used automatically to enforce consistent program layout.

Theoretically, effective organisation and presentation of source code should facilitate the identification of beacons, the invocation of plans and the building of chunks, all of which are central to program understanding. The use of indentation to emphasise the logical structure of a program is an example of a 'structure beacon'. When used in this way, the structure:

- provides clues which programmers use to formulate, confirm and refine hypotheses during understanding (as seen in Brooks' model);

- provides clues that guide programmers in the invocation of suitable plans; and

- promotes the formation of a program chunk. The chunk is then compared with the plans contained in the programmers' knowledge base - a repertoire of programming skills and techniques.

There is also evidence which suggests that well-structured programs take less time to understand [38, 238].

Bearing in mind the significance of program layout in understanding, programs should be organised and presented in a manner that facilitates the formation of mental models.

> *"effective program presentation makes good programs more understandable and bad programs more obvious"*
>
> Baecker & Marcus ([13], p.ix).

6.9.5 Comprehension Support Tools

There are tools which can be used to organise and present source code in a way that makes it more legible, more readable and hence more understandable. These include the 'Book Paradigm' [208, 207], the pretty-printer, the static analyser [108, 295] and the browser.

Many comprehension tools are designed to serve as aids to enable the understander to speed up the understanding process. The output from these tools, however, does not provide explanation of the functionality of the subject system. Here we describe the Book Paradigm and some of its features.

6.9.5.1 Book Paradigm

This tool is based on the 'book metaphor'. It involves documenting source code using publishing features and style traditionally found in books - sentencing, paragraphing, sectioning, pagination, chapter division, prefaces, indexing and a contents page - in a fashion that facilitates comprehension. Figure 6.9 shows an example of the source code book for one of the ACME Health Clinic's medical information systems called Mobile Clinic. Organisation of source code in this way promotes understanding by:

- allowing programmers the freedom to use a variety of strategies and access paths that they would not normally use when reading programs;
- providing high-level organisational clues about the code and low-level organisational chunks and beacons;
- presenting information in a form that a programmer can easily recognise, thus expediting invocation of plans from the programmer's repertoire.

126 Software Maintenance: Concepts and Practice

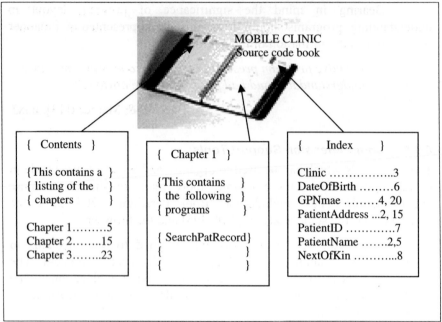

Figure 6.9 **An example of a source code book**

6.9.6 *Evolving Requirements*

It has been known since the early days of the discipline of software engineering that the issue of requirements can be make or break for a software system.

In the early days, requirements were treated as though they were static, but of course, like all elements of a system, they evolve.

For years, we have talked about "capturing requirements", but more recently the language has shifted as the true nature of requirements becomes better appreciated.

Projects large and small have struggled or foundered through problems with requirements - misunderstandings, conflicts, failure to adapt as contexts changed. An estimated 45% of resources goes on system failures. A project, for example, that takes years to bring to fruition, is bound to change as a result of changing requirements. An instructive case to study in this respect is that of the building (eventually!) of the channel rail tunnel linking England and France.

We have all become comfortable with the stages in the evolution of a software system - e.g. requirements, design, implementation, testing, and so on. However, there was truth in the words of Allen Fairbairn (Systems Engineering manager on the channel tunnel link) who said that the true phases of a project are enthusiasm, disillusionment, blame for the innocent and reward for the uninvolved (i.e. the lawyers)[11].

In terms of requirements we need to think in more flexible terms:

- Impact analysis is key, because changing requirements implies the addition, modification and deletion of requirements, which means that we have to introduce change as an integral part of building and maintaining systems.

- Written requirements cannot be treated as though written in stone, just because they have been recorded. They will evolve.

- The evolution of requirements will lead to requirements that conflict. Resolution of conflict will become a part of requirements analysis.

- Requirements have always been an unofficial matter of negotiation. This will need to be recognised more formally.

Vision is perfect with hindsight and we should use this to learn about evolving requirements and how to deal with them. A simple (with hindsight) example is that reactions by the opposition to a new system are a predictable source of changing context and requirements. During the building of the channel tunnel rail link, the "opposition", the ferry operators equipped themselves with better and faster ferries, that could challenge the speed and stability of the railway.

> **Exercise 6.7** Enumerate and explain briefly the factors that can affect your understanding of a program.
>
> **Exercise 6.8** What measures would you take to improve the understandability of the program in Figure 6.10?
>
> **Exercise 6.9** List all the maintenance tools available in your local system. Try out three of these and for each, explain the following: its use, its key features and how it improves understanding.

---

[11] Allen Fairbairn was addressing the December 2001 meeting of the Interdisciplinary Software Engineering Network at The Royal Society.

```
MODULE AddNumbers

FROM BasicIO IMPORT WriteReal, WriteString, WriteLn, ReadInt, WriteInt;
CONST max = 20;
VAR a : ARRAY [1..max] OF INTEGER; number : INTEGER; total : INTEGER;

BEGIN
  WriteString("Type in 20 numbers "); number := 0;
  WHILE number <> 20 DO number := number + 1; ReadInt (a[number]); END;

  WriteString ("The 20 numbers in reverse are "); WriteLn; number := 20;
  REPEAT WriteInt (a[number]),max); WriteLn; number := number – 1
  UNTIL number = 0;

  number := 20 total := 0;
  WHILE  number <> 0 DO total := total + a[number]; DEC (number); END;
  WriteString ("The average for the 20 numbers is ");
  WriteReal (FLOAT (total) / FLOAT (max), 12);

END AddNumbers
```

Figure 6.10 A program to add numbers

6.10 Implications of Comprehension Theories and Studies

There is as yet no empirical evidence as to which of the program understanding strategies discussed is the best. Nonetheless, it is important to be aware of the effect that these strategies or other cognitive issues can have on various critical activities of software maintenance. These closely related activities include: knowledge acquisition and performance; education and training; the designing of programming languages, maintenance tools and documentation standards; and issuing guidelines and making recommendations.

6.10.1 Knowledge Acquisition and Performance

The knowledge that a maintainer requires for modifying a program depends on the nature of the change. For example, with an enhancement that does not impact on other sections of the program, a local view of the program will suffice. On the other hand, if the modification affects other parts of the system, then a global view and the cause-effect relation for the system are needed. The strategy used to study the program can determine both the speed and accuracy with which the required information is obtained and also the ultimate success of the modification.

For example, in a study to investigate the relationship between the comprehension strategy used, the knowledge acquired and the programmers' performance on a modification task, it was observed that the strategy used determined the knowledge acquired and also affected performance on a modification task [180]. The subjects who used a systematic strategy (similar to the opportunistic) were successful in making modifications because they gathered knowledge about the cause-effect relation of the system's functional units. However, the subjects who used the as-needed strategy (similar to bottom-up) failed to do the same because they did not obtain the cause-effect relation.

6.10.2 Education and Training

Maintainers need to be taught about program understanding. If they are aware of the different approaches and the effect of each on understanding, it is conjectured that they would be in a better position to judge which is the most suitable one for a given task and environment. They can also reflect on the appropriateness of the strategy that they usually use. The maintainers should, however, be allowed to work with the strategies with which they feel comfortable if they so wish.

6.10.3 Design Principles

Comprehension hinges on the ability to form an accurate mental model of the target program. This being the case, a sound understanding of how a programmer goes about comprehending a program can provide useful insights. Lessons can be learnt about appropriate principles for designing programs, programming languages, documentation standards and support tools that facilitate the formation of mental models. Tools developed to support comprehension should make provision for top-down, bottom-up and opportunistic models, but without imposing any of them on maintainers.

6.10.4 Guidelines and Recommendations

Results from empirical studies provide a basis for software maintainers to set guidelines for programming and documentation practices. For example, based on the psychological argument and empirical evidence that a modular program is better suited to maintainers' cognitive structures and cognitive processes than a non-modular program [155], organisations and their personnel should be more willing to take the guidelines seriously. Empirical evidence can also be deployed as a basis for recommendations in areas such as documentation standards [175] and choice of techniques, methods and tools.

> **Exercise 6.10** Why is it important for maintainers to obtain a good understanding of the various program comprehension strategies and other cognitive issues?

6.11 Summary

The key points that have been covered in this chapter are:

- The process of understanding software products in general and programs in particular is at the heart of virtually all maintenance activities and it accounts for over half of the time and effort spent on effecting change.

- Program comprehension involves abstracting information about certain aspects of the software system.

- The information needs of maintenance personnel vary with their responsibilities.

- During comprehension of a system, the understander forms an internal representation, which serves as a working model of the system. At the outset, the model may be incomplete but becomes more complete and more accurate as additional information about the system is obtained.

- Three principal strategies for program comprehension are top-down, bottom-up and opportunistic.

- Factors that impinge on program comprehension include: (i) language expertise and domain knowledge of the maintenance personnel; (ii) programming practice and implementation issues; (iii) availability of documentation; (iv) organisation and presentation of programs; (v) inherent complexity of the original problem; and (vi) programming environment and availability of automated tools.

- Suitable expertise and experience in the problem and programming domains, consistency of style, adherence to local coding and documentation standards, up-to-date and accurate systems and internal program documentation, good program presentation and good support tools are necessary to enhance understanding and thereby facilitate maintenance work.

The underlying objective in trying to enhance our understanding of the cognitive requirements and processes of maintainers is to improve performance on maintenance jobs, thereby paving the way for higher productivity and successful evolution of software products. These ideals, no matter how useful and desirable they may be, will not be realised without the availability of suitable techniques. The following chapters examine a number of currently available techniques that are used to support software change.

7

Reverse Engineering

"If you don't know where you are, you can't be sure you're not travelling in circles"

Pickard & Carter ([223], p A-36)

This chapter aims to

1. Discuss reverse engineering, forward engineering, reengineering and restructuring.
2. Explain the concepts of redocumentation and design recovery.
3. Describe the purpose, objectives and benefits of the above techniques with respect to effecting software change.
4. Discuss reverse engineering tools and identify some of their limitations.
5. Discuss the application of reverse engineering techniques to maintenance problems.
6. Discuss the weaknesses associated with the techniques covered in this chapter.

7.1 Introduction

As shown in the previous chapter, understanding a software system precedes any type of change. The comprehension process takes up a great deal of the total time spent on carrying out the change. The reasons for this include incorrect, out-of-date or non-existent documentation, the complexity of the system and a lack of sufficient domain knowledge on the part of the maintainer. One way to alleviate these problems is to abstract from the source code relevant information about the system, such as the specification and design, in a form that promotes understanding.

Reverse engineering is a technique that can be used to do this. Reverse engineering alone does not lead to a change in the program; it simply paves the way for easier implementation of the desired changes. Changes are implemented using techniques such as forward engineering, restructuring, and reengineering. The issues underpinning these techniques form the theme of this chapter.

7.2 Definitions

Abstraction – a "model that summarises the detail of the subject it is representing" [72 p.201].

Forward engineering – the traditional software engineering approach starting with requirements analysis and progressing to implementation of a system.

Reengineering – the process of examination and alteration whereby a system is altered by first reverse engineering and then forward engineering.

Restructuring – the transformation of a system from one representational form to another.

Reverse engineering – the process of analysing a subject system to:
- identify the system's components and their interrelationships and
- create representations of the system in another form or at higher levels of abstraction. [60 p.15]

7.3 Abstraction

Abstraction is achieved by highlighting the important features of the subject system and ignoring the irrelevant ones. There are three types of abstraction that can be performed on software systems: function, data and process abstraction.

7.3.1 Function Abstraction

This is also known as procedural abstraction and means eliciting functions from the target system - those aspects which operate on data objects and produce the corresponding output. Functions are usually described using verbs such as **add, check, pop**, etc. Functions are often characterised by an input-output relation; a function f takes x as input and produces $f(x)$ as output. During the abstraction process, we are interested in what the function does and not how it operates.

7.3.2 Data Abstraction

This means eliciting from the target system data objects as well as the functions that operate on them. The main focus here is on the data objects. The implementation details are considered irrelevant. A typical example of data abstraction is the production of an abstract data type for a stack with operations **CreateStack, Push, IsEmptyStack** and **Pop**. An example of data abstraction at the design level in object-oriented systems is the encapsulation of an object type and its associated operations in a module or class. Procedural languages such as Ada and Modula-2 offer the package and module respectively. These separate the definition of entities from their implementation which enables the programmer to separate the specification of data types from the details of the operations carried out on them. Data and function abstraction can take place at different levels depending on the phase of the life-cycle.

7.3.3 Process Abstraction

This is the abstracting from the target system of the exact order in which operations are performed. There are two classes of process that can be abstracted: concurrent and distributed processes. **Concurrent** processes communicate via shared data that is stored in a designated memory space. **Distributed** processes usually communicate through 'message-passing' and have no shared data area. A detailed discussion of this form of abstraction is outside the scope of this book (see [283] for further discussion).

7.4 Purpose and Objectives of Reverse Engineering

The concept of reverse engineering is borrowed from established engineering disciplines such as manufacturing. It is popular within the domain of software engineering in general and software maintenance in particular, especially for its potential in helping program understanding.

A system's components are the products from different phases of the software life-cycle, for example the requirements specification, the architectural and detailed design, and the actual source code [255]. Although reverse engineering can start from any of these products, the most common starting point is the program source code, primarily because after several years of evolution, the specification or design information for the system may be inaccurate or not be available. This is usually because previous maintenance tasks have been inadequately documented. Accordingly, unless otherwise stated, it should be assumed that reverse engineering starts from the source code.

The goal of reverse engineering is to facilitate change by allowing a software system to be understood in terms of what it does, how it works and its architectural representation. The objectives in pursuit of this goal are to recover lost information, to facilitate migration between platforms, to improve and/or provide new documentation, to extract reusable components, to reduce maintenance effort, to cope with complexity, to detect side effects, to assist migration to a CASE environment [72, 101], and to develop similar or competitive products [241]. A summary of these objectives is contained in Table 7.1.

- *To recover lost information:* With time, a system undergoes a series of changes. Because of such things as management pressure and time constraints, the corresponding documentation for the requirements specification and design may not be kept up to date and may not even exist. This makes the code the only source of information about the system. Reverse engineering tools allow this information (requirements specification and design) to be recovered. For example, reverse engineering has been used to capture the specification and design of Cobol application programs [158]. The recovered specification would be in a specification language such as Z, and the design represented as data flow diagrams, control flow diagrams, and entity-relationship diagrams.

- *To facilitate migration between platforms:* In order to take advantage of a new software platform. (for example, a CASE environment [110]) or hardware platform (for example, a parallel architecture [52, 64]) a combination of reverse and forward engineering can be used.

The specification and design are abstracted using reverse engineering tools. Forward engineering is then applied to the specification according to the standards of the new platform. An example is the migration of Fortran programs to new parallel environments using the toolset *pRETS* [124].

- *To improve or provide documentation:* As previously mentioned, one of the major problems with legacy systems is insufficient, out-of-date or non-existent documentation. During redocumentation, tools can be used to augment inadequate documentation or to provide new.

- *To provide alternative views:* Redocumentation tools can be used to provide alternative documentation such as data flow diagrams, control flow diagrams and entity-relationship diagrams in addition to the existing documentation. This is a means whereby other views of the system can be obtained. For example, data flow diagrams portray the system from the point of view of data flow within the system and outside. Control flow diagrams, on the other hand, show the system from the perspective of the flow of control between the different components.

- *To extract reusable components:* Based on the premise that the use of existing program components can lead to an increase in productivity and improvement in product quality [29], the concept of reuse has increasingly become popular amongst software engineers. Success in reusing components depends in part on their availability. Reverse engineering tools and methods offer the opportunity to access and extract program components. Software reuse is discussed in the next chapter.

- *To cope with complexity:* One of the major problems with legacy systems is that as they evolve, their complexity increases. In the event of a modification, this complexity must be dealt with by abstracting system information relevant to the change and ignoring that which is irrelevant. Reverse engineering tools together with CASE tools provide the maintainer with some form of automated support for both function and data abstractions.

- *To detect side effects:* In cases where the maintainer lacks a global view of the system, ripple effects are a common result of change. That is, undesired side effects are caused and anomalies go unnoticed. Reverse engineering tools can make the general architecture of the system visible, thereby making it easier to predict the effect of change and detect logic and data flow problems.

- *To reduce maintenance effort:* This has been one of the main driving forces behind the increasing interest in reverse engineering. A large percentage of the total time required to make a change [69, 214] goes into understanding programs. The two main reasons for this are lack of appropriate documentation and insufficient domain knowledge [202]. Reverse engineering has the potential to alleviate these problems and thus reduce maintenance effort because it provides a means of obtaining the missing information.

Table 7.1 Summary of objectives and benefits of reverse engineering

Objectives	Benefits
1. To recover lost information	1. Maintenance
2. To facilitate migration between platforms	(a) enhances understanding, which assists identification of errors
3. To improve and/or provide documentation	(b) facilitates identification and extraction of components affected by adaptive and perfective changes
4. To provide alternative views	
5. To extract reusable components	(c) provides documentation or alternative views of the system
6. To cope with complexity	
7. To detect side effects	2. Reuse: Supports identification and extraction of reusable components
8. To reduce maintenance effort	
	3. Improved quality of system

7.5 Levels of Reverse Engineering

Reverse engineering involves performing one or more of the above types of abstraction, in a bottom-up and incremental manner [239]. It entails detecting low-level implementation constructs and replacing them with their high-level counterparts. The process eventually results in an incremental formation of an overall architecture of the program. It should, nonetheless, be noted that the product of a reverse engineering process does not necessarily have to be at a higher level of abstraction. If it is at the same level as the original system, the operation is commonly known as 'redocumentation' [60]. If on the other hand, the resulting product is at a higher level of abstraction, the operation is known as 'design recovery' [29, 60] or 'specification recovery' (Figure 7.1).

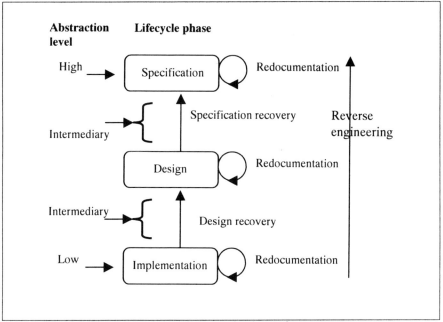

Figure 7.1 **Levels of abstraction in a software system**

7.5.1 Redocumentation

Redocumentation is the recreation of a semantically equivalent representation within the same relative abstraction level [60]. The goals of this process are threefold [159]. Firstly, to create alternative views of the system so as to enhance understanding, for example the generation of a hierarchical data flow [24] or control flow diagram (for example, Figure 7.2) from source code. Secondly, to improve current documentation. Ideally, such documentation should have been produced during the development of the system and updated as the system changed. This, unfortunately, is not usually the case. Thirdly, to generate documentation for a newly modified program. This is aimed at facilitating future maintenance work on the system – preventive maintenance.

140 Software Maintenance: Concepts and Practice

```
PROCEDURE CommandSelector;

BEGIN
        Statement 1;
        IF <boolean expression 1> THEN
                Statement sequence 1
        ELSIF <boolean expression 2> THEN
                Statement sequence 2
        ELSE
                Statement sequence 3
        END {IF}
        Statement 2;
END Command Selector;
```

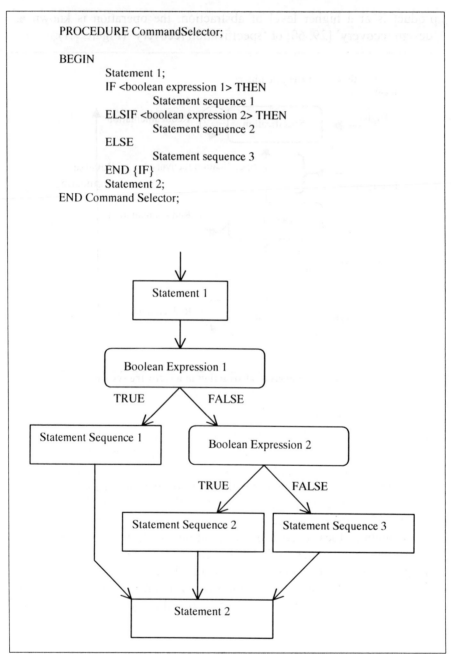

Figure 7.2 A program and its corresponding control flow diagram

7.5.2 Design Recovery

Design recovery entails identifying and extracting meaningful higher-level abstractions beyond those obtained directly from examination of the source code [60]. This may be achieved from a combination of code, existing design documentation, personal experience, and knowledge of the problem and application domains [29]. The recovered design - which is not necessarily the original design - can then be used for redeveloping the system. In other words, the resulting design forms a baseline for future system modifications [110]. The design could also be used to develop similar but non-identical applications. For example, after recovering the design of a spelling checker application, it can used in the design of a spell checking module in a new word processing package.

Different approaches, which vary in their focus, can be used to recover these designs. Some draw heavily on programming language constructs contained in the program text as seen in the model by Rugaber et al. [239]. They argue that an important aspect of design recovery is being able to recognise, understand and represent design decisions present in a given source code. Program constructs, which vary between programming languages, enable recognition of design decisions. Examples of such constructs are control and data structures, variables, procedures and functions, definition and implementation modules, and class hierarchies.

Other approaches rely on knowledge about the problem and application domains. An example here is the use of 'automated cliché recognition' offered by The Programmer's Apprentice [235]. Clichés are standard problem solving techniques, such as searching and sorting, that can easily be identified by inspection. This assumes that an experienced programmer can reconstruct the design of a program by recognising the clichés used. This is based on the premise that success in recovering design relies more heavily on knowledge about the domain than knowledge about general and widely applicable components such as sorts and searches [29].

A number of models for recovering design have been proposed [7, 29]. Choi and Scacchi propose an approach to extract and restructure the design of large systems, where the term 'large systems' refers to those systems with intermodular relations.

7.5.3 Specification Recovery

In some situations reverse engineering that only leads to the recovery of the design of the system may not be of much use to an organisation or a software engineer. A typical example is where there is a paradigm shift and the design of the new paradigm has little or nothing in common with the design of the original paradigm, for instance moving from structured programming to object-oriented programming. In this case, an appropriate approach is to obtain the original specification of the system through **specification recovery**. This involves identifying, abstracting and representing meaningful higher levels of abstractions beyond those obtained simply by inspecting the design or source code of the software system. During this process, the specification can be derived directly from the source code or from existing design representations through backward transformations. Information obtained from other sources such as system and design documentation, previous experience, and problem and application domain knowledge can greatly facilitate the recovery process.

Ideally the recovered specification should be represented in a form that can be reimplemented easily in another programming language or paradigm. An example of such forms is a mathematical function in a language such as Z^{++}. Usually such representations preserve the precise semantics of the source code (see Lano and Haughton [159] for some useful examples). The specification recovered can also be represented as 'object classes' [205, 296]. Object class representation is particularly useful when reverse engineering is performed with the intent of migrating the current system to an object-oriented platform. In this case the system is represented as a set of objects and operations (a detailed treatment of the object-oriented paradigm and case studies is given in chapter 13).

The specification recovered during reverse engineering can be put to a number of uses. Firstly, a fairly representative specification of a system can be used to support software maintenance without necessarily requiring access to the source code. Secondly, the specification assists the maintainer in acquiring the appropriate level of understanding required to effect a change to a software system. And thirdly, if the specification is suitably represented it can be used in the development or maintenance of similar software systems. The use of a specification in this way can sometimes have more benefits than a similar use of source code [202].

7.5.4 Conditions for Reverse Engineering

There are no hard and fast rules as to what criteria a program must fulfil before it may usefully be subject to reverse engineering. There are, however, some features (see, for example, [45, 101, 281]) which may serve as warning signs or indicators. The motives for reverse engineering are usually commercial [241]. A summary of these indicators is given in Table 7.2.

Table 7.2 Factors that motivate the application of reverse engineering

Indicator	Motivation
1. Missing or incomplete design/specification	Product / environment related
2. Out-of-date, incorrect or missing documentation	
3. Increased program complexity	
4. Poorly structured source code	
5. Need to translate programs into a different programming language	
6. Need to make compatible products	
7. Need to migrate between different software or hardware platforms	
8. Static or increasing bug backlog	Maintenance process related
9. Decreasing personnel productivity	
10. Need for continuous and excessive corrective change	
11. Need to extend economic life of system	
12. Need to make similar but non-identical product	Commercially related

Reverse engineering in itself does not directly lead to modification of a system. It simply enables an understanding of a system by representing it at an equivalent or higher abstraction level. The desired change can then be effected by one or more of the following supporting techniques.

7.6 Supporting Techniques

The understanding obtained through reverse engineering can support the implementation of change through techniques such as forward engineering, restructuring, and reengineering. This section considers these techniques. Some examples will be used to highlight their significance in improving the maintainability of programs.

7.6.1 Forward Engineering

Forward engineering, as the term suggests, is the opposite of reverse engineering. It refers to the traditional software development approach - proceeding from requirements to detailed implementation via the design of the system. Forward engineering will not be covered in this chapter as it has been covered extensively elsewhere (see publications such as [229, 255, 274]).

7.6.2 Restructuring

This involves transforming a system from one representational form to another at the same relative level of abstraction without a change in its functionality or semantics [60]. The transformation would usually be to a more desirable format. This activity is based on the premise that after a string of modifications, the structure of programs tends to degrade.

> *"The addition of any function not visualized in the original design will inevitably degenerate structure. Repairs, also, will tend to cause deviation from structural regularity since, except under conditions of the strictest control any repair or patch will be made in the simplest and quickest way. No search will be made for a fix that maintains structural integrity."*
>
> Lehman & Belady ([23], p.113)

As the degeneration continues, the programs become more complex and difficult to understand. To control this increase in complexity, the source code needs to be restructured. Seen in this light, restructuring is a form of preventive maintenance aimed at improving the physical state of the target system in conformance with a given standard [60]. There are various types of restructuring which differ in the part of the system affected and the manner in which this is done.

1. *Control-flow-driven restructuring:* This involves the imposition of a clear control structure within the source code [61] and can be either intermodular or intramodular in nature. Choi and Scacchi term these 'restructuring in the small' and 'restructuring in the large' respectively [61]. An example of restructuring in the small is restructuring a 'spaghetti-like' module's code so as to comply with structured programming concepts. An example of restructuring in the large is regrouping physically distant routines - located in different modules - so as to give the system a more

coherent structure. This is particularly useful in cases where some old compilers forced conceptually close routines to be physically far apart - due to memory considerations - thus making it difficult to understand the functionality of the code.

2. *Efficiency-driven restructuring:* This involves restructuring a function or algorithm to make it more efficient. A simple example of this form of restructuring is the replacement of an IF-THEN-ELSIF-ELSE construct with a CASE construct (Figure 7.3). With the CASE statement, only one Boolean is evaluated, whereas with the IF-THEN-ELSIF-ELSE construct, more than one of the Boolean expressions may need to be tested during execution thereby making it less efficient. Note however, that for this particular example, an optimising compiler would do this restructuring automatically.

```
IF ExamScore >= 75 THEN              CASE ExamScore OF
   Grade := 'A'                         75..100 : Grade := 'A'
ELSIF ExamScore >= 60 THEN              60..74 : Grade := 'B'
   Grade := 'B'                         50..59 : Grade := 'C'
ELSIF ExamScore >= 50 THEN              40..49 : Grade := 'D'
   Grade := 'C'                      ELSE
ELSIF ExamScore >= 40 THEN              Grade := 'F'
   Grade := 'D'                      ENDCASE
ELSE
   Grade := 'F'
ENDIF
```

Figure 7.3 Restructuring a program to improve efficiency

3. *Adaption-driven restructuring:* This involves changing the coding style in order to adapt the program to a new programming language or new operating environment, for instance changing an imperative program in Pascal into a functional program in Lisp. Another example is the transformation of program functions in a sequential environment to an equivalent but totally different form of processing in a parallel environment [52, 116, 124].

In addition to the source code, other representations of a software system can be restructured. These include requirements specifications, data models and design plans. Although it is difficult to automate the restructuring process completely, there exist some automatic restructuring tools [115].

7.6.3 Reengineering

This is the process of examining and altering a target system to implement a desired modification. Reengineering consists of two steps. Firstly, reverse engineering is applied to the target system so as to understand it and represent it in a new form [60]. Secondly, forward engineering is applied, implementing and integrating any new requirements, thereby giving rise to a new and enhanced system.

These two steps can be further broken down as, for example, in the 8-layer Source Code Reengineering Model (SCORE/RM) proposed by Colbrook *et al.* [64]. This model supports retrospective abstraction of data from source code. The first five layers - encapsulation, transformation, normalisation, interpretation and abstraction - constitute reverse engineering. The remaining three layers - causation, regeneration and certification make up forward engineering. The authors argue that the model has a number of applications. Firstly, it provides a mechanism which enables the maintainer to work through the code and understand its purpose, produce documentation and modify the code in a way that enhances its maintainability. Secondly, it supports retrospective specification of a system from the available source code.

7.7 Benefits

The successful achievement of these objectives translates into a number of benefits in the areas of maintenance and software quality assurance. The output of reverse engineering can also be beneficial to software reuse – reapplication of existing software code or design [102].

7.7.1 Maintenance

Generally, the ability to use reverse engineering tools to recapture design history and provide documentation facilitates understanding of a system [159]. Considering the time devoted to program understanding, reverse engineering tools offer real scope for reducing maintenance costs. For example, data collected from a study of the effect of reengineering upon software maintainability indicated that reengineering can decrease complexity and increase maintainability [254]. The basic understanding gained through reverse engineering can benefit maintenance activities in various ways:

- *Corrective change:* The abstraction of unnecessary detail gives greater insight into the parts of the program to be corrected. This makes it easier to identify defective program components and the source of residual errors. The availability of cross-reference tables, structure charts, data flow and control flow diagrams resulting from reverse engineering - can assist in tracing and identifying the variables to be changed as well as the areas likely to be affected by the change.

- *Adaptive/perfective change:* The broad picture made available by reverse engineering eases the process of understanding the major components of the system and their interrelationships, thereby showing where new requirements fit and how they relate to existing components. Extracted specification and design information can be used during enhancement of the system or for the development of another product.

- *Preventive change:* Reverse engineering has been recognised as being of specific benefit to future maintenance of a system:

  "... the greatest benefits of reverse engineering tools can be realised after the changes are implemented in any of the categories of maintenance... These include the automatic regeneration of numerous graphical representations of the software to assist future maintenance."

  Cross *et al* ([72], p.264)

7.7.2 Software Reuse

In general terms, software reuse refers to the application of knowledge about a software system - usually the source and object code - to develop or maintain other software systems. The software components that result from a reverse engineering process can be reused. Quite often these components need to be modified in one way or another before they can be reused. The issue of reuse is dealt with in the next chapter.

7.7.3 Reverse Engineering and Associated Techniques in Practice

Reverse engineering and associated techniques such as reengineering and restructuring have had practical applications within different sectors of the computing industry [282]. The techniques described in this chapter have been used successfully in a number of organisations for very large and complex software systems [3, 185, 205, 296, 278]. The following case study in which reverse engineering was successfully employed is the reengineering of a large inventory of US Department of Defense information systems [3]. Other cases in which the techniques described in this chapter played a pivotal role are described in chapter 13.

7.8 Case Study: US Department of Defense Inventory

The US Department of Defense (DoD) is involved with the maintenance of a large inventory of heterogeneous, non-combat information systems at more than 1700 data centres totalling over 1.4 billion lines of code [185]. There are two key problems that the DoD faces in connection with these systems. Firstly, their operation consumes an enormous part of the department's budget - more than $9 billion each year. And secondly, due to lack of standardised data and data structures across these systems, the DoD is often unable to obtain correct information from the data available in the existing databases. For example, issuing the same query to several payroll systems can produce different kinds of responses that are sometimes impossible to reconcile.

As a result of these problems, there was a need to integrate the different computer systems used by the DoD. This led to a project known as Joint Operations Planning and Execution Systems (JOPES) with special emphasis on the data requirements of the systems, that is, 'reverse engineering data requirements'. Some of the main activities of this project were:

- the extraction of business rules and data entities from the software systems and data structures;
- derivation and management data models of the systems;
- configuration management of the different systems.

Due to the bulky nature of the data structures and associated code, a divide-and-conquer approach was used to extract the business rules and data entities embedded in them before these were organised in categories. The approach was top-down followed by bottom-up. During the top-down phase, draft versions of high-level 'as-is' business process and data models were derived from analysis of user screens, reports and policy statements. The draft data model consisted of a draft 'as-is' business model and a draft mixed - physical, conceptual and external - 'as-is' schema. Reverse engineering and data dependency analysis tools were then applied to these models as well as software, data dictionary and data files. The schema levels of the draft data model were then separated, validated and inconsistencies resolved. The latter was repeated until the data was normalised.

Apart from the logical data models and data elements, some other deliverables from this project were: high-level model view decomposition hierarchies; traceability matrix (which could be used to perform impact analysis in the event of a change); system and data migration plans (directives on how to facilitate future expansion and migration of the existing system); reusable software requirements; DoD standard data model; DoD standard data elements; and an integrated enterprise database.

Some of the lessons learned from this project were:

- Getting the commitment and authorisation of senior management, though not easy, was critical to the success of the project.
- The discovery and recovery of data requirements embedded in the systems required a great deal of analysis undertaken by humans with the support of commercial and customised software tools.
- It was difficult to estimate the cost of the reengineering effort. This was partly due to the unstructured nature of one of the systems being reengineered.
- A single reverse engineering CASE tool was insufficient to support all the reverse engineering activities involved in the project. It also came to light that many of the tools focused on code analysis with little or no support for extraction of business rules.
- Integration, modernisation, restructuring and/or augmentation of the existing information infrastructure appeared to be the current ways of dealing with information integration problems.

7.9 Current Problems

As discussed in the preceding sections, reverse engineering promises to be particularly useful in addressing the problems of understanding legacy systems. There are, however, a number of problem areas that still need to be addressed. These stem primarily from the difficulty of extracting high-level descriptions of a system from its source code alone [40].

- *The automation problem:* It is not yet feasible to automate fully at a very high level. Technology is not yet mature enough to provide the level of automation that software engineers would like. Complete automation may never be feasible because the process of understanding a system - in which reverse engineering plays a part - requires the use of domain-specific information. This may always be reliant upon domain experts. Biggerstaff notes that "the degree of automation is unlikely to go beyond the notion of an assistant that can perform wide-ranging searches and suggest domain-based recovery strategies to the software engineer" [29 p.38].

- *The naming problem:* Even if it were possible to automate the extraction of high-level descriptions from source code, naming would still pose a problem. Take as an example the source code for a binary sort algorithm. Extracting the specification is one thing, but automatically naming it (with a meaningful name such as BinarySort as opposed to the less meaningful identifier, p3, say) is quite another. Boldyreff and Zhang [40] have done some work to address this problem. Their approach, called the transformational approach, involves functional decomposition of the program. Code segments are transformed into recursive procedures. The programmer then names and comments each procedure interactively. A collection of these comments then forms a higher-level abstraction of the program.

Exercise 7.1 Explain the differences between the different types of reverse engineering techniques and give examples where appropriate.

Exercise 7.2 Carry out specification and design recovery on all or parts of a software system that you are not familiar with (the system should be at least 2K lines of code in length).

- What technique(s) do you use to identify the specification and design and why?

- What form of representation do you consider suitable for these tasks? Indicate your reasons.

- What lessons did you learn from this work?

Exercise 7.3 A bank has a substantial investment in a Cobol software system that is at least one million lines of code in length and has been running for over 20 years. It is used on a daily basis to perform various operations such as managing customer accounts and loans. After several years of modification - both planned and *ad hoc* - the system has become too expensive to maintain. As a result, the bank wants some advice on the next step to take. Suppose that you have been employed as a software maintenance consultant. What advice would you give the bank? Indicate the reasons for any recommendations you make.

7.10 Summary

The key points that have been covered in this chapter are:

- Reverse engineering is a technique used to obtain an overview understanding of a program prior to its being changed. Forward engineering, restructuring and reengineering are techniques which may be employed subsequently to implement a desired modification.

- Redocumentation and design recovery are two forms of reverse engineering. Redocumentation is the representation of a program in a semantically equivalent form but at the same relative level of abstraction. Design recovery is the extraction of higher-level abstractions of the program.

- The objectives of reverse engineering include: the recovery of lost information; easing the migration between platforms; providing new or alternative documentation; extracting reusable components; coping with complexity; and detecting side effects.

- Achievement of these objectives can bring about benefits such as reduction in maintenance effort, provision of reusable components and enhancement of software quality.

- Automation of reverse engineering processes can expedite maintenance, but complete automation is not yet possible.

- Although reverse engineering-related techniques promise to help maintenance problems, the lack of automation prevents their full potential being realised.

As already pointed out in this chapter, techniques such as forward engineering, restructuring and reengineering can be used to effect changes to a software system. It is, however, important to note that in the process of implementing these changes, every attempt must be made to increase productivity, and to improve the maintainability and quality of the software system. One way of achieving these objectives is to use existing software components, a process known as software reuse, and this is the subject of the next chapter.

8

Reuse and Reusability

"In an era of competitive software marketing, if a program is good enough to be of interest to many people, it is good enough to be marketed commercially for a profit. Does this mean that the only kind of software being donated to public repositories is software of limited use to others, and therefore not worth reusing?"

Aharonian [2]

This chapter aims to

1. Discuss the concepts of software reuse and reusability.

2. Explain the goals and benefits of employing reusable software components during software maintenance.

3. Discuss the technical and non technical issues underpinning software reuse and reusability.

4. Explore ways of maximising the potential of software reuse.

5. Discuss the use of appropriate techniques to design and construct solutions given a change request and a set of reusable components.

6. Explain weaknesses of current reuse techniques and possible ways of addressing these weaknesses.

8.1 Introduction

The problems of low productivity and poor software quality are still commonplace within the software industry [134]. This is true of software maintenance projects in particular despite an increase in expenditure on software maintenance activities and the availability of more sophisticated methodologies, techniques and tools. One way to minimise the effects of these problems is to use previously developed software, rather than 're-inventing the wheel' by writing all the code from scratch. This is the concept of **software reuse** [31, 43, 133, 150].

Productivity can be increased by software reuse because less time and effort is required to specify, design, implement and test the new system. The quality of the new product tends to be higher, primarily because the reused components will have already been through cycles of rigorous testing. Reuse results in a more reliable, more robust and higher quality product. The telling observation has been made that 60-85% of programs used to build systems already exist and can be standardised and reused [157, 148]. It must be stressed that benefits come from the reuse of good software components - that is, components that have been well engineered, rigorously tested and are demonstrably secure and reliable. The reuse of badly engineered, insecure and unreliable components will give no benefit.

Software reuse, though initially targeted at software development projects, is more and more being applied to maintenance problems. It has been reported that software reuse can bring about a significant reduction in maintenance costs [242] and an increase in productivity of maintenance personnel [157]. In order to reap the benefits of software reuse, it is important that the software has been designed to be reused. This is still not the norm although there are moves in this direction. Thus, there is often a need to adapt the software prior to its being reused. This chapter discusses the issues concerned with the concept and practice of software reuse as it pertains to software maintenance.

8.2 Definitions

Data – factual information such as measurements used as a basis for calculation, discussion, or reasoning.

Personnel – the individuals involved in a software project.

Product – a "concrete documentation or artefact created during a software project" ([15], p.3).

Program –- code components, at the source and object code level, such as modules, packages, procedures, functions, routines, etc. Also commercial packages such as spreadsheets and databases.

Reuse – "the reapplication of a variety of kinds of knowledge about one system to another similar system in order to reduce the effort of development or maintenance of that other system" [31 p.xv]

8.3 The Targets for Reuse

A number of different definitions of software reuse exist in the literature [31, 88, 133, 150]. There is the simplistic view which defines the term as the simple reuse of code. This fails to take into consideration other forms of software-related knowledge that can be reused. Both knowledge and program artefacts can be reused. The extent to which items such as procedures, modules and packages can be reused (with or without adaptation) is known as reusability [133]. Some of the attributes that are used to assess reusability are structure, functionality, level of testing, complexity and frequency of reuse. The knowledge that can be reused comes from three main sources: the process, the personnel and the product [20, 15, 267].

8.3.1 Process

Process reuse may be the application of a given methodology to different problems. The application of methodologies such as formal methods, or object-oriented design in the development of different products is an example of process reuse. Another example of reusing a process is the use of a cost estimation model - such as Boehm's COCOMO II [37] model - when estimating the cost of a maintenance project. There is a growing body of empirical evidence demonstrating the extent to which the reuse of a process impacts on productivity and product quality. In general terms, an operation which is repeated becomes familiar and thus easier to perform; problems are discovered and addressed and thus the benefit from repetition tends to increase.

8.3.2 Personnel

The reuse of personnel implies reusing the knowledge that they acquire in a previous similar problem or application area. This expertise is known as domain knowledge. An example of this is 'lesson learned' knowledge – the knowledge acquired through meeting and addressing a particular situation in practice. This is notoriously difficult to teach as theory. Owing to the difficulty in archiving this kind of knowledge and the turnover of personnel within the software industry; reusable personnel knowledge is volatile. As such, it cannot be considered a fixed asset of the host organisation. The expertise gained in one project is often taken away to other projects or to a different organisation [108]. Ways to minimise the effect of this problem are through the application of domain analysis to capture this knowledge in a reusable form (see chapter 6) or through measures to combat high staff turnover (see chapter 10) or tools such as software experience bases (see chapter 5).

8.3.3 Product

Product reuse involves using artefacts that were the products arising from similar projects. Examples include the reuse of data, designs and programs.

8.3.4 Data

Reusable data enables data sharing between applications and also promotes widespread program reusability. Reusable data plays an important role in database systems. For different applications to share the data held in these databases, the data needs to be in a format that facilitates data transfer between applications. Although there is still no universal format for data interchange, it is becoming ever more common for different applications to share data. An example of data that needs to be reusable is patient data in medical information systems, primarily because different individuals are often involved in the care of a patient - the family doctor, the hospital consultant, the pathology laboratory, etc. All these health professionals may have different application programs, but nonetheless require access to the same data.

8.3.4.1 Design

The second reusable aspect of a software product is its design - architectural and detailed design. The architectural design is an abstract or diagrammatic representation of the main components of the software system, usually a collection of modules. The detailed design is a refinement of the architectural design. Reuse of architectural design has a greater payoff than reuse of detailed design [202].

The design of a system can be represented in many ways, for example using context diagrams, data flow diagrams, entity-relationship diagrams, state transition diagrams and object models. The redeployment of pre-existing designs during the development of similar products can increase productivity and improve product quality. Despite this potential, there is little evidence of widespread design reuse, characterised by the general lack of any form of standard software design catalogue. One exception is in the area of compiler construction. Compilers are usually developed from fairly well-known and documented components such as lexical analysers, parsers, symbol tables and code generators. This is still a long way from established areas, such as the automobile industry or home construction where the design of existing products is routinely reused.

8.3.4.2 Program

Program reuse is the reuse of code components that can be integrated into a software system with little or no prior adaptation; for example, libraries (containing scientific functions and well-known algorithms such as binary sort), high-level languages and problem-oriented languages. As regards commercial packages, spreadsheet programs have been hailed as one of the most successful examples of a reusable product [148]. They can be used by a wide variety of users to perform a wide variety of tasks. For instance, a specific function such as automatic recalculation permits users to change one or more variables and see the result of automatic recomputation of all values.

> **Exercise 8.1** What do you understand by the terms reuse and reusability with regard to software development and maintenance?
>
> **Exercise 8.2** Describe the different sources of knowledge that can be reused and give examples.

8.4 Objectives and Benefits of Reuse

There are three major driving forces behind the concept of reuse: to increase productivity, to improve quality and to facilitate code transportation [66].

- *To increase productivity:* By reusing product, process and personnel knowledge to implement changes rather than writing code from scratch, the software engineer's productivity can be greatly increased because of the reduction in the time and effort that would have been spent on specification, design, implementation and testing the changes. Reuse can, accordingly, reduce the time and costs required to maintain software products. For reuse to be justified, the time taken to search the reuse library and to understand, adapt and incorporate the reusable component needs to be significantly less than that needed to write the component from scratch.

- *To increase quality:* Since reusable programs have usually been well tested and already shown to satisfy the desired requirements, they tend to have fewer residual errors. This leads to greater reliability and robustness. It is this feature which makes software reuse attractive to software engineers interested in improving (or at least maintaining) the quality of software products. Note once again that we are talking about the reuse of *good* programs and program components.

- *To facilitate code transportation:* The aim of code transportation is to produce code that can easily be transported across machines or software environments with little or no modification. This excludes activities which are aimed at adapting the same product to changes in its software or hardware operating environment. Producing machine-independent components can be achieved through the use of in-house, national or international standards. Portability reduces the time and resource required to adapt the components to a different machine or software environment.

It is not always possible to achieve all the above objectives at any given time or on any given project. However, success in achieving them can bring about benefits such as a reduction in maintenance time and effort and an increase in maintainability.

- *Reduction in maintenance time and effort:* One benefit of reuse is a reduction in maintenance time and effort [157, 148]. Owing to the generality, manageable size and consistency in style of reusable components, it is much easier to read, understand and modify them when effecting a software change, there is also a reduction in the learning time as a result of the increasing familiarity with the reused code that the user gains with time.

The greatest benefit of reuse to maintenance is obtained during perfective change for two reasons. Firstly, because perfective change requires incorporation of new components that can be obtained from reuse libraries, and secondly because perfective change consumes about 50% of maintenance costs (Figure 4.2). Schach [242] has shown that in situations where more than 51% of the budget is devoted to maintenance, the cost savings during maintenance due to software reuse is significantly greater than those during development due to software reuse.

- *To improve maintainability:* Another benefit of reuse is that it can improve maintainability. Reusable components tend to exhibit such characteristics as generality, high cohesion and low coupling, consistency of programming style, modularity and standards. These are also characteristics that maintainable programs ought to manifest. Thus, an attempt to improve the reusability of software components can contribute significantly to enhancing their maintainability [108].

Exercise 8.3 Give reasons why it is important to reuse programs instead of writing them from scratch.

Exercise 8.4 What benefits can be derived from reusing software?

8.5 Approaches to Reuse

Biggerstaff [30, 32] provides a very good framework for approaches to reuse. There are two main approaches depending on the nature of the component that is being reused, either static building blocks or dynamic patterns (Table 8.1). Coincidentally, this impinges on how the target system is obtained - through composition or generation [30, 32].

In this section, these approaches to reuse are discussed and some examples given.

Table 8.1 Approaches to reuse

Features	Approaches to reuse			
Name of component	Atomic building blocks		Patterns	
Principle of reuse	Composition		Generation	
Type	Black-box	White-box	Application generator based	Transformation based
Example systems	Mathematical functions UNIX commands	Object oriented classes	Draco	SETL

8.5.1 Composition-Based Reuse

In the composition approach, the components being reused are atomic building blocks that are assembled to compose the target system. The components retain their basic characteristics even after they have been reused. Examples of such building blocks are program modules, routines, functions and objects. A number of well-defined composition mechanisms are used to 'glue' these components together.

A simple example of such a mechanism is the UNIX pipe [153]. It is a way of connecting the output of one program to the input of another, and as such, it can be used to create a large program by combining smaller ones. Consider the problem of determining the number of files in a subdirectory This task can be split into two subtasks: list the files and then count them. The *ls* command lists files. The *wc -w* command counts the number of words in a file. So to count the number of files in a subdirectory, these two programs can be combined using the pipe (represented by the symbol '|') thereby giving 'ls wc | w'.

In object-oriented programming, the composition mechanism is achieved through the principle of inheritance [266]. This allows the construction of new components from existing ones. By the use of inheritance we can obtain components that are either a modification of another component or a collection of other components. Take, for instance, the example presented in Figure 8.1, where we define an object called MEMBER (of a University) and also specify its attributes such as Name, Address and DateOfBirth. A student in the University is a member and has the attributes of the object MEMBER, but has the additional features of enrol and examine. Similarly, a lecturer is a member of the University but has the additional features of employed and lectures. In a situation where we already have the component MEMBER and its associated attributes, and we want an additional component, STUDENT or LECTURER, all that is required is to construct STUDENT or LECTURER using MEMBER and implement only their additional features. Inheritance in this instance promotes efficient reuse of existing code and expedites the development process.

In order to increase their reusability, software components need to exhibit certain design and implementation characteristics. These characteristics are considered in chapter 6. During composition, if the components are reused without modification, as in the above example, this is black-box reuse. On the other hand, if the components require modification prior to being reused, this is white-box reuse.

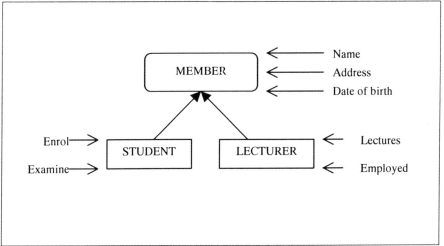

Figure 8.1 Inheritance as a composition mechanism

- *Black-box reuse:* In black-box reuse, the component is reused without modification. Since the user does not need to modify the component prior to reusing it, only information on what it does is made available. The use of routines from standard libraries such as *MathLib0* and *InOut* in Modula-2 are examples of this form of reuse. Only the definition modules of these libraries are made available to the user, thereby ensuring that the user cannot change the implementation of the component. This type of reuse can be very successful [202], especially in application domains that are well understood and where there exist standard interfaces between reusable components. Examples of well-understood reusable components can be found in UNIX and mathematical applications in Fortran, as reflected in the high proportion of software engineers reusing them.

- *White-box reuse:* In white-box reuse, the component is reused after modification. This approach to reuse requires that the user be supplied with information on both what the component does and how it works. In a language such as Modula-2, information on what the program does is contained in the definition module and information on how the program works is contained in the implementation module. Access to the source code of the implementation module permits the user to modify the component in accordance with the requirements of the target system.

8.5.2 Generation-Based Reuse

In the generation approach, the reusable components are active entities that are used to generate the target system. Here, the reused component is the program that generates the target product. Unlike the composition approach, the output generated does not necessarily bear any resemblance to the generator program. Examples are application generators, transformation-based systems and language based systems.

Although our discussion is based on Biggerstaff's framework, we consider language-based systems and transformation-based systems to be similar, and as such, both have been treated under transformation-based systems. The reason for this is that language-based generation systems exhibit some transformation features, except that during the transformation process the target system is expressed in a well-defined language.

8.5.2.1 Application Generator Systems

Application generators are software systems that are used to generate other applications. Provided the specification of the application to be generated is expressed in some notation, it is generated automatically. Parts of the application generator such as its architectural design are reused during the generation of the output product, thereby giving rise to some similarities between the generator system and the output application [31].

Different mechanisms are used to capture the specification of the target product. Examples are formal specification [226], logic specification, knowledge-based specification, grammatical specification and algorithmic specification [232]. Application generators are usually domain-specific. A typical example of an application generator is yacc[12] in UNIX [153]. This is a program that generates a parser when given an appropriate grammatical specification.

Another example is Neigbors' Draco system [202]. It enables the construction of domain-specific software products from reusable components. The approach on which this system is based requires that a set of domains with which an organisation is familiar be identified and modelled by a specialist in those domains. When a change request is received by the organisation's analyst, an attempt is made to match the requirements of the change to existing domains. If this is possible, then the specification is expressed in an appropriate notation and then refined into executable code.

8.5.2.2 Transformation-Based Systems

Transformation-based systems are products that are developed using an approach whereby high-level specifications of the system are converted through a number of stages into operational programs. There are two types of transformation that can be used during this conversion process: step-wise refinement and linguistic transformation.

- Step-wise refinement involves continuously refining the high-level specification by adding more detail until the operational programs are obtained.

- During linguistic transformation the operational programs are derived by transforming the system through different stages. At each of these stages, the system is represented using an intermediate language which may be translated into some other intermediate language until the final implementation of the system - in a given programming language - is obtained.

---

[12] yacc: 'yet another compiler compiler'.

The key feature of linguistic transformation-based systems is that the detailed implementation is hidden from the user. This method is particularly important in situations where the user simply wants to specify the abstract details of the system to be developed while suppressing as many design or implementation details as possible.

An example of a transformation system is the SETL language [81, 85]. This is an imperative sequential language. Its philosophy is that computations can be represented as operations on mathematical sets. The program specified in SETL is then translated into a lower-level language called LITTLE - with semantics that lie between Fortran and C.

8.5.2.3 Evaluation of the Generator-Based Systems

The notion of reuse in the above types of generator is that they themselves are the reusable component because they are used to generate different programs. In principle it is easy to classify systems according to the above generation-based taxonomy. In practice, however, it is difficult to classify a generated system as belonging to any specific category. Quite often, the systems are hybrid in nature, borrowing concepts from more than one of the categories. For example, Neigbors' Draco system [202] has features of both an application generator and a transformation system.

8.6 *Domain Analysis*

There are two categories of component that can be reused: horizontally reusable and vertically reusable components [133]. Horizontal reuse is reuse of components that can be used in a wide variety of domains, for example algorithms and data structures. Vertical reuse is reuse of components that are targeted at applications within a given problem area.

Due to the application domain oriented nature of vertical reuse, there is often a need to identify common problems within the domain and attempt to produce 'standard' solutions to these problems. This can be achieved through **domain analysis**: a process by which information used in developing and maintaining software systems is identified, captured, and organised with the purpose of making it reusable when maintaining existing systems (adapted from R Prieto-Diaz [230]).

This is achieved by studying the needs and requirements of a collection of applications from a given domain [202]. The objects (for example; existing and future requirements, and the current implementation) and operations pertinent to this domain are identified and described. The constraints on the interactions between these objects and the operations are also described [134]. These descriptions are then implemented as code modules in a given programming language ready to be reused. The inputs and outputs involved in the whole process are illustrated in Figure 8.2. The Draco system [202] is a good example of a system that provides support for domain analysis.

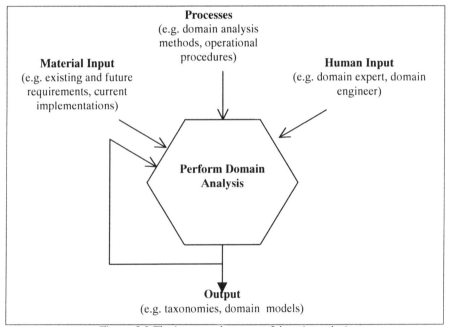

Figure 8.2 The inputs and outputs of domain analysis

Domain analysis is best performed by a domain expert who has experience of developing many systems in the same domain. It is especially important to organisations that are specialised in particular software systems for a designated problem set. The advantages of domain analysis include the following:

- The repository of information produced serves as an invaluable asset to an organisation. The information can be used for training other personnel about the development and maintenance of software systems belonging to the domain in question [132].

- One of the problems with the data processing industry is the high turnover of personnel - especially in maintenance departments - thus depriving organisations of the valuable expertise gained from previous projects. With domain analysis, the impact of such turnover can be minimised.

Domain analysis has a wide range of benefits to software organisations, especially those interested in reuse. There are, however, a number of factors that may prevent organisations from undertaking it [132]:

- It requires a substantial upfront investment. This can be a risky venture for the organisation because there is no absolute guarantee that the results of the domain analysis will justify its cost.
- It is a long-term investment whose benefit will not be realised until the organisation observes some increase in productivity and a reduction in the cost of maintenance as a result of reuse.

8.7 Components Engineering

The composition-based approach to reuse involves composing a new system partly from existing components. There are two main ways in which these components can be obtained. The first is through a process known as design for reuse. This involves developing components with the intention of using them on more than one occasion. The second way is through reverse engineering.

8.7.1 Design for Reuse

8.7.1.1 Characteristics of Reusable Components

To accommodate the evolutionary nature of a software system during its lifetime, it is essential to anticipate change. This means designing and implementing modules that are susceptible to modification. Similarly, with reuse, candidate components should be designed and implemented in a way that shields them from too many changes when they need to be reused. That is, if significant benefits are to be reaped from reusing a component, the issue of its reusability should not be a matter of mere coincidence or an afterthought. Its development and maintenance must be guided by sound design principles. In general the design principles aimed at enhancing evolvability apply equally to reusability. In this section, only those principles which we believe impact strongly on reusability are discussed. Readers interested in the others should consult texts such as Ghezzi *et al* [108] and van Vliet [274].

- *Generality:* This means the potential use of a component for a wide spectrum of application or problem domains. Typical examples of software systems which exhibit generality are database and spreadsheet packages which have been designed to accommodate the needs of a wide variety of users. This is in contrast to much more domain-specific applications, for instance, air traffic control systems or clinical prescribing packages. Consider a simple example: a program to sort 75 items. A generic approach where the sort routine does not rely on the number or type of the items has more reuse potential than an approach which uses a fixed size array and builds specific item comparisons into the sort routine.

    Generality presents a problem for reusability. It has been observed that solutions that are targeted at a wider problem domain (for example, formal specification) tend to have lower pay-off than those that are targeted at a narrower problem domain (for example, problem-oriented languages) [32]. Thus, prior to deciding on the degree of generality needed, it is essential to achieve the right balance between generality and pay-off.

- *Cohesion versus coupling:* Cohesion is an internal property which describes the degree to which elements such as program statements and declarations are related. A module with high cohesion denotes a high affinity between its constituent elements. Coupling, on the other hand, is an external property which characterises the interdependence between two or more modules in a given system. High coupling signifies a strong interrelationship between modules in a program. In the event of a change to one module, high coupling implies that several other modules are likely to be affected. Loosely coupled modules, on the other hand, are more independent and thus easier to understand and adapt for reuse. Increasing the degree of reusability of a software component therefore implies high cohesion and loose coupling since the component can be reused without worrying too much about which other modules accompany it.

- *Interaction:* The interaction with the user in terms of the number of read-write statements per line of source code should be minimised but there should be more interaction with utility functions - those that can be used for several purposes [148]. The aim is to reduce the impact of change on the front end of the system.

- *Uniformity and standardisation:* The use of standards across different levels of the software [227] is likely to promote reusability of software components. Standards exist for such things as user interface design, programming style, data structure design and documentation. For example, standards help towards uniformity in the techniques used to invoke, control and terminate functions as well as in the methods used for getting help during use of the software [148]. The increasing use of international standards such as the ISO 9000 quality series [141] should accelerate the move towards reusability of software products by ensuring commonality in the documents and operational procedures pertaining to a software system.

- *Data and control abstractions:* Data abstraction encompasses abstract data types, encapsulation and inheritance. Control abstraction embraces external modules and iterators [227]. To allow effective reuse, it is essential to have a clear separation between the programs that manipulate data and the data itself.

- *Interoperability*: The increasing popularity of interoperability will aid reuse by allowing systems to take advantage of remote services. Consider for example the issue of patient identification in clinical systems. Work on Patient/Person Identification Servers [68] will both aid system building/maintenance and make the whole issue of identification more reliable.

8.7.1.2 Problems with Reuse Libraries

The components library plays a central role in composition-based reuse. There are, however, a number of problems associated with designing the library and also obtaining candidate components from it [202]:

- *The granularity and size dilemma:* When designing a components library, it is important to have appropriately sized fragments so as to facilitate understandability and increase the generic potential. This implies that the library will contain many small components, which poses problems with classifying and searching. The classification and search problems can be minimised by having a smaller number of large library fragments, but this increases the problems of understandability and genericity. Thus, there is a conflict [202].

- *The search problem:* Without an appropriate mechanism for describing the contents of a components library, it will be difficult for a user to find components that match the requirements of the system to be composed. It may take more time than would be required to write the code from scratch. This would discourage the reuse of existing software and encourage individuals to resort to writing their own code. The knowledge-based technique by Basili and Abd-El-Hafiz [15] and the behaviour sampling technique by Podgurski and Pierce [224] address this problem.

- *The classification problem:* It is important to store information in the components library on what components it contains. However, it is not always obvious how to specify this information. Some research has been undertaken to address this issue. For example, the use of functional specifications has been suggested as a means of representing components in the library [143]. Another example of a classification scheme is that by Prieto-Diaz and Freeman [231]. They classify the components based on three factors: functionality (what the component does), environment (where it does it) and implementation details (how it does it).

- *The specification and flexibility problems:* Not only is it difficult to specify, in the library, what the system does, it can also be difficult to specify how it works and the constraints on its usage. This poses problems for a user intending to undertake white-box reuse. Another problem faced during white-box reuse is not being able to tell which design and implementation decisions are fixed and which are flexible.

8.7.2 Reverse Engineering

The second way in which reusable components can be made available is by identifying and extracting them from existing systems that were not originally designed for reuse but nonetheless have reusability potential. One of the techniques that is commonly employed for this purpose is reverse engineering. This technique enables

> *"... the extraction of components from existing software, through the analysis of both code and documentation, possibly helped by*

software engineers, abstracting and generalising these so that they become widely reusable."

Dusink & Hall ([88], p.7)

See chapter 7 for further discussion on reverse engineering.

Exercise 8.5 Compare and contrast the different approaches to reuse, giving examples of systems that can be obtained from each of these approaches.

8.7.2.1 Case Study – Patient Identification

In the early days of medical information systems in the 1950's and 1960's, systems identified patients by name or by locally generated ID number. Each system invented its own method.

Staff at the ACME Health Clinic evaluated a system that was in many respects well ahead of its time, but had to reject it because its patient identification method meant it could not distinguish between two patients at the clinic who happened to be same sex twins with the same first initial.

Locally generated IDs were a solution for a while, but created problems when patients moved.

In the UK, in an effort to find a solution all systems could use, there was a move to have all patients electronically registered by their NHS numbers. This initiative brought to light previously unnoticed clerical errors in the allocation of NHS numbers. The numbers could not be guaranteed to be unique. This was a solvable problem but it did not get to the heart of the issue of patient identification.

Populations are far more mobile than they used to be. People cross international borders. There is a brisk illicit trade in false IDs for many purposes. NHS numbers and their equivalents in other countries do not necessarily provide accurate identification and are not always available when needed.

There are occasions (and they tend to be the emergency situations) where the patient is unable to provide any clue as to their identity e.g. they may be unconscious. Smartcards can help, but may be stolen and misused.

> Retina and fingerprints are more reliable but imply that by taking such a print, a person's relevant medical history is available. Does this imply a huge database holding a populations' identification and medical details? This opens up an enormous can of worms in terms of civil liberties. History does not give much hope that such a collection of data would not be misused. How do we weigh the risks for potential for harm from the misuse of detailed medical information against the risks of, say, an allergy being missed when a patient is brought in unconscious?
>
> The security issues surrounding personal and medical data are far from being solved. Should we be looking to medical advances whereby a quick test of a patient's DNA and vital signs will show up all relevant medical data, allowing appropriate treatment to be administered without necessarily knowing who the patient is?
>
> The apparently 'simple' issue of identifying a patient soon mushrooms far beyond the immediate issues. It is an interesting demonstration of the fact that building and maintaining software often reaches far beyond the solving of a technical problem.

8.7.3 Components-Based Processes

A potential advantage to components-based processes is in tackling the over-concentration of expertise. Maintenance of traditional software tends to result in a small number of people developing in-depth specific technological or business expertise. These people then become indispensable in the maintenance of a system. This is due largely to scarcity of resource. Often there is no time available for training new personnel, and even where there is, the experts cannot be spared because their time is dedicated to maintaining the system.

Components-based processes counteract this effect. Components by their nature cross technological and business areas. The focus of required skills changes. Components services skills are needed as there will be a components library to be maintained.

Both domain-specific and generic components-based frameworks for software products have been developed. The Object Management Group (OMG), in their Model-Driven Architectures initiatives are significant contributors to standardisation in this area [203]. As well as formal standards, there are *de facto* standards such as Java [259]. An international standard for process engineering models, also developed by the OMG, is the Software Process Engineering Metamodel [204].

8.8 Reuse Process Model

Traditional top-down life-cycle models (see chapter 5) do not specifically address ways by which reuse activities can be accommodated at each phase of the life-cycle [283]. This is a result of several factors [133]:

- Software reuse is not inherently top-down, as are some of the life-cycle models (for example, the waterfall model).
- In software reuse, the developer or maintainer takes a view that extends beyond single projects or systems.
- Reuse involves the exploitation of commonality at many levels of abstraction besides that easily captured in code.
- Reuse depends, to a large extent, on the ability to analyse specific domains in order to extract maximally reusable components. Structured methodologies designed for top-down life-cycle models, however, rarely provide specific techniques to analyse domains.

Despite the above weaknesses, traditional life-cycle models may serve as frameworks within which reuse can be accommodated. In response to the need for 'reuse-conscious' life-cycle models, a number of propositions for refinement of current life-cycle models have been put forward [19, 151, 231, 253]. For instance, Simos suggests that:

"What is needed is a process model that allows for iteration between the top-down, 'problem-driven' approach and a bottom-up, 'parts-driven' perspective.... Such a process model would correspond more closely to the real state of practice in software development than the current model, and would at least initially have a less prescriptive, more descriptive flavour."

Simos (cited in [133], p.38)

Although Simos makes particular reference to development, in principle the above characteristics would also apply to any reuse model targeted at maintenance activities. To exploit the potential of software reuse successfully, there must be a mechanism to integrate it into existing software engineering process models rather than considering it as an add-on. Hooper and Chester [133] provide a good review of other propositions and reuse models. One of these is that of Prieto-Diaz and Freeman [231]. Their view of a reuse model is summarised in the algorithm in Figure 8.3. It assumes that the software engineer has already understood the problem to be solved and the specifications that are available. A model with no such assumption is a four-step generic reuse/reusability model proposed by Kang [150].

```
given a set of specs
BEGIN
    search library for component
    IF identical match then terminate
    ELSE
        collect similar components
        FOR each component
          compute degree of match
        END (*FOR*)
        rank and select best component
        modify component
    END(*IF*)
END
```

Figure 8.3 A reuse process algorithm

8.8.1 Generic Reuse/Reusability Model

Proposals for many of the reuse process models stem from the failure of orthodox process models, e.g. waterfall and spiral life-cycle models, to address reuse issues. Kang's [150] refinement of the DOD-STD2167A life-cycle (similar to the waterfall life-cycle) led to a four-step 'generic reuse/reusability model' developed at the Software Engineering Institute in the Carnegie Mellon University, Pittsburg. His idea was to identify reuse activities applicable to each phase of the DOD-STD-2167A life-cycle based on the generic model. This model is further refined by Hooper and Chester [133] to include an evaluation phase, thereby extending it to a five-step model (Figure 8.4).

174   Software Maintenance: Concepts and Practice

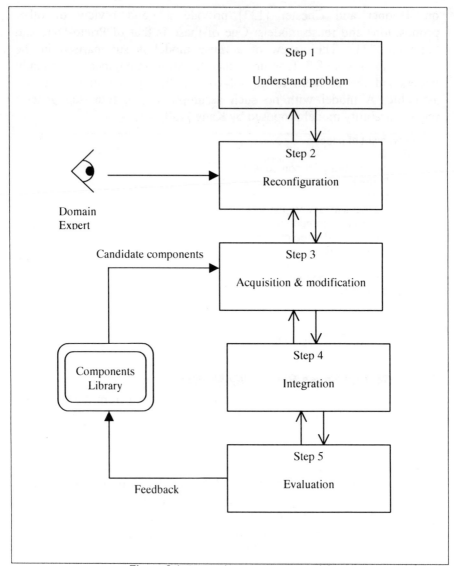

Figure 8.4 A generic reuse process model

The steps of this generic reuse model are summarised below:

- Step 1: This step involves understanding the problem to be solved and then identifying a solution structure based on predefined components available.

- Step 2: The solution structure is then reconfigured in order to maximise the potential of reuse at the current and the next phase. This means involving the domain experts of the next phase who will study the proposed solution of the current phase and identify reusable components available at the next phase. Several techniques can be used to identify reusable components [15]. The criteria for selection are based on factors such as functionality, logic and pre- and post-conditions.

- Step 3: The major task at this stage is preparing the reusable components identified in the solution structure in readiness for integration. This involves acquiring reusable components, modifying and/or instantiating them for the problem being solved. For those components that cannot be acquired or that are uneconomic to adapt, new ones are developed.

- Step 4: The main aim at this stage is integrating the completed components into the product(s) required for the next phase of the software life-cycle.

- Step 5: In this step, the experience from the preceding steps is used to evaluate the reusability prospects of two categories of component. The first category is those components that need to be developed for the sub-problems for which no reusable components exist. The second category is those components that have been obtained from the adaptation of predefined components. The result of this evaluation exercise is then used to update the current library of reusable components.

The main advantage of the generic model, as Hooper and Chester note, is that it takes a multi-project view of development and maintenance whereby products from one project are expected to be used for other projects.

Like the refinements proposed by Simos, Kang's model does not make specific reference to maintenance activities. This, however, does not prevent it from being applied during the implementation of software change since the steps he lists also apply to maintenance.

8.8.2 *Accommodating a Reuse Process Model*

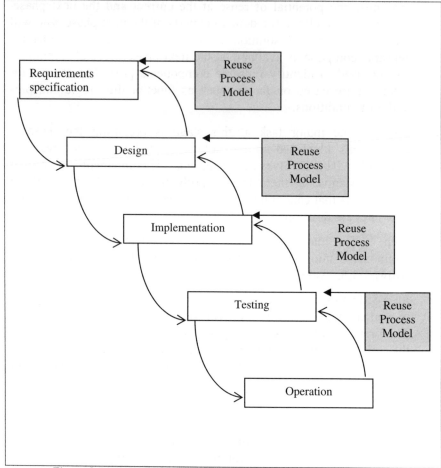

Figure 8.5 Incorporating a reuse process model into a waterfall lifecycle

One of the reasons that may discourage organisations from adopting software reuse is the difficulty of accommodating it in an existing software engineering process model. Without an appropriate mechanism such a change may destabilise the organisational culture which in turn may encourage resistance to the incorporation of reuse into the organisation's process model. One way to encourage the adoption of reuse is to assist personnel in applying reuse at the various phases of the software life-cycle they are already using. The integration of a reuse model such as Kang's may help soften any resistance from personnel since it does not require the existing software engineering process model to be abandoned (Figure 8.5). There are of course many other issues that need to be addressed in order to accommodate reuse into an organisation (see the following section and [133]).

8.9 Factors that Impact upon Reuse

Hooper and Chester note that:

> "... *if reuse is to occur in an effective way, it must be integrated into the software process in such a way that we consider reusing software as the means to satisfy requirements before we consider developing new software.*"
>
> Hooper & Chester ([133], p.36)

As noted earlier, reuse has the potential to increase personnel productivity and improve product quality. This potential, however, has not yet been fully realised. This is due to both technical and non-technical factors. These are discussed below.

8.9.1 Technical Factors

8.9.1.1 Programming Languages

The use of several programming languages to develop software within a company hinders attempts to develop reusable components [66]. One way to address this problem is to choose a programming language and mandate its use for projects within an organisation.

8.9.1.2 Representation of Information

Another impediment to reuse is the representation of design information in a form that does not promote reuse. The reuse of design can be automated. Biggerstaff and Perlis [31] suggest that one way to achieve this is by representing knowledge about the implementation structures in a form that allows a designer to separate individual design factors. For example, given a program that converts an infix expression to Reverse Polish Notation, the designer should be able to factor out the concept of a stack, which is data structure based, from a mathematical expression which is application domain based.

8.9.1.3 Reuse Library

For ease of reuse, large libraries of reusable components must be populated and easily accessible. There is a need for adequate retrieval techniques for managing the libraries. This is an expensive and time-consuming venture upon which some companies are not willing to embark [66].

8.9.1.4 Reuse-Maintenance Vicious Cycle

In the course of applying reuse techniques to alleviate maintenance, it is essential to populate the component library with as many reusable fragments as possible. However, as the library gets bigger, managing it can present another maintenance problem. This can lead to a 'reuse-maintenance vicious cycle'. One way to minimise the effect of this is to use good design principles when designing the components as well as the library in which they will be stored.

8.9.2 Non-Technical Factors

Non-technical factors play a large part in inhibiting the smooth adoption of reuse. Bott and Ratcliffe [43] contend that the cumulative effect of the non-technical problems presents a greater obstacle than the technical ones, a view also shared by Aharonian [2].

8.9.2.1 Initial Capital Outlay

Reuse depends, to a large extent, on the availability of large libraries of reusable components. The initial setting up and managing of such libraries is an expensive business. Added to this is the general reluctance of some companies to make a commitment and investment in reuse without some form of incentive [66]. Biggerstaff [29] points to a number of reasons for this. Firstly, the financial infrastructure of the company may not be capable of supporting such a level of investment. Secondly, some companies do not understand the extent to which they will depend on software technology in the long term. And thirdly, it takes a while for the process of technologies to be reflected in organisational policies. For example, it took a long time for successful technologies such as workstations to be widely used in many companies. In comparison, an advanced technology will take time to be widely adopted.

8.9.2.2 Not Invented Here Factor

It has been shown that there is a tendency amongst software engineers to avoid the use of programs not developed in-house [32, 66]. The not-invented-here (NIH) factor is a cultural issue [32]. Programmers traditionally prefer to develop their own code rather than use other people's and there can be a prevailing mood which makes the production of code from scratch a matter of pride. These problems will be overcome by the establishment of a different culture. There is evidence that this is already happening, probably as a factor of the maturing field, and reuse is being viewed in a more positive light.

8.9.2.3 Commercial Interest

One way to encourage software reuse is to give software components a wide circulation, for instance making them available in the public domain. However, a product that is worth reusing by other individuals or companies may well be marketed commercially for profit. This can prevent authors of software from putting products in the public domain for reuse by others, especially where they would be reused for commercial gain.

8.9.2.4 Education

It is sometimes the case that managers, who are in a position to play a significant role in reuse programmes, lack an adequate level of software engineering education. This may impede their ability to recognise the potential financial and productivity benefits of reuse [66].

8.9.2.5 Project Co-ordination

In some companies there is little or no co-ordination between projects. This leads to duplication [66]. Putting in place a reuse programme would facilitate the reuse of knowledge gained and should yield cost and productivity benefits. One way of doing this is for the company to take a multi-project view of development and maintenance. This entails treating the deliverables – artefacts and other forms of knowledge - from every project as potential input to other projects.

8.9.2.6 Legal Issues

The notion of reusing someone else's software, especially a public software library, raises a series of legal questions which are yet to be addressed. For example, Aharonian [2] asks:

- *"Does reusing software in certain configurations violate known and unknown patents? Will companies be liable for actions of uninformed programmers? Will companies need lawyers as part of their software reuse staff?*
- *Who is liable for faults attributed to acquired repository software components? At which point in modifying external software, does the burden of reliability pass from the original developer to the modifying company?"*

Until these questions have been carefully considered and ambiguities resolved, the potential of software reuse may never be realised regardless of technological breakthroughs and potential benefits.

Exercise 8.6 You have just joined a team of software engineers in which you are the only one who has studied and practised software reuse and reusability. The company you work for has no reuse programme although they are willing to start one. You are asked to implement the reuse programme.

- What is the first step you would take?
- Outline the technical, managerial and organisational steps you would go through.
- What tactics do you need to employ in order for the programme to succeed?
- What difficulties do you anticipate and how would you overcome them?

Exercise 8.7 A mechanical engineering contractor has been using a large and complex Fortran software system for over 12 years. There is no documentation for the system and the maintenance programmers have moved to a different company. In order to take advantage of state-of-the-art parallel machines, the contractor wants the software to be reimplemented on a parallel platform.

- Briefly describe the techniques that will be needed to accomplish the task.
- How would you go about performing the job, bearing in mind the merits of software reuse?

8.10 Summary
The key points that have been covered in this chapter are:

- Software reuse involves the redeployment of software products from one system to maintain or develop another system in an attempt to reduce effort and to improve quality and productivity. Reusability is the ease with which this goal can be achieved.

- The key driving forces behind the reuse of software components during maintenance are: to increase productivity and product quality, to improve maintainability and to reduce maintenance costs. The key benefit of reuse to maintenance is "...to allow high speed and low-cost replacement of ageing systems, whose functions and data requirements have become well known" [148 p.493].

- Reuse process models may be applied at each phase of the life-cycle [19, 151, 253].

- Software reuse is a multi-faceted issue that embraces several concepts - domain analysis, development and refinement of components, classification / packaging, searching, evaluation / assessment and integration.

- The two main approaches to reuse are composition and generation. Using the composition methods, a product is constructed from a combination of atomic building blocks. With the generation method, programs are used in the generation of other programs.

- Several technical and non-technical factors impinge on reuse. Examples of the technical factors include generality, cohesion and coupling, component interaction, uniformity, level of data and function abstraction and availability of internal documentation. Examples of non-technical factors include initial capital outlay, the NIH factor, commercial interests, inadequate education, project co-ordination and legal concerns.

- There are a number of ways to maximise the potential of reuse. Management support is especially important, as are planning and investing for reuse, and having adequate tool support.

Specific maintenance techniques have been examined in this and previous chapters. Once the system has been changed, it will be released to users. However, it cannot just be assumed that everything will work according to specification. To minimise residual errors, the software is tested. Testing is the subject of the next chapter.

9

Testing

"The best tester isn't the one who finds the most bugs or who embarrasses the most programmers. The best tester is the one who gets the most bugs fixed."

Kaner *et al* ([149], p15]

This chapter aims to

1. Discuss the concept of software testing, looking at why and how it is done.

2. Look at the key aspects of a software tester's job.

3. Discuss different types and categories of test.

4. Look at test plans.

9.1 Introduction

What is testing and why do we do it?

Testing is the examination of a software system in the context of a given specification set. You will find texts that tell you we test in order to verify that a software system conforms to an agreed specification. However, this is wrong. The purpose of testing is to find errors in software systems i.e. to identify ways in which it does *not* conform to an agreed specification. It may seem pedantic to emphasise the latter purpose over the former. Aren't they the same anyway? At one level perhaps, but there are important differences that we will explore later.

In many ways, testing is analogous to software maintenance as a whole. It is a vital component in the development of software systems; it is required throughout the lifetime of a system; it is rarely budgeted for sufficiently; its status is far below its importance etc.

There is a large body of theory behind testing. As with maintenance as a whole, the theoretical concepts sometimes seem a world away from the real life situations that testers are faced with. However, software testers with a good knowledge of the theoretical background will be better equipped to cope with the problems that will arise, for example, as a result of lack of resource to carry out sufficient testing.

9.2 Definitions

Proof – the process of establishing validity in accordance with principles of mathematical reasoning.

Test – a critical examination by submission of an entity to conditions or operations that will lead to its acceptance or rejection against a set of agreed criteria.

9.3 Why Test Software

Before looking at the details of testing, it is important to have a clear and comprehensive grasp of why we test software. Think back to the overview section of Part II. You were asked to discuss the following question and answer in terms of why the answer missed the point of the question.

Question: Why do we test software? Answer: To see if it works?

Another question and answer was given to compare:

Question: Why did you drive across town today? Answer: To look at the *opening hours* notice on the shop, to see if it will be open on the 3rd Saturday in June next year.

What are the problems in the second example? For one thing, it's a long way to drive to get information that would be more easily obtained by a phone call. As well as taking longer, it's not very reliable. What if the shop is shut and the information is not posted on the door? What if the information is posted? Does that really answer the question about what will happen on the 3rd Saturday in June next year? At best, it gives an indication.

Testing software to see if it works is much the same. Unless you can comprehensively test every eventuality, every context of every input (which you can't, the possibilities are infinite) the best you can do by testing is to say that it works in this finite set of circumstances, and gives an indication of how it might work in others.

If you wanted to say that a software system worked, you would do it by proof, not test.

Compare software with the situation where proof is possible. The equation $y=mx+c$ (where m and c are constants) gives a straight line when plotted on a graph. We know this is the equation of a straight line because we can prove it mathematically. We certainly don't test it (by plugging in different values for m and c) to find this out.

Thus, a fundamental answer to the question of why we test software is that <u>we test software because we cannot prove it.</u>

Much work has been done on formal methods and different approaches to testing (see for example [44, 147]), but there is no software system proving tool on the horizon, and there may never be.

But isn't the purpose of testing, as mentioned above, to verify that the system works? No, it isn't, because the system does not work. Because we cannot prove software, we cannot build software without errors. Thus to test software to verify that it works, is to aim for the impossible. You will never get the best out of your personnel if they are set up to fail – as are testers who are trying to show that a system works. The successful tester finds bugs in a system.

Given that the best that testing can ever do is verify operation in a tiny set of the possible operating contexts, is it worth doing at all? The answer to that is a resounding Yes. Testing is vital to the safety and correct operation of software systems. The reality is that programmers find and fix most bugs. Given that estimated bugs run at an average of more than 1 per program statement, enormous numbers of them are fixed in order to release software at an estimated 3 or less per 100 program statements [22].

Finding the bugs is only half the story. Finding the error doesn't fix it, only identifies it. And for a variety of reasons, not all bugs can be fixed. Good software testers can identify, categorise and prioritise the errors they find.

Systematic testing, following principles researched for effective software production relies on the software development and maintenance processes having themselves been carried out systematically and to appropriately high standards. Obviously, in many cases this will not have been done.

Very often, systems to be tested will have been developed in ways that are far from ideal. It is as pointless to pretend that systems to be tested will have been produced according to ideal conditions as it is to pretend that testing conditions will be ideal. However, recognising the best case scenario is also valuable, because no-one should become so resigned to developing and maintaining software to inadequate standards that they stop trying to improve things. A maintenance programmer needs to know about the theoretical models of development and maintenance in order to be a good maintenance programmer even in less than ideal conditions. In the same way, knowledge of the theory of testing is a vital component of a tester's toolkit.

9.4 What is a Software Tester's Job

A tester's job is more than to find errors in software. It is also to design tests that find errors and then find further errors (to avoid allowing the release of software with serious bugs), and to get errors corrected. Testers will recognise the severity of errors, and there will be debate between programmers and testers as to which errors can and should be fixed.

Myers [199 ch.2] compares the tester and program to be tested with a doctor and sick patient. If a test run shows no errors, it should not be deemed 'successful' any more than a doctor's examination of a sick patient that failed to find the cause of the sickness, be deemed a success.

Remember that bug fixing is corrective maintenance, with all its attendant problems of ripple effects and so on. The sensible course of action is sometimes NOT to correct an error e.g. if the software is close to release and there is no time to investigate possible ripple effects.

Testing costs money, therefore it has to show a return for its investment by adding value to the program under test. The better improved and more reliable a program is, the more likely it is to repay this investment [199 ch.2].

If the expectation is that the tester will verify a program as error-free, he/she will always fail to meet expectation, or worse, will start to design tests that allow the program to 'succeed'. The finding of yet another serious bug after the programmer thought that all was well may be extremely annoying, not just to the programmer, but also to the manager who is working to a tight schedule to get the system shipped. But however irritating, the finding of a serious bug by a tester is a good piece of work and should be treated as such.

9.5 What to Test and How

Even a program that takes in two 2-digit numbers, multiplies them together and stores the answer, has an infinity of possible test cases. Each of the two inputs can be any number in the range -99 to 99. That gives 39,601 possible pairs of numbers. A finite set of inputs? No, you cannot assume that the user will hit the keys he is told to. Any combination of available keys is a viable test case, and this includes the ctrl+alt+del sequence as well as the reset button and the on-off switch. Add to this the test of how the system reacts when a heavy handed doctor inputs data by descending upon the keys with great force, or when lightning strikes during data input. These latter two cases exercised maintenance staff looking after systems at the ACME Health Clinic. In the first case, the system had to be modified (by flushing the input buffer) to cope with the heavy-handed user. In the second, extensive integrity checks were necessary to verify the extent of the damage to the data. Neither case had been covered in system tests. The former was subsequently included as a routine test of system modifications.

9.5.1 Who Chooses Test Data

Ideally, programs will have sets of test data that have been designed from their specifications, although this shouldn't be assumed to be sufficient. It is possible for a program to pass all the tests in its agreed test data set, but still not operate correctly. Test cases can be decided by looking at what the program is supposed to do i.e. by examining the specification, or by examining the listing or by examining the program as it runs. Different sets of tests will result.

There are some basics to choosing test cases including the following:

- Valid as well as invalid inputs must be checked.

- Classes of test data can be distinguished to cut down the overall set of tests i.e. inputs that should give the same or similar results and where a successful test on one member of the class may justifiably be extrapolated to assume success for all members of the class. Hence, boundary conditions should be subject to greater scrutiny. In the example of a program taking inputs in the range −99 to 99, test cases should include both limits as well as values just below and just above.

- It is important to know where problems are likely to occur. For example, at boundaries, both anticipated and unexpected. Combinations of events, factors or inputs must be looked at, and not just the anticipated ones. If a circumstance is possible, no matter how remote the possibility seems, it may happen.

- Never assume that you are testing ideal code, however much easier that makes the job.

Since you can never test everything, where do you stop? What determines that a test phase is finished? This question is answered by looking at what is at stake. A system controlling a medical device for example, should be subject to more rigorous testing than say a games program. This is not to play down the importance of testing games programs. The release of error-ridden games may destroy a company's competitive edge and thus the livelihoods of its employees.

Exercise 9.1 Pick two software systems and consider how you would go about designing test cases. Do the systems have formal specifications that you can use as a basis? Can you identify test sets from which to extrapolate a whole series of results? Where are the boundary conditions?

9.6 Categorising Tests

Testing software systems is a complex discipline in its own right. It is not, and should not be treated as an *ad hoc* bolt-on to deal with problems when they occur. The discipline has evolved to provide a framework within which we can now rely upon software-controlled aircraft, nuclear power stations, medical robots and so on. This isn't to say that we always get it right, but the discipline has evolved to the degree that properly designed test strategies allied to properly engineered software systems have the potential to provide software systems we can rely on.

We cannot provide a system that is safe from catastrophic failure, but properly implemented test strategies and risk analyses can allow us to predict with confidence that catastrophic software failure will occur no more than once in X years. As long as X is many times larger than the lifetime of the system, we have a close approximation to safe software.

A comprehensive treatment of software testing is beyond the scope of this book, but many excellent texts exist that deal with the subject from different perspectives [149].

This chapter will look at a simple categorisation of tests to provide an overview.

Testing can and should take place at all stages of the development and maintenance life cycle. We can categorise by stage e.g. requirements, design, coding. Within this we can look at top down, bottom up, unit or whole, static or dynamic tests. Whether one way is better than another, and the best ways of conducting specific types of test are argued in the literature [86, 92, 198, 199, 297], but the general consensus is for a mix of strategies tailored to a specific situation. We can also test aspects such as portability e.g. will the system work on another platform or in another language and will it produce data that retains its integrity when processed by a different system.

The many aspects of software systems from source code details to high level managerial policy can all be tested. However, as the maintenance programmer spends a lot of time dealing with other people's code, we will look at some aspects of testing code.

9.6.1 Testing Code

What constitutes a serious software bug? There are bugs that do not cause the program to fail e.g. the program prints an instruction on the wrong part of the screen. An interesting example is a Windows program that uses the key sequence Alt+F4 for some common action. This could cause untold havoc for its users because that is the sequence that closes down most Windows programs. Yet it could be argued that it was not an error in the program itself.

Code can be tested at many different levels – do individual statements execute according to specification, do procedures provide expected output for given input, does the program as a whole perform in a particular way? Within this are many issues to be borne in mind. For example, it is possible to execute each statement without touching upon certain conditions. However, test cases should try to take account of all possible conditions and combinations of conditions, with special emphasis on boundary conditions and values where behaviour is often erroneous.

9.6.1.1 Black Box and White Box Testing

In black box testing, the system acts as a black box – we don't see inside it, we just see what goes in and what comes out. Test cases are derived from the specification, and take no account of the internal operation of the program.

In white box testing we 'see inside the box' and look at the detail of the code.

A program giving the correct result to a black box test, is not necessarily executing its code correctly. Similarly, a program statement executing correctly does not mean that it conforms to its specification.

9.6.1.2 Structured Testing

An aim of structured testing is to maximise the number of errors found by the test cases used and to avoid redundant test cases. Consider the program that takes two integers as input and outputs their product, 39,600 different combinations could be tested and still miss some of the boundary conditions. Redundant testing is inefficient.

Good and properly structured test cases are valuable entities. They should be kept. Test cases should not just be invented on the fly and discarded. This doesn't imply that everything must be formally recorded, or that every test case for every program will be of lasting value. But it is frustrating and counterproductive to find yourself sitting at a terminal for hours creating test cases because the last person to test this software didn't record what they had done. It saves a lot of time to have a set of test cases, to know the circumstances in which they were used, and what results they produced.

It seems obvious to say so, but you must know the expected outcomes of each test case. If you don't, you won't know if you have found a problem or not.

Testing should be planned by assuming that the program contains errors. It's a very safe assumption to make, yet all too often, testing strategies are built upon the premise that the program works.

9.6.1.3 Integration Testing

Testing a program starting with tests of its elements and then combining them to test larger elements is known as integration testing. A procedure, function or module may work on its own, but fail to execute correctly when tested together with other elements. Consider a function that takes two numbers and returns the result of subtracting one from the other. The order in which the numbers are supplied to the function is vital to correct operation, but incorrect ordering won't necessarily show up until the function is tested in conjunction with other elements of the program that use it.

Testing program elements requires program stubs to be written. These are small programs that execute the element under test. Program stubs do not appear in the final product, but are in themselves a powerful and reusable testing tool.

9.6.1.4 Regression Testing

Testing finds errors and also checks that amended code has fixed the problem. However, software has a tendency to instability. We have discussed for example the ripple effect that modifications can produce. Thus an amendment that fixes one error may introduce or reintroduce others. Regression testing is the running of tests both to see that the identified bug has been fixed and to check that other errors have not been introduced.

A set of regression tests can be built up to cover tests for every bug ever discovered in a piece of code. These tests can then be run every time the code is modified.

9.7 Verification and Validation

The verification and validation of software is key in building systems that can be trusted. Verification, ensuring accuracy against an agreed set of requirements and specifications, is largely what this chapter has been about. Validation is external certification that a system can demonstrate a level of compliance, perhaps to a legal requirement such as a specific safety standard.

Carrying out verification and validation activities is not enough. They must be documented. Without adequate documentation, it will not be possible to demonstrate compliance (referenced in [51]).

The aims of verification and validation are to achieve better systems i.e. systems with improved reliability, performance, quality and cost effectiveness. Ratikin [234] provides guidance on essential techniques in software verification and validation, showing also how to reconcile conflicting demands e.g. of quality versus tight deadlines. The impact on cost and scheduling of verification and validation processes is a legitimate concern, and it is important to get the balance right. However, undue criticism on grounds of cost should not be allowed to shortcut necessary verification and validation work [10].

Verification and validation methodologies provide a robust framework for the creation of quality software systems [279], and are more effective when performed independently of the team building or maintaining the system [89, 279].

A useful guide, as in many areas, is to look at the guidelines and standards already developed [138, 139].

9.8 Test Plans

A test plan can vary from a short informal document to a multi-volume series, depending upon the purpose for which it is intended.

The IEEE standard defines a test plan as

"A document describing the scope, approach, resources, and schedule of intended testing activities. It identifies test items, the features to be tested, the testing tasks, who will do each task, and any risks requiring contingency planning."

[ANSI/IEEE Standard 829-1983 for Software Test Documentation]

A test plan can either be a tool or a product [149 ch.12]

Kaner advises that a test plan whose purpose is to act as a tool is *"valuable ... to the extent that it helps you manage your testing project and find bugs. Beyond that, it is a diversion of resources"* [149 p.205].

Test plans can become products. A company taking over a large software system with a view to maintaining it into the future will also be interested in a test plan that will help them to do this. Developing test plans as products may require strict adherence to specific specifications e.g. military standards, and will require the same attention to detail and clarity as full-blown user/system documentation.

Good test plans facilitate testing in many ways including:

- providing lists of useful test cases identifying such things as boundary conditions and classes of test data. This improves efficiency and means important test cases are less likely to be missed.

- providing information on what the scale of the job is likely to be and what resources will be needed.

- providing information to identify and prioritise tasks, thus aiding organisation of the testing team and identifying roles and responsibilities.

9.8.1 Points to Note

From test plans ranging from the very informal to the very sophisticated, there are general points that hold true. These are largely a matter of common sense, but forgetting them can waste inordinate amounts of time and resources.

Deal with errors and try out solutions one at a time. Otherwise you won't know which error is causing the problem or which solution fixed it or caused a further problem.

If it can happen, it will happen, and should be tested. Ill-informed managers or software developers may become impatient at tests of apparently 'unlikely' scenarios, but not taking account of these can be very costly when things go wrong.

Don't test your own software. There are numerous examples of the most glaring of problems overlooked because people have tested their own code. The code writer's preconceptions get in the way. The creators of the enigma codes in the 1930/40s provide a lesson software testers would do well to heed. They relied upon statistical analyses as an assurance of how un-crackable the codes were. Had they set teams of people onto the task of cracking them, they may have realised sooner just how vulnerable they were. [286].

The use of a good test plan can avoid these problems.

Exercise 9.2 Write a test plan for a program (of a reasonable size – at least 100 LOC) that was not developed by you. If you are undertaking a course that has involved a substantive piece of software development, swap your code with a fellow student and write test plans for each others code. The originators of the code should study the test plans produced for their code and discuss the strengths and weaknesses. In particular, look for anything unexpected that has come to light about your code.

Exercise 9.3 Look at the following case study. List all the problems that concern error messages. Consider how these might have been avoided and formulate some general rules that would prevent these problems occurring in other systems.

9.9 Case Study – Therac 25

This case study relates to incidents in the 1980's. The software system problems it highlights were catastrophic in their effects, causing death and injury. Had all the lessons been learnt, and had the problems disappeared from the modern world of software, there would be no place for the case study in this book. However, the underlying issues – for example, testing, levels and means of communication, procedures for follow-up of reported problems, technical issues and good programming practice – are still relevant today.

The Therac Machines

The Therac-25 radiotherapy machine evolved from the less sophisticated Therac-6 and Therac-20. The Therac-6 delivered only x-rays. Theracs-20 and 25 operated in both x-ray and electron mode. Put simply, these machines could deliver either low dose or high dose radiation. The high-dose beam was blocked so as to deliver a diffuse and not a concentrated beam. The Therac-25 software was adapted from Therac-6 and used subroutines from the Therac-20 to handle electron mode. Typical therapeutic doses are around 200 rads for a single treatment. 500 rads and above can be fatal.

A Chronology of the Problem Incidents

A hospital in Marietta, Georgia had been operating a Therac-25 since the beginning of 1985. Other places had been using the machines since 1983. In June 1985, a patient in the Marietta hospital complained of being burnt during treatment. No fault could be found with the machine. The manufacturer, when contacted, insisted that machine malfunction could not be the cause. Nonetheless, the patient filed a lawsuit against the manufacturer in the November. This was settled out of court with no liability admitted. Little can be known for certain about this first incident, but later reconstructions estimated that the patient had probably received two doses of between 15,000 and 20,000 rads.

July 1985, in Ontario Canada, saw the next probable Therac-25 accident. The operator reported that when the machine was activated, it shut down with a cryptic error message and indicated that no dose had been delivered. Operators were accustomed to frequent malfunctions and simply pressed a 'proceed' key to continue. Because of severe skin reddening when the patient returned three days later, the machine was taken out of service. Regulatory authorities and Therac-25 users were informed that there was a problem, but were not told that a patient had been injured. The patient died in the November of cancer, but the autopsy revealed serious radiation overdose.

The manufacturer could not reproduce the malfunction. They suspected a hardware fault and made some changes, which they claimed led to an improvement of 5 orders of magnitude.

Again, users were told there was a problem, told to make visual checks and not to proceed if a certain series of error messages appeared. Once again, however, they were not told of the injury to the patient.

Gordon Symonds, head of Advanced X-ray Systems at the Canadian Radiation Protection Bureau led an analysis of the Therac-25 and listed four modifications necessary for minimum compliance with the Canadian 1971 Radiation Emitting Devices Act. As well as the hardware modifications that were made, the report said treatment should be suspended, not just paused, on dose-rate malfunction, removing the possibility of proceeding via the proceed key. In response to this, the manufacturer decreased the number of tries from five to three, but the recommended modification was still pending some months later when further incidents occurred. Additionally, the manufacturer was asked to install an independent system to verify the turntable position (to ensure that an unblocked electron beam could not be delivered). This was not done and the machine continued to rely on software verification alone.

In common with other machines, one in Yakima, Washington was modified in response to the incident in Ontario. In December of the same year, a patient developed severe skin reddening in a pattern later shown to match the open slots in the Therac-25 blocking trays. The cause was not attributed to the machine at the time, although the hospital later contacted the manufacturer to ask if machine malfunction could have been the cause. The reply was unequivocally that it could not. Many technical reasons were given. On this occasion, the patient suffered injury, but survived. It was later estimated that the accidental overdose was substantially less than that in a more serious incident at the same facility a year later.

Despite mounting evidence of fundamental problems, and system modifications, the death toll was still to rise. In March 1986, an accidental overdose in Tyler, Texas was investigated in detail. This proved something of a turning point in unearthing the real problems.

The Tyler Incidents

Patient and machine operator are separated and usually communicate via video and audio links. On the occasion in question, the video was not turned on and the audio wasn't working.

The patient, who was half way through a treatment programme and knew what to expect, knew at once that something was wrong. He described the sensation as having a hot cup of coffee poured over his back, and immediately started to get up to alert the operator.

The sequence of events was that the operator, who was experienced with the machine, entered the patient's prescription details, but typed 'x' for x-ray, instead of 'e' for 'electron'. This was a common mistake because the majority of treatments were x-ray. She used the cursor-up key to edit the entry to 'e'.

When she pressed the 'beam on' key to begin the treatment, the machine displayed 'malfunction 54' and 'treatment pause'. Treatment pause indicated a low priority problem, i.e. not serious enough to suspend treatment. The dose monitor display indicated that 6 monitor units had been delivered, as opposed to the 202 intended. It was later established that, far from under-dosing the patient, the machine had delivered between 16,000 and 25,000 rads.

The operator was accustomed to frequent malfunctions causing the machine to pause, and did what she usually did in pressing the proceed key to continue. The machine then paused again with the same error and dosage messages. In fact, another huge overdose had been delivered as the patient was getting off the table to report the first problem. This time, the beam hit his arm.

Examination of the patient showed intense skin reddening, and was initially put down to electric shock. The hospital physicist examined the machine and found no apparent problem. He did not know the meaning of the malfunction message because it was not detailed in the documentation provided with the machine.

The day after the incident, the machine was shut down for testing. A day of tests failed to reproduce malfunction 54. The manufacturer reported that there had been no other similar incidents.

After further investigation, including testing for anything that could have given the patient an electric shock, the machine was put back into service. About a week later - three weeks after the previous incident - the next overdose occurred.

The same operator making the same error in inputting 'x' rather than 'e', edited the prescription as usual and, when the machine indicated ready, she pressed the 'beam on' key. The machine immediately paused and showed malfunction 54. The audio link to the patient was working, and the operator heard the patient shout for help. This patient had been having treatment for a skin cancer on the side of his face. As a result of the overdose - an estimated 25,000 rads - he died three weeks later of acute radiation injury to the right temporal lobe of his brain.

The condition of the first patient worsened in the weeks following the incident. He was admitted to hospital some weeks afterwards with radiation-induced myelitis. Amongst many problems, he lost the use of his left arm and both legs. Paralysis of his vocal cords left him unable to speak. He died five months after the accident.

The hospital physicist took the machine out of service immediately after the second incident and contacted the manufacturer. He then began his own investigation. It was not easy to replicate the conditions for a malfunction 54, but with the operator's help, he managed it. Once he could reproduce the error, he began working out what dosages the patients had actually received.

Finding the Errors and the Solutions

In the Therac software, completion of data entry was detected by the presence of the cursor on the command line. It was possible for an operator to move the cursor back up the screen, edit the entries, and move it back down to the command line, without the edit being detected by the software. The changes would not always go undetected. Speed of data entry was a key factor. Even then, not all malfunctions were critical. The real problem was the specific speed and sequence that left the blocking trays open when the machine was set to deliver an electron beam.

In May, the FDA took action and declared the Therac-25 defective under the Radiation Control for Health and Safety Act. The manufacturer was ordered to inform all users, investigate the problem, find a solution and issue a corrective action plan which would have to be approved by the FDA. The manufacturer issued a temporary fix which was in essence to instruct users to disable the cursor up key, so that data could not be edited in the way that could cause the problem.

Between May and the end of 1986, a corrective action plan and a revised version were produced, but the FDA was still voicing concerns on several areas including the lack of a rigorous testing plan for future modifications.

In January 1987, another patient was accidentally overdosed in Yakima, Washington and died three months later. This accident was also traced to a software fault, but a different one. Put simply, the program used a particular variable to indicate whether or not everything was okay to deliver a treatment. A zero value indicated okay. Any other value indicated a problem and the treatment would be paused or suspended. The variable was set to zero when everything was in place, but another of the subroutines incremented it every time it executed. During machine setup, this subroutine might be executed several hundred times. The variable was stored in a single byte. Thus on the 256th increment, the variable would overflow and become zero. If the operator pressed a particular button at the point the variable overflowed, a setup problem would not be detected, which is what happened in the second Yakima incident, and led to the fatal overdose.

After this incident, the manufacturer was instructed by the regulatory authorities in the USA and Canada to discontinue operation.

The corrective action plan went through several iterations and included hardware as well as software safety features, correction of the identified software bugs and logic errors, a means by which operators could visually verify the positioning of the blocking trays, the provision of meaningful error and dose rate messages, limiting of editing keys, a type of dead man's handle to prevent unwanted changes, and updated documentation.

Some Key Points

A lack of procedures for follow-up is evident even from the first incident. Despite having a lawsuit filed against it, the manufacturer was telling its customers for a long time afterwards (and even after further incidents) that there were no reported problems. No law at the time required reporting to regulatory authorities in the USA. This was amended in 1990.

Following hardware changes made after the incident in Ontario, the manufacturer claimed improvements of 5 orders of magnitude. There was no evidence to back this claim. They had not even been able to reproduce the fault.

Staff at the Yakima facility were unable to mount an effective investigation after the incident in December 1985. Documentation on machine malfunction was inadequate, they were misled by an absolute assurance backed up by much technical evidence that the machine was not at fault, and were told that no similar incidents had previously occurred.

It was Fritz Hager, the hospital physicist in Tyler, Texas, who carried out a detailed investigation with the help of the Therac-25 operator. It was largely as a result of his work that the software errors were discovered as soon as they were. Without his investigation, more patients might have been injured or died.

The crib sheet supplied with the Therac-25 showed 'malfunction 54' to be a 'dose input 2' error, with no further explanation. What it actually indicated was the delivery of a dose that was either too high or too low.

The Therac-20 was tested once problems with the Therac-25 became known. It proved to exhibit the same software problem, but was not a danger to patients because it incorporated mechanical interlocks to monitor the machine and did not rely solely on software, as did the Therac-25.

Where did the Fault Lie?

Software errors were undoubtedly a primary cause of the Therac-25 accidents, but software error alone was not the cause. As well as technical problems at several levels - logic and programming errors - there were managerial and procedural errors. There was no proper process for follow-up of reported problems, no effective testing strategy, as evidenced by the errors in the software and the lack of any plans for testing future modifications. Testing problems were also evident in the manufacturer's inability to reproduce the reported malfunctions. This goes hand in hand with trying to base tests on the assumption that there are no faults.

> The absolute elimination of the software errors that could result in fatal overdose was not then (and would not now be) possible. However, the added safety features, including both software and hardware, were successful in preventing further catastrophic failure for the rest of the lifetime of the Therac-25.

Software is one component of a more complex system involving hardware, users, managers etc. This dimension should always be borne in mind. A serious operational error is unlikely to be just a software error. It will be a combination of many things. Even a software error, or the software component of the error, is rarely an explicit coding error. The Therac-25 is a notable exception, where a coding error can be said to have led to fatalities. However, even here the situation was far more complex involving errors at many levels including in design decisions, managerial decisions and quality assurance procedures.

Exercise 9.4 Reports and analyses of the Therac-25 incidents are easily obtainable. The case study given earlier is a brief summary. It does not cover, for example the true extent to which the users were key in unearthing the problems, nor does it go into any depth on the issue of reuse of software subroutines from the earlier versions of the software. Other well-documented events are the cracking of the enigma codes in the 2nd world war [286] and the failure of the Ariane 5 spacecraft, flight 501 in 1996 [8]. Choose one of the following to investigate in depth:

- Concentrating on the users of the systems, compare the roles played by the users of the enigma machines (code creators and code breakers) with the role played by the users of the Therac machines.
- Compare the reuse of software subroutines, and the problems this caused, in the Therac-25 machine and the Ariane 5 spacecraft.

9.10 Summary

The key points that have been covered in this chapter are:

- We test software because we cannot prove it. The purpose of testing is to find errors.
- A tester not only finds, but also prioritises errors. Not all bugs can or should be fixed.
- It is important to design tests that find the maximum number of software bugs without expending resources on redundant tests.
- There are many ways of categorising software testing and many different strategies for testing. The "best" test strategy is usually a mix of several techniques.
- Test plans can facilitate efficient and effective testing.

We have now looked at what happens during maintenance and how software is made to evolve. However, we have not considered in depth the issue of whether or not a change should be carried out. The management and organisational side of this question is the subject of the next chapter.

10

Management and Organisational Issues

"Characterising and understanding software maintenance processes and organisations are necessary, if effective management decisions are to be made and adequate resource allocation is to be provided."

Briand, Kim, Melo, Seaman & Basili [46]

This chapter aims to

1. Explain the criteria for choosing the right calibre of maintenance personnel.
2. Distinguish between the qualities of development and maintenance staff.
3. Describe ways of motivating maintenance staff.
4. Discuss approaches that can be used to increase maintenance productivity.
5. Explain the concept of a maintenance team and its importance.
6. Distinguish between the types of team, their strengths and weaknesses.
7. Explain the importance of educating and training maintenance personnel.
8. Discuss the different organisational modes for maintenance activities.

> 9. Describe the types of education and training programmes available to maintenance personnel.

10.1 Introduction

During the very early days of Information Technology, when computers were very expensive and less powerful than they are today only large organisations and a few individuals used them to write programs. These were usually small programs aimed at performing relatively simple tasks, and as such, could be maintained by individuals. As the computer's capability soared and price fell, it become available in a wide variety of work settings. One of the consequences was that the demand for complex software systems became commonplace. This led to a radical change in the context in which software was developed and maintained. In turn, this implied a need for radically different management and organisation. In effect, there has been a shift of emphasis in software maintenance; that is, a transition from small special-purpose programs - e.g. mathematical functions - to very complex applications - e.g. real-time systems and embedded systems; and from one-person tasks to team tasks (i.e. to project level) primarily because the complexity surpassed that which could be managed by a single individual [42].

The outcome of these changes is evident in the problems of the software crisis. The demand for high quality sophisticated software systems far outstrips the supply of such systems. The net result is that management-related issues have taken on a greater significance, as has the organisation of activities so as to deliver the goods. The management of personnel and the organisation of maintenance tasks relates closely to the equivalent activities in development projects. Nonetheless, there are significant differences. Management in maintenance can be viewed in terms of managing change in the software system and managing personnel. The management of change is the subject of chapter 11.

This chapter is aimed at providing an overall context for personnel management with respect to the required qualities, motivational factors, team dynamics, improving productivity and provision of adequate education and training. It is also the aim of this chapter to discuss the different approaches that can be used to organise maintenance tasks.

10.2 Definitions

Management – the act or art of exercising executive, administrative and supervisory direction.

Team working – a number of people associated together in carrying out a task.

10.3 Management Responsibilities

Small systems that can be developed and maintained single-handedly, and that usually have short life spans, are of no interest to us; their successful operation does not need any significant management control. Large and complex software systems are the ones that present challenges for management because:

- they form an integral part of an organisation,
- their ability to evolve is at the heart of their operation, and
- their maintenance requires the services of large numbers of personnel.

With such complex software systems, the role of maintenance personnel is central to their successful operation. It is the job of management to enable maintenance personnel to live up to this expectation. In this respect, management has the responsibility of ensuring that the software system under maintenance is of a satisfactory quality, and that desired changes are effected with the minimum possible delay at the least possible cost. This can be achieved by:

- devising a means of managing maintenance personnel in order to increase their productivity, ensure job satisfaction and improve system quality, all of which can be facilitated through choice of personnel, motivation, a suitable team structure and education and training;
- selecting a suitable way of organising maintenance tasks so as to increase productivity, control maintenance effort and cost, and most importantly deliver a high quality system. This depends very much on the organisational modes employed for maintenance tasks.

10.4 Enhancing Maintenance Productivity

It is an aim of management to maximise productivity. There are several ways in which this can be done. It is a management task to find the right people for the job, then to see that they are motivated, and given the necessary information and resources to do the job well. It is incumbent also upon the management team to equip itself with sufficient knowledge of the area it is managing.

10.4.1 Choosing the Right People

The COCOMO analysis of 24 maintenance projects and 63 development projects [35] indicated that the single most important factor in increasing productivity is to get the right people for the job. This means tackling the problem of low status of maintenance personnel and working towards improving the general image of maintenance work, an image not enhanced by the low status and low financial rewards traditionally given to maintenance staff. Another way of attracting high calibre people to maintenance work is by tying the overall aims of the organisation to the aims of maintenance [36]. It should be noted that the model referenced above has been refined by COCOMO II [37] and a number of extensions, but the results in terms of personnel remain the same.

Choosing the right people for the job in terms of specific skills and experience is only half the story, Once a team is in place, the single most important factor influencing productivity is motivation.

10.4.2 Motivating Maintenance Personnel

In the overview of this section of the book, the problem was posed of possible loss of experienced personnel. A team should never be solely reliant on one or two "stars" whose loss would cause the enterprise to collapse. Nonetheless, it is hard to overestimate the value to a team of its experienced personnel. A motivated team is far more likely to stay. In the problem posed, serious consideration should be given to allowing the experienced team to take on the new project. The up-front costs of employing new experienced personnel may be greater, but the long-term investment will be worthwhile. Keeping the team means their experience of the old project is still available, even if they are not working directly on it.

Software maintenance still has an image problem. As a result, management has a much more difficult task motivating maintenance personnel than motivating development personnel. Attitudes of management can affect the quantity and quality of work that subordinates achieve, and the way that work is completed [57].

Some ways of motivating personnel are through rewards, appropriate supervision, assignment patterns and recognition:

- *Rewards*: Maintenance work often requires extraordinary bursts of effort, for example to keep operational a vital system that crashes unexpectedly, to add in extra functionality to tight deadlines, to 'rescue' commercial credibility. It is important that maintenance personnel feel valued and rewarded for their hard work. One intuitively thinks of reward in financial terms – the one-off bonus payment for a particularly good piece of work. However, ill-thought-out bonus schemes can be counter-productive. A structured reward system such as promotion is often more effective. If someone is capable of good enough work to earn bonus payments, he or she is likely to be someone worth retaining in a maintenance team. Promotion brings not only financial reward, but also enhanced status. It is a statement of confidence in a person, it allows them to feel valued and that their efforts are recognised. It engenders loyalty to a team far more than the one-off bonus system. Good maintenance programmers can easily be poached by promises of better bonuses. Status, recognition, and a good working environment, however, are not so easily duplicated. Never underestimate the value of a good maintenance team. Lower basic pay and one-off bonuses may look, to the paymasters, like a more effective deal than steady salary increases, but reducing staff turnover by retaining good people saves enormous amounts of money. Consider this in the light of program comprehension and the costs involved.

  A maintainer can master a system so well that the operation of the system revolves around him or her. In such cases, it becomes difficult to move the maintainer elsewhere in the organisation. This may or may not prove problematic and can be dealt with by choosing a suitable organisational mode (see section 10.7).

- *Supervision:* It is not always possible to have highly experienced maintenance staff. There is a need to assign inexperienced staff to maintenance tasks. It is essential to ensure that they get the right level of technical supervision and support from senior members of staff, otherwise they become demotivated through attempts to accomplish tasks beyond their skills and expertise.

- *Assignment patterns:* From time to time it is important to rotate maintenance personnel between maintenance and development tasks. One advantage is that they do not feel stuck with the maintenance tasks. Secondly, their maintenance experience can help them develop more maintainable systems.

- *Recognition:* Getting proper acknowledgement for the very real benefits that maintenance brings to an organisation [7] can assist maintainers to recognise their importance within the organisation.

- *Career structure:* Providing an effective maintenance career structure equivalent to that for development will help to engender a culture where maintenance is seen as a valuable activity by staff and management. It is important also that maintenance is viewed as an activity that enhances the assets of a company and not just as a drain on resources.

The problem is often not that the relevant motivating factors are absent, but that they are not visible. It should be a management aim to improve the image of maintenance work to make these factors more apparent and thus attract high calibre personnel. Also central to motivation is the ability to ensure effective communication between management and personnel.

10.4.3 Communication

It is important that management keep maintenance personnel informed. If staff are unaware of what the procedures are, for example for document control, and why they have been put in place, they will be unable to follow them effectively or give competent feedback on problems associated with them. Information must flow in both directions in order that the maintenance process may be properly controlled, and information may be gathered on the processes carried out so that benefits may be documented and quantified.

This means, in essence, that maintenance personnel must give management information on progress 'at the coal face' in order that the management process can be effective. Note, however, that it is for management to put in place the framework needed for effective communication.

10.4.3.1 Adequate Resources

Resources can be viewed in terms of tools – software and hardware – and working environment. In a study of maintenance programmers, they put state-of-the-art software tools at the top of their list of things most likely to increase productivity. It is important that investment in tools for maintenance is not secondary to investment in tools for development as this gives a clear signal of the perceived relative status of the two activities.

The issue of investing enough in maintenance staff also includes employing the appropriate number of staff. Over-stretching too few good people can lead to dissatisfaction with the working environment.

It is incumbent upon management to be aware of new developments in the field. Otherwise their managerial authority can stifle innovation at a lower level which will lead to a dissatisfied team. The morale of a team that wants to work with state-of-the-art tools and techniques but cannot is unlikely to be high. Perceived low status is also one of the reasons for the high turnover of staff – especially skilled personnel – in maintenance jobs.

10.4.3.2 Domain Knowledge

Managers, in order to be effective, must have adequate knowledge of the maintenance process. In particular, they need to be aware of the cost implications of the various maintenance stages in order to be able to guide the maintenance process effectively. For example, management needs to know that the analysis of existing code is one of the most expensive phases. This area is covered in detail in Chapter 6. Without this knowledge, it is difficult to make effective decisions as to how to tackle problems or how best to invest resources.

> **Exercise 10.1** You are a maintenance manager with the task of persuading top management to increase the budget for the maintenance department. In drawing up your report, what are the points you would emphasise in trying to achieve your aim?

Exercise 10.2 High calibre personnel would rather do software development work than software maintenance work. Explain why this is so and how, if you were a maintenance manager, you would try to attract high calibre people to work in your department.

10.5 Maintenance Teams

The structure of the maintenance team itself is an important factor in determining the level of productivity. For example, a team where personnel are constantly changing will be bad for productivity because of the lag time involved in bringing new staff up to speed on a project.

Two types of team commonly used in development are egoless programming and the chief programmer team [187, 191].

The **egoless programming** team is an organisational structure of individuals whose operation is based on the philosophy that everyone involved in a project should work together to develop the best possible software system. It requires a collegiate setting where team members are open to criticism and do not allow their ego to undermine the project objective.

The **chief programmer** team imposes an organisational structure in which discipline, clear leadership and functional separation play a major role [14]. Its objectives are to organise software maintenance into clearly-defined tasks, to create an environment that promotes the use of state-of-the-art tools, and to ensure that at least two people understand every line of code. It differs sharply from egoless programming in the lack of a comparable level of democracy.

These two well-known team types can be deployed in software maintenance. The major difficulty is that software maintenance tends to be change-driven without the overall timetable and budget considerations given to development projects. The maintenance process is initiated when there is a change to be made. This change may be too small to warrant the services of a team. At other times though, there could be a request for a major maintenance task thereby justifying a team effort. To address the differences, Martin and McClure have suggested two types of maintenance team: the short-term (temporary) team and the long-term (permanent) team [187].

10.5.1 Temporary Team

A temporary team is created on an informal basis when there is a need to perform a specific task, for example a code review. The programmers work together to solve the problem at hand. Leadership is not fixed; it rotates between the team members. The main problem with this arrangement is that program quality, programmer morale and user satisfaction can be compromised.

10.5.2 Permanent Team

A permanent team is a more formal arrangement. It allows for specialisation, creates communication channels, promotes an egoless, collegiate atmosphere, reduces dependency on individuals and allows for periodic audit checks. This team is created on a permanent basis to oversee the successful evolution of a software system throughout its lifetime. The team consists of a maintenance leader, a co-leader, a user-liaison person, a maintenance administrator and other programmers.

The **maintenance leader** provides technical support to the whole team. He or she is responsible to the maintenance administrator. The **co-leader** is an assistant to the maintenance leader. The **user-liaison** person is charged with linking the users and the maintenance team. The **maintenance administrator** is the administrator with a range of responsibilities such as hiring, firing and promotion of staff. The **maintenance programmers** perform problem diagnosis and implement change under the supervision of the maintenance leader.

It is worth pointing out that regardless of the maintenance team adopted, it is important for it to have a mix of experienced and junior personnel. To this end, it is incumbent upon management to take positive steps towards encouraging high calibre people into maintenance work.

10.6 Personnel Education and Training

The personnel of an organisation are central to its successful operation. Their full potential and contribution, however, may be undermined by the lack of an appropriate level of education and training. Education and training in software maintenance is a traditionally neglected area. Few software engineering degrees even devote a full lecture course to the topic and training has tended to be *ad hoc*. However, there is evidence now of a changing trend. A growing academic market for textbooks aimed at degree level and beyond is becoming evident. Note, for example, the need implied by the production of this book. A few Universities, for example the University of Durham, UK, and the University of Maryland, USA, devote a significant proportion of their degree programme to maintenance issues [26]. In this section the objectives and strategies of software maintenance education are discussed.

10.6.1 Objectives

10.6.1.1 To Raise the Level of Awareness

Maintenance personnel need to understand the processes and procedures of maintenance – especially the key differences and relationship between development and maintenance – in order to be able to do their job effectively. The reasons for this are as follows:

- From a management perspective, maintenance managers must understand the specific needs of the maintenance environment in which they operate, for example to recognise the need to set attainable goals in a field which is notorious for the imposition of unrealistic deadlines. Failure to meet deadlines can be demoralising and can impede future productivity. A thorough appreciation of the issues concerned with maintenance can assist in better management – planning and control – of maintenance activities.

- From a maintenance programmer's point of view, it is important for the programmer to recognise that maintenance is not just a peripheral activity in an organisation, it is at the heart of the organisation's functioning. This is a key point and needs to be recognised as such. The more highly computerised an organisation is, the more vital is recognition for this. Remove maintenance as a key activity from an organisation like a bank or a Stock Exchange, and the effect would be catastrophic.

- In circumstances where inexperienced staff (e.g. newly recruited graduates) are assigned to maintenance jobs, it is not uncommon for them to notice that the task they are working on is remote from what was taught to them in University or College courses. Intensifying the level of software maintenance concerns in software engineering-related courses in Universities and Colleges can significantly improve the maintenance skill levels of computer science and software engineering graduates.

- Despite recent improvements, software maintenance still has an image problem. One of the reasons for this is lack of understanding of what software maintenance really is; it is often perceived as simply effecting corrective change. It is important to enlighten those – directly or indirectly – concerned with software maintenance to recognise the activity in its true light.

10.6.1.2 To Enhance Recognition

In organisations whose operation depends on the successful evolution of their software systems, it needs to be recognised within the management structure that maintenance is a vital and valuable activity. When carried out effectively it can ensure successful running of systems and lead to increased customer satisfaction [170].

10.6.2 Education and Training Strategies

There are a number of ways in which the education and training of maintainers can be undertaken. These include University education, in-service training, self-tuition, conferences and workshops.

- *University education:* A large number of Universities currently run courses in software engineering, most of which touch upon software maintenance issues. Considering the increasing importance of software maintenance in industry and academia [9, 282], it is important that software maintenance be elevated from just a 'tag-on' to software engineering to a fully fledged course or be integrated fully within the software engineering course. This is particularly important for graduates who intend to pursue a career in programming. The trend in this respect is in the right direction.

- *Conferences and workshops:* Attending conferences and workshops nationally or internationally – e.g. those organised by bodies such as the IEEE Computer Society (http://www.computer.org/) and the Durham Research Institute in Software Evolution (http://www.dur.ac.uk/CSM/) – offer maintenance personnel the chance to meet others with similar experiences. One of the advantages of such meetings is that the delegates can exchange ideas and identify areas for future collaborative work. One of the drawbacks is that due to the high cost, it may not possible for every member of a maintenance team to gain such exposure.

- *Hands-on experience:* No matter what level of education and formal training software maintenance personnel receive, it will only be reinforced by having the opportunity to do real maintenance work on large software systems. This remains the most valuable way to acquire the appropriate level of knowledge and skill required to undertake successful software maintenance.

10.7 Organisational Modes

After having settled on the type of team to deploy, the next concern is organisational mode. There is a choice between combining development and maintenance activities or having a separate department. The decision to separate or combine the activities depends on factors such as the size of the organisation and the maintenance portfolio with which it has to deal. Large organisations which have a wide range of products and large capital reserves can afford to finance two separate departments. If there is a large software systems portfolio to maintain alongside other development projects, there would be an expectation that there would be separate departments. In practice, however, many organisations combine development and maintenance activities.

The following sections look at the different modes of organising maintenance activities in more detail.

10.7.1 Combined Development and Maintenance

The combination of development and maintenance activities may depend on the type of change (change ownership), program modules (module ownership), activity domains (W-Type), application domains (A-Type) and life-cycle phase (L-Type).

10.7.1.1 Module Ownership

The module ownership mode requires that each member of the team is assigned ownership of a module. The owner of a module is responsible for effecting any changes that need to be implemented in that module. The main advantage with this mode of organisation is that the module owner develops a high level of expertise in the module. Its weaknesses are:

- Nobody is responsible for the overall software system.
- The workload may not be evenly distributed.
- It is difficult to implement enhancements due to unknown dependencies.
- It is difficult to enforce coding standards.

10.7.1.2 Change Ownership

In the change ownership mode each person is responsible for one or more change no matter which modules are affected. That is, the person is also responsible for the analysis, specification, design, implementation and testing of the change. The strengths of the change ownership mode are:

- There is a tendency to adhere to standards set for the whole software system.
- Integrity of the change is ensured.
- Changes can be coded and tested independently.
- Code inspection tends to be taken seriously.

Its weaknesses are:

- Training of new personnel takes much more time than it would for the module ownership mode. This is primarily because knowledge of the entire system is required.
- Individuals do not have long-lasting responsibilities, but instead have a series of transient responsibilities.

10.7.1.3 Work-Type

The key feature of Work-Type mode is that there is 'departmentalisation' by work type; analysis, specification, etc. Those in the different departments work as a team but with clearly defined responsibilities and roles. The main strength of this arrangement is that members in each department develop specialised knowledge and skills. The drawback is the cost of co-ordinating the different departments.

10.7.1.4 Application-Type

With the Application-Type mode, division is based on application areas such as health information systems or office automation. The advantage with this mode is that members of the team develop specialised application knowledge. Like the Work-Type mode, its drawback is the cost of co-ordinating of the various application domains.

10.7.2 Separate Maintenance Department

This mode of organisation requires a separate maintenance department. It is based on the need to maintain a large number of system portfolios, and the increasing business need of keeping software systems operational at all times.

Its strengths are:

- There is clear accountability.
- It allows development staff to concentrate on development of new software systems.
- It facilitates and motivates acceptance testing just after development.
- It encourages high quality end-user service.

Its weaknesses are:

- There is a danger of demotivation due to status differences (see earlier discussion).
- The developers tend to lose system knowledge after the system is installed.
- There is a high cost involved in the co-ordination of development and maintenance when needed.
- There may be duplication of communication channels.

In the cases where there is a separate maintenance department, some organisations take measures to minimise the effect of the dichotomy by providing the maintenance team with support. This support can be provided by assigning some members of the development team to join the maintenance team on installation of the system. Lientz and Swanson have called these members the **maintenance escort** [176]. This is usually a temporary measure; the maintenance escorts return to development work after ensuring that the system functions according to the agreed specification. At times, the maintenance escorts may become permanent members of the maintenance team by virtue of their familiarity with the system during its development.

> **Exercise 10.3** Software maintenance is a traditionally neglected area in computer science and software engineering degree courses. Say why the differing environments of the University degree course and the industrial maintenance department could have been a major cause of this neglect.

10.8 Summary

The key points that have been covered in this chapter are:

- A major software maintenance management responsibility is control of personnel issues.

- Software maintenance productivity may be enhanced by choosing the right people, motivating them and giving them adequate resources to do the job.

- Tackling the problem of low status of maintenance personnel and working towards enhancing the general image of maintenance work is largely a task for those responsible for educating and training maintenance personnel.

- A good maintenance team is a very important and valuable asset to an organisation.

- The need for education and training is paramount and education strategies are gradually changing to become more appropriate to maintenance issues.

Software maintenance is a complicated business that dwarfs software development in terms of the complexities of looking after multiple versions, supporting users and prioritising tasks. Without some structured means of keeping track of it all, it would be impossible to manage, and impossible to know for certain that the job was being carried out effectively. These issues form the basis of the next section of the book.

PART III: Keeping Track of the Maintenance Process

Overview

Maintaining software is a complex field and it is not easy to keep track of everything that is happening. Nonetheless, it is vital to do so. In this part of the book, we look at how to keep track of all the complexities of the maintenance process and, related to this, how to be sure that what we are doing is effective.

- **Configuration Management**

IT systems grow and change. The more successful a system, the better used it will be and the more it will evolve. Uncontrolled change leads to less order within a system and eventually to a system that is so degraded and disordered it can no longer change. With software at the heart of so many systems in the modern world, it is ever more vital that software change and evolution is controlled so that systems can grow in functionality and usefulness, rather than defaulting to an uncontrolled slide towards disordered complexity.

Even if you will never be called upon to take charge of the management of complex software change, you need a good understanding of what controlling software is all about. It will underpin much of what you do and the decisions you make as a maintenance programmer.

- **Maintenance Measures**

The development of good, maintainable systems is a laudable aim, but what exactly does good and maintainable mean? How can you judge if one system is better than another? Measures such as user satisfaction are important, but not always enough. "The users like system A better than system B" does not mean that system A is necessarily a better system. It might collapse irretrievably at the next attempted upgrade, making the users perforce switch their allegiance to system B. On the other hand, well-structured, maintainable code does not automatically mean great 'look and feel' and high user satisfaction. The issues are related, but not the same.

In striving to build 'good' systems, maintainability is a key factor. A maintainable system has a chance of being developed into a good system. A non-maintainable system has nowhere to go.

The ideal would be to judge systems by a maintainability factor – a meaningful and rigorously calculated measure that would apply to all software and give a true measurement of how maintainable it was. As yet, no-one has figured out a way of doing this. Maybe they never will, but that doesn't mean that we can't measure software. We can, and the understanding of how software measures can be applied is key in building up an in-depth understanding of how software systems evolve.

Discussion Points

These points are intended to stimulate thinking and discussion on fundamental issues in software maintenance. The issues raised are explored in the chapters of this section, but it is a beneficial to think around these areas and try to draw conclusions yourself, before looking for answers in the text.

- **The Paper Trail**

The following example is of people facing a situation where the right or wrong decision is not immediately obvious. Think through the issues, the underlying ones as well as the superficial. Analyse if and where these people are getting it wrong, what they might have done better and how they might be motivated to get it right.

Keeping Track of the Maintenance Process

Programmer A has been maintaining system X since it was developed. A major upgrade is to be undertaken, and new programmers are being brought in to work with programmer A.

Programmer A is discussing with his manager how best to spend the time remaining before the new team starts. There are one or two minor modifications that users have requested. These will not take long, and could be cleared up before the new team arrives, thus giving it a clean start. On the other hand, a couple of minor straightforward modifications might be just the thing to get the new programmers familiar with the system. Programmer A feels he should use the time to comment the existing code and bring the system documentation up to date. Being the sole maintainer, he has been a bit lax at times. His manager thinks that getting started on documenting the requirements for the major upgrade might be a better use of the time, to give the new team a flying start. The old code will eventually be ported to another language. Is there any point in updating its documentation? If there is any catching up of paperwork to be done, programmer A could update his QA backup forms – the forms that all personnel are expected to keep to show how, when and where electronic data is backed up. Programmer A defends his position of keeping his own personal records as he is the only one with access to, or ability to use, the data he has responsibility for backing up. Furthermore, he points out, the whole system will be changed when the new team starts. The manager agrees, but points out that a QA review would still put a black mark against the non-existence of this paperwork.

They debate the pros and cons. What is to be gained or lost by the timing of each of the suggested tasks?

- **Hidden Benefit**

As part of a job interview, Candidate A and Candidate B are given a programming task. They must make a simple modification to a piece of software. The system comprises tens of thousands of lines of code. There is insufficient time to tell them the details of what the system does. All they know is that at certain identifiable points, the code makes a 5% adjustment to a total. For the new version, the adjustment must be 7.5% under one set of conditions, 3% under another, and must stay at 5% for the rest of the time.

Candidate A's objectives are speed and the least possible modification of the source code. The points that might require modification are easily identifiable. Constants within the existing code already exist for the values 3, 5 and 7.5. Candidate A uses these, adds conditional statements only at the places where the new conditions could occur and turns in a working version that requires little new compilation. Together with this, Candidate A makes the recommendation that the modification be re-done when time allows, such that the calculations are no longer reliant on the constant values, and the testing of conditions expanded to include all possible points.

Candidate B's objective is to make the modification in a reasonable time, but with due regard to code structure. This involves removal of any use of constant declarations. The required values will be read in from an external table. Conditional statements are placed at all identified points, on the grounds that even if this modification does not require it, a future one might. Together with the working version, requiring full recompilation, Candidate B turns in a recommendation that the objects subject to these percentage shifts be better encapsulated, such that calculations are invisible in the main source code, and that the conditional statements themselves are no longer necessary.

When required to argue for their own solution against the other candidate's, A claims to have demonstrated the ability to perform a quick and workable amendment. Preventive maintenance, by way of code amendment, can easily follow when time allows. This solution gets a working version back on the clients' desk in the quickest time. Although not the best structured code, speed of delivery might give a commercial advantage.

B says that A has taken this argument too far. There might be need for another quick fix before the necessary preventive maintenance can be done. A quick-fix on top of A's solution might, for example, change the value of one of the constant declarations with catastrophic effect. B claims a solution that, although not perfect, has provided a working system in a reasonable time and one that can bear the weight of another quick-fix without disastrous results.

Try to argue the case from both sides, and see if you can make a convincing case for employing either candidate.

11

Configuration Management

Good practice comes down to common sense, but if it were as easy as it sounds, far fewer projects would get it wrong.

This chapter aims to

1. Describe what configuration management is and the major processes that make it up.
2. Discuss configuration management as vital to the integrity of the end product.
3. Define change control and explain its role in configuration management.
4. Explain the role and importance of documentation in maintenance.
5. Give examples of software support tools.
6. Explore some differences between configuration management in software maintenance and in software development.

11.1 Introduction

Configuration management is a means of keeping a hold of the process of software change, and of having confidence in the implementation of change. Configuration management looks at the overall system process and its constituent parts down to a certain level of detail. Below this level, we enter the realms of software measurement which is covered in the next chapter.

As we have seen, software maintenance consumes up to 75% of the total life-cycle cost and is by far the biggest concern of those who develop and maintain commercial software. At the heart of maintenance is an evolving software product.

In the field of software engineering, there is an added complication when dealing with system configuration and change. This is that the software component of the product which is released is in the form of executable code whereas the corresponding 'product' within the supplier organisation is source code. This source code is the representation of an executable equivalent, but which one? Source code can be modified without there being any effect upon executable versions in use and, if strict controls are not kept, the source code which is the exact representation of a particular executable version may no longer exist. Additionally, source code alone is insufficient documentation to enable understanding of the system, as is explored fully in chapter 6, and tight documentation controls are necessary.

The means by which the process of software development and evolution is controlled is called **configuration management.** When so much hangs on a continually changing product, it is vital that the process of change be controlled. Without proper control, we cannot keep a handle on what the product is or does. Configuration management in software maintenance differs from configuration management in software development because of the different environments in which the activities are carried out. Software maintenance is undertaken in the environment of a live system in use by a probably large user base. Potential effects upon a live system are much more immediate than those upon a system still under development.

Control of the process of change in the software industry has been less rigorous than in other engineering disciplines. Yet without control, product integrity is lost. Suppose that a customer reports a bug in a software system. In order to address this situation, to assess the severity of the problem, it is necessary to know which product the customer is using. The executable code that the customer is running must be matched with the appropriate source code. This is not always going to be possible if changes and updates to the software have not been properly controlled. Maybe the source code for this version (and perhaps several subsequent versions) was not kept. Perhaps the bug is a serious one and perhaps the customer cannot upgrade to the current version; it may be inappropriate for the customer's hardware. A serious bug may be costing the customer money in lost business. Who will pay ultimately? A court may well decide that it was unforgivably lax on the part of the software supplier to fail to keep the necessary information on a live system. The lack of control may cost the software company dear and may even put it out of business.

Putting procedures in place for the effective control of software maintenance has an attached cost. However, any short-term saving from neglecting to install such procedures is very soon wiped out when problems occur.

11.2 Definitions

Baseline – The arrangement of related entities that make up a particular software configuration. Any change made to a software system relates to a specific baseline. Baselines can be defined at each stage of the software life-cycle, for example functional baseline, design baseline, product baseline, etc.

Change – the act, process or result of being altered.

Change control – keeping track of the process of making a modification.

Configuration – A mode of arrangement, confirmation or outline; the relative position of the component parts of a system, for example the relative positions of the stars and planets in the solar system.

Configuration management – "The discipline of developing uniform descriptions of a complex product at discrete points in its life-cycle with a view to controlling systematically the manner in which the product evolves" [200].

Software change control – keeping track of the process of making modifications to a software system.

Software configuration – The current state of the software system and the interrelationship between the constituent components. These would typically be the source code, the data files and the documentation.

Software configuration management – Configuration management related specifically to software systems.

Software documentation – the written record of facts about a software system recorded with the intent to convey purpose, content and clarity[13].

Variant – Source and object specialised to different platforms. For example, Microsoft Word for Windows for the PC and Microsoft Word for Windows for the Macintosh are variants of the same product.

Version – A version represents a small change to a software configuration. In software configuration management terms one refers to versions of a given baseline rather than dealing with a proliferation of baselines.

Version control – Keeping track of baselines, versions of baselines and the relationships between them.

11.3 Configuration Management

Configuration management was established as a field in its own right in the 1950's with the primary purpose of guaranteeing reproducibility of products. It is now recognised as an activity that is critical to the management and maintenance of any large system, including one that is software based.

Using the definition given in the previous section, configuration management activities fall into four broad categories:

1. The identification of the components and changes;
2. The control of the way the changes are made;
3. Auditing the changes – making the current state visible so that adherence to requirements can be assessed;
4. Status accounting – recording and documenting all the activities that have taken place.

Depending upon the size of the organisation there might or might not be someone with sole responsibility for configuration management. In a large organisation, there might be a configuration management team with a configuration manager. In a small organisation, the duties of a configuration manager might be taken on by others along with other

---

[13] Adapted from Tausworthe's definition of 'concurrent documentation' ([264], pp.32-9).

duties. But however the task is organised, it is the same job that needs to be done.

All components of the system's configuration are recorded along with all relationships and dependencies between them. Any change – addition, deletion, modification – must be recorded and its effects upon the rest of the system's components checked. After a change has been made, a new configuration is recorded. There is a need to know who is responsible for every procedure and process along the way. It is a management task both to assign these responsibilities and to conduct audits to see that they are carried out.

A programmer, for example, might make a modification to a software module in accordance with instructions received. Another programmer requiring this modification for interface to another module might, if unaware of the work already done, redo the modification. Similarly, if the first programmer is unaware of the wider requirements, he or she might make the modification in a way that is inappropriate to other modules which depend upon it. It is the programmer's job to program. It is a management job to have a clear view of the system as a whole at all levels.

Mini Case Study – Giving Appropriate Guidance and Direction

The management task of assigning appropriate responsibility applies at many levels. Problems in non-software-related tasks can affect software development and vice versa. At the research institute attached to the ACME Health Clinic, a large research project involved the conducting of a wide-ranging survey during its first year. In the second year of the project, there were complaints that a software development group's work was held up because the results of the survey were not available. In fact, the survey had been done and the information gathered but no one had been able to give guidance to the survey team about how to collate and present their results. The staff and resource had been available to do the work but because no one had explicit responsibility for overseeing the interface between the survey team and the rest of the project, delays were caused.

A major aim in configuration management and change control is reproducibility. We might wish to reproduce an older version of a system if a new one has serious shortcomings or we might wish to reproduce specific functionality in a particular environment. In fact, the need may arise to reconstitute both the product and the process at any stage in its evolution.

In pursuit of this aim, three objectives of configuration management are control, consistency and minimising cost.

- *Control:* The very essence of software maintenance is the evolutionary nature of software systems. If the process by which such systems evolve is not controlled, chaos can result.

    Configuration management is necessary because software systems have a long lifetime and are subject to change. Constant change to workable live software systems is bound to lead to problems without a proper means of control.

- *Consistency:* Configuration management is necessary to ensure the production of consistent sets of software products:

    - Consistent sets of documents

        Software projects in their development will produce reams of documents. Some will be vital to the maintenance phase and these need to be identified. However, many documents which are vital during the development process might not be needed subsequently. Often, where these contain vital information it will have been subsumed into other documents – for example, final deliverables and manuals. It is very important to identify which these documents are, and decide what procedures are to be applied to keeping track of them.

        As well as standardised document identification which allows for versioning and indexing, standard reporting mechanisms should be put in place [229]. The whole area of documentation is an important and often neglected one. Section 11.5 is devoted to a detailed discussion of documentation and its importance to the maintenance process.

    - Consistent software releases

        A large area of responsibility is the management of the release of changed systems into the world. Standardised version and product release control is needed to keep track of what is where. Version control is discussed later.

- *Cost:* A major aim in configuration management is to ensure that the changes are made such that overall costs are minimised. This means cost in terms of future maintenance as well as the cost of the immediate change.

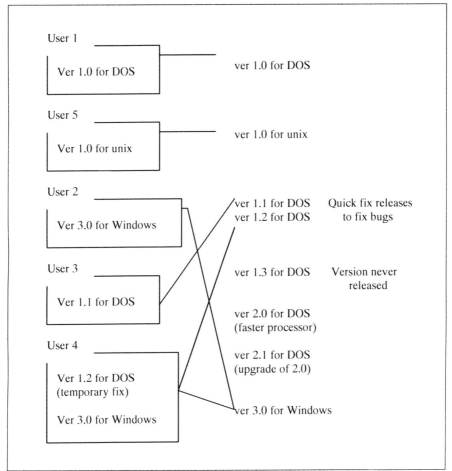

Figure 11.1 Different versions of a software product

Figure 11.1 shows a small section of a company's user base and the different versions of a software product currently in use. Suppose that user 3 has a problem with the system because of a newly discovered bug. There are several options open to the system supplier. The most attractive from the point of view of the supplier would be to persuade the user to upgrade to a newer version, perhaps version 2.0 or even 3.0.

However, this might not be possible. Hardware constraints may prevent it. An upgrade to version 1.2 or 1.3 is another possibility but these are interim releases, one of which was a temporary short-term solution for a specific user. The company will not wish to increase its user base on these interim releases now that these have been superseded by newer versions. It might be that the best, or only, solution is to produce another quick-fix solution, perhaps a version 1.2a which addresses both the newly found error and any serious problems which have come to light with the temporary version 1.2.

It is easy to see that without consistent and accurate records and documentation, it will be all but impossible to keep track of this, whereas proper procedures will enable the identification of

- the software version in use by a particular user – attempting a repair of the wrong version will only make things worse;
- the options for upgrade – it is necessary to know which options are viable in the user's environment;
- the levels at which different versions are compatible – the structure of data files, for example, might change between versions or releases, and attempting to run an inappropriate version might lead to corruption of the user's data;
- the source code corresponding to a specific version – if, as in the example, the only option is a new release of version 1.2 as version 1.2a, it is vital to be able to trace and reproduce the source code for version 1.2 despite the fact this might not correspond to any executable version currently in use.

Without a structured approach it is impossible to guarantee

i. the integrity of the system,
ii. that the course of evolution is traceable or
iii. that correlation between all the different parts of the system is identifiable.

Configuration management is more than just a set of methodologies and tools. An organisation will select configuration management methodologies appropriate to its specific needs but considerable skill is needed in both selection of the right techniques and methodologies and the effective imposition of them upon the software development and maintenance process.

Exercise 11.1 What is meant by the configuration of a software system? Illustrate your answer by detailing the configuration of a software system on which you have worked or are currently working.

Exercise 11.2 Why might it be important to be able to reproduce a software configuration for a version of a system which has no users?

11.3.1 A Specific View of Software Configuration Management

There are many different ways of tackling the specifics of software configuration management and no single system will suit all projects. The choice of specific procedures depends upon many things, for example the working environment and the resources available.

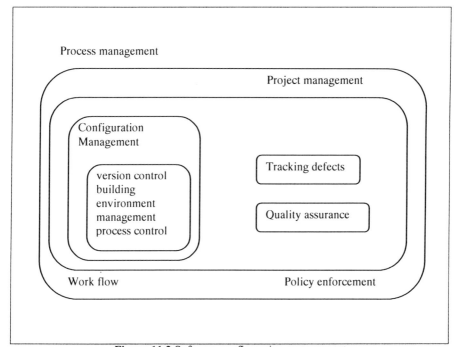

Figure 11.2 Software configuration management

In this section we will look in detail at one view of software configuration management. Leblang [164] views it as a four-part process broadly in line with the four-category definition of Narayanaswamy and Scacchi [200]:

1. version control
2. building
3. environment management and
4. process control

These categories sit within an overall process where collective control is the task of process management (Figure 11.2).

11.3.1.1 Version Control

A company that has developed and supplied a software product will find itself having to maintain this product in many different versions. There are many reasons for this. Not all users will upgrade to the latest version simultaneously. The latest version might imply a change in operating system. A company cannot abandon a product and with it a large customer base just because it has developed a better version that runs on a more up-to-date platform. Similarly a company cannot abandon users of a previous version just because a newer version has been released. In the main, a company will be supporting many versions of a product. Control of the evolution of a single system is no trivial task. When multiple versions and upgrades have to be considered, the task becomes a mammoth one.

During the process of software evolution, many objects are produced, for example files, electronic documents, paper documents, source code, executable code and bitmap graphics.

A version control system keeps track of all the changes to every object and can also support parallel development by allowing branching of versions. Figure 11.3 shows version control at its simplest where the current version of the whole system is given by version 2 of object 1, version 3 of object 2, version 4 of object 3 and version 2 of object 4.

In a more complex system where, for example, parallel development must be supported, branching may occur (Figure 11.4). It is now not such a simple matter to identify the latest version of the object.

Version 2.2 might be a later version than version 4.0, for example. The version control system must control the creation of these variants as well as the merging of the different versions to form a complete system. Version control tools exist and are discussed further in Chapter 14.

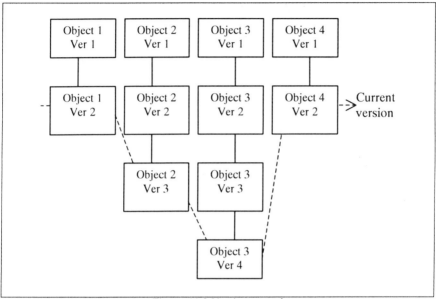

Figure 11.3 Version control

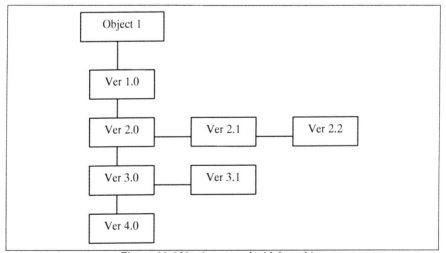

Figure 11.4 Version control with branching

11.3.1.2 Building

Software systems must be built and rebuilt from the objects of which they are made. These objects will evolve and change and the management of building the system must ensure that the correct product can be produced reliably. Automatic build tools might involve **minimal rebuilding** – reusing objects where possible and rebuilding only where an object has changed or has had a dependency change. Documentation is vital and build tools should produce the documentation necessary to recreate the complete file system environment for any specific build.

Objects must be built from the appropriate versions of the sources using the appropriate tools. Automated systems which might ensure that the correct version of the sources is used do not always ensure that the correct tools, for example the right version of the compiler, are used. Traditional tools require that the user specifies module dependencies via some sort of system model like a makefile. The manual updating of a system model is unsatisfactory as it is all too easy to fail to declare all dependencies, especially as the system configuration changes. System model generators automate this process but might be language specific, can be slow, and are not always reliable in all circumstances. However, as their use has become more widespread, their reliability has improved.

11.3.1.3 Environment Management

This is the means by which the file system is managed. The aim here is to ensure that the appropriate versions of files are selected and that the environment at any stage may be reproduced. Environment management must take account of the need both to share objects and to keep objects apart from each other. For example, a maintenance programmer must be able to make changes to an object without the changes having any effect upon the system as a whole prior to such change being completed, verified and accepted as part of the system. On the other hand, it must be possible to test the results of change upon the system as a whole and to test one change against another. An environment management system must be what Leblang [164] describes as a time machine which allows everything in the environment to appear as it did at some given point in time.

11.3.1.4 Process Control

Process control is the means by which configuration management interacts with the wider aspects of the organisation and controls the way that other processes interact with each other. The configuration management process must interact with all the processes and methodologies used, for example the design and analysis methodologies.

> **Exercise 11.3** The example in Figure 11.3 uses integer numbers to label different versions. Why would this be inadequate for branching versions such as those shown in the example in Figure 11.4?

11.4 Change Control

Change control concerns the specific area comprising the sequence of events starting with a request for a change to a live software system and ending with either the approval of a system incorporating the change or a rejection of the request for change.

Bennett *et al.* [26] define the activities which comprise change control as:

- Selection from the top of a priority list.
- Reproduction of the problem (if there is one).
- Analysis of code (and specifications if available).
- Incorporation of change.
- Design of changes and tests.
- Quality assurance.

Change control ensures that changes to a system are made in a controlled way such that their effects can be predicted. Full change control procedures can be time-consuming and are not necessarily appropriate at every stage of the evolution of a system. There are cases where the process of deciding and approving change can be done less formally. For example, pressing reasons might emerge for the use of one algorithm over another or for a module to be structured in a different way from the one originally envisaged. An experienced team is quite capable of making these decisions without putting such changes to a full-blown change control process.

> ### Mini Case Study – When is a Less Formal Change Control Process Appropriate?
>
> For the ACME Health Clinic's original Windows-based Medical Information System, program development was carried out in Microsoft's Visual Basic 3.0. Design of the data and modules had aimed at an optimal way of passing medical record structures to and from subroutines. Subsequently it was discovered that the run-time stack of Visual Basic 3.0 is very small and could not cope with the data structures as designed. Thus a new means of passing data was designed. The problem and the solution were discussed within the project team and documented but did not need a full-blown change control process which would have been counter-productive because of the time it would have taken. Had the solution to this problem been a change in the actual data structures, then far more structured procedures would have been followed, as this would have implied a major change in the system design. And had either of these solutions been carried out after the system had gone live in the clinic, then a proper change control process would have been followed. Once a system is live, the possible effects of any change are far-reaching and can affect the user base as well as the live system, which in this example is interacting with patients and therefore has the potential to cause harm.

11.4.1 The Responsibilities of Management in Change Control

- *Deciding if the change should be made:* This is the job of a Change Control Board. A request for change must be analysed to see if it is valid. Is it a requirement for a genuine change or does it stem perhaps from a user's misunderstanding of existing functionality? A potential change must be costed. The cost of making the change must be balanced against the benefit that will accrue from it.

    It is the job of the Change Control Board to decide whether or not to accept a request for change. It is usual to institute a change request form that gives details of the change requested and the action taken. Change request forms are a very useful form of documentation. The definition of the exact format of a change request form and the information contained within it is a job for the configuration management team although in some cases it will be necessary to conform to client standards. An example is given in Figure 11.5. The Change Control Board considers the effect of a change from a strategic and organisational viewpoint rather than a technical one and decides whether or not the change would be cost-effective.

- *Managing the implementation of the change:* The ramifications of making a change must be assessed. This assessment will have begun as part of the costing process.

- *Verifying the quality:* Implementation of a change should be subject to quality control. A new version of the system should not be released until it has satisfied a quality control process.

Change Request Form
Name of system
Version
Revision
Date
Requested by
Summary of change
Reasons for change
Software components requiring change
Documents requiring change
Estimated cost

Figure 11.5 An example of a change request form

A key component in the general control of change and specific control of the processes of software evolution is documentation. A major aim in configuration management and change control is reproducibility. We might wish to reproduce an older version of a system if a new one has serious shortcomings or we might wish to reproduce specific functionality in a particular environment. Without a written record of what the situation was previously and is now; and why and how it changed, reproduction is impossible with any guarantee of accuracy.

Nowadays the move is towards teams working in parallel on the maintenance of systems. This calls for far more sophisticated means of control; for example, the need for strict procedures on the checking out, editing and checking in of entities such as source code modules from a components library.

> **Exercise 11.4** Investigate the concept of the change control form and design a detailed change control form for use in an organisation which supports many different versions of many different software products for a large user base. Give a reason for the inclusion of each field on the form. Useful detail can be found in [255].

It is essential to be able to retain and manage the system components. In order to do this, accurate and up-to-date information about them must always be available. The means of making such information available is through documentation. In the next section, the categories, role, production and maintenance of documentation are discussed.

11.5 Documentation

Documentation is integral to the whole process of management and control. It has a major role to play in making processes and procedures visible and thereby allowing effective control.

The recording process usually begins when the need for the system is conceived and continues until the system is no longer in use.

11.5.1 Categories of Software Documentation

There are two main categories of software documentation: user documentation and system documentation.

User documentation refers to those documents containing descriptions of the functions of a system without reference to how these functions are implemented [255].

System documentation contains documents which describe all facets of the system, including analysis, specification, design, implementation, testing, security, error diagnosis and recovery.

The user documentation and system documentation are further split into separate documents, each of which contains a description of some aspect of the software system (see, for example, Table 7.1).

Table 7.1 Types and functions of documentation

Type		Constituent document	Function
User documentation	1.	System overview	Provides general description of system functions
	2.	Installation guide	Describes how to set up the system, customise it to local needs, and configure it to particular hardware and other software systems
	3.	Beginner's guide / tutorial	Provides simple explanations of how to start using the system
	4.	Reference guide	Provides in-depth description of each system facility and how it can be used
	5.	Enhancement booklet	Contains a summary of new features
	6.	Quick reference card	Serves as a factual lookup
	7.	System administration	Provides information on services such as networking, security and upgrading
System documentation	1.	System rationale	Describes the objective of the entire system
	2.	Requirements analysis / specification	Provides information on the exact requirements for the system as agreed between the user and the developer / maintainer
	3.	Specification / design	Provides description: (i) of how the system requirements are implemented (ii) of how the system is decomposed into a set of interacting program units (iii) the function of each program unit
	4.	Implementation	Provides description of: (i) how the detailed system design is expressed in some formal programming language (ii) program actions in the form of intra-program comments
	5.	System test plan	Provides description of how program units are tested individually and how the whole system is tested after integration
	6.	Acceptance test plan	Describes the tests that the system must pass before users accept it
	7.	Data dictionaries	Contains descriptions of all terms that relate to the software system in question

There are other ways in which documentation may be classified. For example, Macro argues that there are three classes of documentation: user manuals, operator manuals and maintenance manuals [184]. The user manual describes what the system does without necessarily going into the details of how it does it or how to get the system to do it.

The operator manual describes how to use the system as well as giving instructions on how to recover from faults. The maintenance manual contains details of the functional specification, software design, high quality code listings, test data and results.

Both classification schemes are identical in the sense that they both include all the information that is contained in software documents (Figure 11.6).

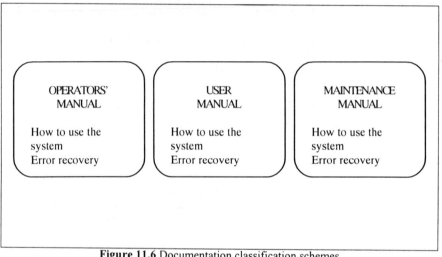

Figure 11.6 Documentation classification schemes

Although the list of software documents presented in Table 7.1 is not exhaustive, it contains many of the documents typically found in a system. The type, content and sometimes name of each document will vary between systems. This variation is caused by a number of factors that include:

- *Development methodology:* The approach used to develop software systems differs from one organisation to another [298]. The type of system documentation produced will depend on the approach used to develop the software.

- *Category of customer:* The relation of an individual or organisation to a software system determines the subset of documents that accompany its copy of the system. For example, a software developer will sell user manuals and object code to software dealers. The same developer might sell system documentation as well as source code listings to a customer who modifies the system to build other products. As such, different customers may receive different documentation sets for the same software system.

- *Version of the system:* System upgrades will be accompanied by additional documents such as enhancement booklets, which convey information on the new features of the system, and other literature on how to upgrade existing systems.

The diversity in the types of documents that come with each software system makes it difficult to give a prescriptive list of documents that must accompany a software system. The nomenclature of documentation varies between systems and organisations. The present scenario is that users must learn to accept the nomenclature of their systems suppliers. The disadvantage of this is that if users have different systems[14] with varying documentation naming conventions, it can be difficult and confusing to switch between systems and find information in an easy and timely fashion. In a time when software maintainers are working hard against the clock to address maintenance backlog problems, the last thing they need is a set of confusing software documentation. The use of international document standards can alleviate this problem.

11.5.2 Role of Software Documentation

There are a number of reasons why it is of paramount importance to have accurate and sufficient documentation about a software system:

- *To facilitate program comprehension:* The function of documentation in the understanding and subsequent modification of the software cannot be overemphasised [255, 284]. Prior to undertaking any software maintenance work, the maintainer should have access to as much information as possible about the whole system. Due to the high turnover of staff within the software industry, it may not always be possible to contact developers of the system for information about it [26]. As such, maintainers need to have access to documents about the system in order to enable them

---

[14] That is, systems from different suppliers, which is usually the case.

to understand the rationale, functionality and other development issues. Each system document has a specific function (see Table 7.1). According to Brooks' top-down theory of program comprehension, program text and the associated documents, each of which is termed an indicator, are used to verify hypotheses about a program's function [48]. However, he warns that 'more documentation is not necessarily better' *(op. cit.,* p.552), one reason for this is that redundancy in documents may result in some documents contradicting others.

- *To act as a guide to the user:* Documentation aimed at users of a system is usually the first contact they have with the system [255]. The user documentation that comes with a system is used for various purposes that include:

    - providing an initial and accurate description of what the system can do. As such, the user can decide whether or not the system can satisfy his or her needs. In order to achieve this, the documents must be written and arranged in such a way that the user can easily find what is required.

    - providing information that enables the user to install the system and customise it to local needs.

    - providing technical information on how to handle malfunctions.

- *To complement the system:* Documentation forms an integral and essential part of the entire software system. Osborne argues that 'without the documentation, there is little assurance that the software satisfies stated requirements or that the organisation will be able to maintain it' [209].

    Exercise 11.5 List the major types of software documentation and explain how each can facilitate maintenance.

11.5.3 Producing and Maintaining Quality Documentation

It is essential to make continuous changes to all facets of documentation affected by maintenance activities. The importance of this is underscored by the fact that the inspection of existing documents may be the only means available to maintenance personnel to understand the details of the software and the reasoning behind its development [11]. Reasonably good[15] documentation will facilitate the achievement of this aim.

Osborne contends that the cost of maintaining a software system is proportional to the **effectiveness** of the documentation which describes what the system does as well as the logic used to accomplish its tasks [209]. It is not only what the documents contain that matters, but how the material is presented. Some authors have suggested a number of guidelines on producing software documents:

1. Writing style: adhering to guidelines for clear and understandable text, for example using the active rather than the passive mode, splitting the text into manageable chunks and repeating complex explanations in different ways.

2. Adhering to document standards: for example, standard cover sheets can ensure traceability of documents. Standard fonts, styles and numbering systems can make it easier for the reader to switch between documents – there will be no need to adapt to different styles for different documents.

3. Standards and quality assessment: putting documents through a quality assessment process will help to ensure conformance to standards.

4. Documentation techniques:

    a) To ensure that documentation is up to date, procedures should be put in place to encourage the use of adequate resource for the updating of documents concurrent with system updates.

    b) The use of good design methodologies, for example good design methods and practices such as structured programming, use of high-level control structures, meaningful identifier names and consistent style, reduces the need for low-level documentation [98]. This is particularly helpful during maintenance.

---

[15] The phrase 'reasonably good' is used to emphasise the importance of striking the right balance between what we expect from software documentation and the information it eventually provides. This is because too much is usually expected from documentation. Weinberg [284] argues that people have different needs when they look at program documentation and no single collection of documentation will satisfy those needs equally well.

5. Documentation support tools: support tools exist to help with the classification and updating of documentation. Appropriate tools can do much towards ensuring consistency in documents.

A common problem that confronts maintainers of software systems is ensuring consistency across all the documents when the software system changes [77, 255]. The usual solution to this problem is to keep a record alongside the documents of the relationships and dependencies of not only the documents, but also parts of the documents [255]. This way, changes to whole or parts of documents can be controlled and managed more effectively The use of structured software development methodologies such as Structured Analysis/Structured Design (SA/SD), Jackson Structured Design (JSD) [298] and Object Modelling Technique (OMT) [240] helps to lend structure to the whole process and makes the effective keeping of documentation an easier task. The advent of software documentation tools, most of which come with the system used to develop the software, is another step along the road to effective and maintainable documentation.

Software systems are modified and enhanced by individuals who were not involved with the initial development. In order to ensure that a system can be updated quickly and reliably, it is necessary to record all information relating to the evolution of the software. When the system is changed, all documents that are affected must be updated as and when the changes occur.

Exercise 11.6 Investigate the Source Code Control System (SCCS) available on your system and explain how you would use it as part of a large software project.

Exercise 11.7 Produce a comprehensive list of the configuration management support tools available on your system. Write a concise note on each summarising its use. On-line help or manual systems are a good starting point.

Exercise 11.8 Explain the limitations of SCCS as regards its use in a parallel development/maintenance environment and explain how these limitations have been overcome in other support tools.

11.6 Summary

The key points that have been covered in this chapter are:

- Configuration management is the management of system evolution by identifying the exact state of a system at discrete points in its life-cycle.
- The major processes that make up configuration management are:
  - the identification of the system components and the changes made to them,
  - the control of these changes,
  - audit,
  - documentation.
- Configuration management is necessary to ensure traceability and reproducibility without which product integrity is compromised.
- Change control, the major part of configuration management, is the management of all the changes that are made as a system evolves.
- Documentation is the written record of facts about a system. Its role in maintenance is to facilitate comprehension and make visible all aspects of what the system does and how it works.
- Software tools exist to support configuration management and it is important to take advantage of such tools to help control the processes of software evolution.
- In essence the management of software maintenance differs from the management of software development because of the different environments in which the activities are carried out.

We have looked at ways of keeping track of the processes of software maintenance. Over and above this, we need to know that what we are doing is useful and effective. Are the processes we are overseeing creating better systems? How can we tell? To be effective, we need to evaluate methods and processes. We need a means of empirical measurement to assess and compare systems and techniques. The subject of measuring software relates not only to making better systems, but also to assessing existing systems. The topic of measurement is studied in the next chapter.

12

Maintenance Measures

> *"...if you can measure what you are speaking about and express it in numbers you know something about it; but when you cannot measure it, when you cannot express it in numbers, your knowledge of it is of a meagre and unsatisfactory kind"*
>
> Lord Kelvin [152]

This chapter aims to

1. Discuss software measurement, software measures and software metrics.
2. Distinguish software measure from software metric.
3. Discuss the importance of measures to maintenance activities.
4. Give examples of maintenance measures and discuss their practical applications.
5. Discuss the limitations of current maintenance measures.
6. Explain the guidelines for choosing maintenance measures.

12.1 Introduction

Software maintenance personnel are faced with the challenge of managing, controlling and making the changes necessary to allow software systems to evolve. The resources required to do this effectively are costly, and a number of ways have been suggested to keep these costs down. For example,

- software personnel should be encouraged towards the '...development of understandable, maintainable software that is easy to revise and validate over the life-cycle' [210 p.22];
- understandable software will help in 'achieving many of the other qualities such as evolvability and verifiability' [108 p.31].

Without doubt, many software engineers would like to develop and maintain software systems with these qualities, not least because such systems will be cost-effective in the long term. There are, however, a number of questions that arise from this. Firstly, what level of understandability, maintainability, evolvability, verifiability or related attributes should a software product manifest in order to be considered acceptable? Secondly, how can one determine whether the tool or method being applied to carry out maintenance work on the product will achieve or has accomplished the desired effect? Thirdly, how can the resources required to undertake any proposed maintenance work on the product be predicted or assessed? In order to address these questions, a sound understanding of the issues concerned with measuring the maintenance-related attributes of software products, processes and resources is needed.

The theme of this chapter is twofold: to discuss the concepts of measurement in general and software measurement in particular, and to explore the scope of measurement in maintenance through the use of some maintenance-related measures.

12.2 Definitions

Empirical – capable of being verified or disproved by observation or experiment.

Entity – either an object (for instance an *athlete* or *chunk of program code*) or an event (for instance *sprinting* or *the design phase* in a software development project).

Measurement – "the process of empirical, objective encoding of some property of a selected class of entities in a formal system of symbols so as to describe them" [152 ch.12 p.4]. This is a commonly accepted inclusive definition, but others have been suggested in the literature [95, 96, 152 ch.12 pp.3-19].

Metric – "a criterion to determine the difference or distance between two entities, like the distance of a query and a document in Information System Retrieval Systems. A well-known metric is the metric of Euclid, which measures the shortest distance between two points" Zuse [299 p.29]. It should be noted that Zuse goes on to say "the term metric, as used for distance metrics, is a misinterpretation in the software research area of software measurement."

Property of an entity – the attribute which is to be measured, for example the speed of sprinting or the complexity of the program.

12.3 The Importance of Integrity in Measurement

A measurement procedure must demonstrate a number of characteristics. It must be

- *Empirical:* The result of measurement should describe empirically established facts. Finkelstein [96] captured the importance of this when he said that the precise, concise, objective and empirical nature of measurement 'gives its primacy in science' (pp. 27-8).

- *Objective:* During measurement, observations should be carried out with integrity, objectively, reliably, efficiently and without bias or ambiguity [152 ch.12 pp.3-19]. If this is done, it should always be possible for someone else to repeat the measurement.

- *Encodable:* An attribute can be encoded or characterised using different symbols such as numbers and graphic representations. In this book, however, encoding will be restricted to numbers. The assignment of numbers in this fashion is aimed at preserving observed relations between entities [236]. For example, the description of the length of programs using lines of code preserves the observed relation 'longer than'.

Based on the above notion of measurement, if two entities possess equivalent levels of an empirically observable attribute, then the same symbol should be assigned to both entities in order to characterise that attribute. An example is using a thermometer to measure the temperature of two freezers, A and B. If freezer A has a temperature of minus 20.5° C and it is as cold as freezer B, then the temperature of freezer B must also be minus 20.5° C.

Similarly, in software development and maintenance, there may be a need to obtain a quantitative description of some attribute of a software product or activity. The domain that deals with such measurement has become known as 'software measurement' [84].

12.3.1 Software Measurement

Measurement concepts and techniques have been widely used in many well-developed science disciplines such as physics [236] and chemistry. In comparison, however, the application of measurement in software engineering is still in its infancy. This is evident in the wide variety of definitions of software measurement in the literature [221, 299]. The definition used here is that software measurement is the 'process of objectively and empirically quantifying an attribute of a software system and the process connected with its development, use, maintenance and evolution' [152 ch.12 p.4].

Although the above definition applies to both development of new systems and maintenance of existing systems, this discussion is centred on maintenance. In general, there are three software maintenance-related entities whose attributes can be subjected to measurement: process, product and resource [95].

- A **process** is any software-related activity such as change analysis, specification, design, coding and testing.
- A **resource** is input to a process, for example personnel, hardware and software.
- A **product** is any intermediate or final output resulting from a software process such as system documentation (for example, specification and design), program listings, test data, source code and object code.

A diagrammatic representation of the relationship between these three entities is presented in Figure 12.1.

In software measurement, two types of attribute can be identified: internal and external [95]. An internal attribute is one which can be measured in terms of the process, product or resource itself. For example, complexity, modularity and reusability are internal attributes of the source code of a program. An external attribute is one which can only be measured with respect to the relation of a process, product or resource to its environment, for example the maintainability of program source code or productivity of software personnel.

According to the above notion of software measurement, we can measure the attribute of a software product, for example the complexity of a program's source code. A common way of estimating the complexity of a program is by counting the number of lines of code (200, say) in the program. We can also measure the attribute of a software process, for instance the effort required in making a change (30 person-hours). Examples of different process, product and resource measurements will be discussed later in the chapter.

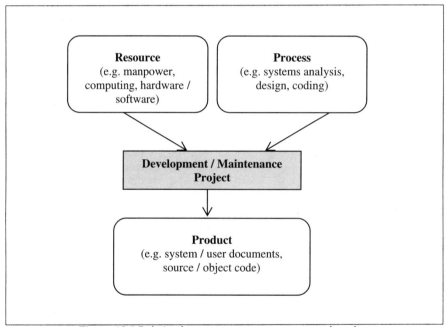

Figure 12.1 Relation between a resource, process and product

12.3.2 Software Measure and Software Metric

The result of a software measurement process is known as a software measure. The measure characterises the property of interest for a class of entities. In the earlier examples of freezers and source code, the numbers

(-20.5° C and 200 LOC respectively) are measures of the temperature and complexity respectively. That is, a measure is the assignment of these numbers (as in the above example) or any other selected symbol during measurement. A measure can also be seen as a mapping of the entity (for example, program source code) to the attribute (for example, complexity). Based on this notion of a measure, an entity can have more than one measure for the same attribute; that is, more than one mapping. This can be illustrated using program maintainability as follows:

Two factors can be used to assess the maintainability of a program, P: understandability and modifiability [223]. Understandability is the time, T1, required per module to determine the changes required. Modifiability is the time, T2, required per module to effect these changes. Any of the times, T1 or T2, can be used to quantify the maintainability of P[16]. In that case there will be two mappings; from P to T1 (measure1) and from P to T2 (measure2). These mappings are illustrated in Figure 12.2.

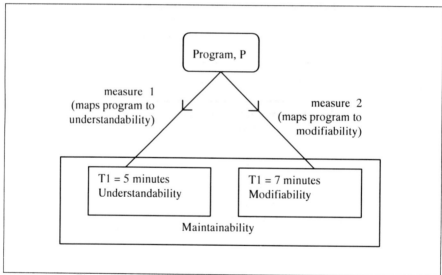

Figure 12.2 Relation between an entity, measure and attribute

Another term that has been widely used in the literature [73, 95, 120, 127] in connection with software measurement is software metric. It

---

[16] Except in a composite measure which combines both understandability and modifiability into a single measure.

Maintenance Measures 253

is sometimes used as a synonym for software measure [299]. The use of metric in this context has been challenged by some authors [95, 299]. They argue that based on its meaning in mathematics (from where the term is derived) it is inappropriate to use it to mean software measure.

The terms measure and metric are still being used interchangeably in the literature [237] but the position taken here is that of Zuse (see section 12.2). The type of measure obtained during software measurement within software maintenance departments depends to some extent on the objective.

12.4 Objectives of Software Measurement

Software measurement can be undertaken for several reasons, notably for evaluation, control, assessment, improvement and prediction.

12.4.1 Evaluation

There is a need for maintainers to evaluate different methods, program libraries and tools before arriving at a decision as to which is best suited to a given task. For instance, during reuse, the maintainer may be faced with the problem of evaluating the suitability of a candidate component obtained from the reuse library.

12.4.2 Control

There is a need to control the process of software change to ensure that change requests are dealt with promptly and within budget. As DeMarco says, "you cannot control what you cannot measure" [79].

12.4.3 Assessment

In order to control a process or product, it is important to be able to assess or to characterise it first. For instance, a manager may need to assess a system to determine whether or not it is economically feasible to continue maintaining it. Also, in order to determine whether or not the maintenance process being used is achieving or will achieve the desired effect, an assessment of the process must be undertaken.

12.4.4 Improvement

There is a need to improve various characteristics of the software system or process such as quality and productivity. It is difficult to assess and monitor such improvements without an objective means of measuring the characteristics. With measures of quality and productivity, management is able to set targets and monitor progress in achieving those targets. If the targets are not met, then corrective actions can be taken.

12.4.5 Prediction

There is a need to make predictions about various aspects of the software product, process and cost. For instance, measures obtained from program code can be used to predict the time required to implement a given change. These measures can assist a manager in the allocation of time, personnel, hardware and software resources to a maintenance project. To a programmer, the measures can serve as indicators of the difficulty associated with understanding a program and can also signify the speed and accuracy with which change can be effected.

In aiming to achieve the above objectives, there is a wide spectrum of measures at the disposal of software maintainers.

12.5 Example Measures

To understand these measures and how they may impact on the maintenance process, it is useful to look at some specifics.

There are several measures that maintainers may need in order do their job. In theory these measures can be derived from the attributes of the software system, the maintenance process and personnel. In practice, however, the most commonly used source of measures is the software system, specifically the source code. The main reason is that very often the only information about a system available to maintainers is the source code. Even in situations where design documentation exists, it may be out of date or inaccurate. Another reason is that algorithms can be used to obtain measures from the source code in an inexpensive and non-intrusive way [299]. Thus, the discussion on maintenance measures will be centred on source code-based measures such as size, complexity, quality, understandability and maintainability.

12.5.1 Size

One of the commonest ways of measuring the size of a program is by counting the number of lines of code. Moller and Paulish define lines of code (LOC) as "the count of program lines of code excluding comment or blank lines" [196 p.67]. This measure is usually expressed in thousands of lines of code (KLOC). During maintenance, the focus is on the 'delta' lines of code: the number of lines of code that have been added or modified during a maintenance process. The advantage of this measure is that it is easy to determine and also correlates strongly with other measures such as effort and error density [292]. It has, nonetheless, been criticised. There are no standards for LOC measurement and it is dependent on the programming language in question [196]. Also it is too simplistic and does not reflect cost or productivity [95]. Despite these criticisms, this measure is still widely used. Halstead's measures – discussed later – can also be used to estimate the size of a program.

12.5.2 Complexity

There is no consensus on a definition for the term 'complexity'. This is evident in the wide variety of complexity measures reported in the literature [112, 299]. In software maintenance, however, it is useful to define program complexity. Zuse defines it as "the difficulty of maintaining, changing and understanding programs" [299 p.28]. One of the major problems that software maintainers face is dealing with the increasing complexity of the source code that they have to modify [292, 169 ch.19 pp.393-449].

Program complexity embraces several notions such as program structure, semantic content, control flow, data flow and algorithmic complexity. As such, it can be argued that computing a single complexity value is misleading; other vital information is hidden in this value. However, there is sometimes a need to compute a single value for complexity which in turn is used as an indicator for other attributes such as understandability, maintainability and the effort required for implementation and testing.

The more complex a program is, the more likely it is for the maintainer to make an error when implementing a change [292]. The higher the complexity value, the more difficult it is to understand the program, hence making it less maintainable. Based on the argument that inherently complex programs require more time to understand and modify than simple programs, complexity can be used to estimate the effort required to make a change to a program.

Over one hundred complexity measures have been proposed in the literature. For example, McCabe's cyclomatic complexity [190], Halstead's difficulty measure [121], Basili-Hutchens' measure [14], and Prather's measure [228]. Zuse provided a useful and comprehensive review of these measures [299]. Work has also been done on the implications of the use of metrics and the selection and interpretation of data [174, 173] to allow greater effectiveness and objectivity in the analysis of software systems. See for example, Turski's work on determining the evolutionary growth of systems [269].

There follows discussion on two of the most popular code complexity measures: McCabe's cyclomatic complexity [190] and Halstead's difficulty measure [121].

12.5.2.1 McCabe's Cyclomatic Complexity

McCabe views a program as a directed graph in which lines of program statements are represented by nodes and the flow of control between the statements is represented by the edges. McCabe's cyclomatic complexity (also known as the **cyclomatic number**) is the number of 'linearly independent' paths through the program (or flow graph) and this value is computed using the formula:

$$v(F) = e - n + 2$$

where n = total number of nodes; e = total number of edges or arcs; and $v(F)$ is the cyclomatic number.

This measure is used as an indicator of the psychological complexity of a program. During maintenance, a program with a very high cyclomatic number (usually above 10) is considered to be very complex. This value can assist the maintainer in a number of ways.

- It helps to identify highly complex programs that may need to be modified in order to reduce complexity.

- The cyclomatic number can be used as an estimate of the amount of time required to understand and modify a program.

- The flow graph generated can be used to identify the possible test paths during testing.

Despite its usefulness and popularity, McCabe's cyclomatic number has limitations [95 pp.277-95]:

- It takes no account of the complexity of the conditions in a program, for example multiple use of Boolean expressions, and over-use of flags.
- In its original form, it failed to take account of the degree of nesting in a program. As such, two programs may have been considered to be equally complex based on cyclomatic number whereas in actual fact, one had a greater level of nesting than the other. There have been a number of improvements to take into consideration the level of nesting [125].

12.5.2.2 Halstead's Measures

In his theory of software science [121, 122, 65], Halstead proposed a number of equations to calculate program attributes such as program length, volume and level, potential volume, language level clarity, implementation time and error rates [121]. Here we shall concentrate on those measures which impact on complexity: program length and program effort. The measures for these attributes can be computed from four basic counts:

n_1 = number of unique operators used

n_2 = number of unique operands used

N_1 = total number of operators used

N_2 = total number of operands used

An operand is a variable or constant. An operator is an entity that can either change the value of an operand or the order in which it is changed. Operators include arithmetic operators (for example, *, /, + and -), keywords (for example, PROCEDURE, WHILE, REPEAT and DO), logical operators (for example, greater than, equal to and less than), and delimiters.

The following formulae can be used to calculate the program length and program effort:

- Observed program length, $N = N_1 + N_2$;
- Calculated program length, $= n_1 \log_2 n_1 + n_2 \log_2 n_2$

- Program effort, $E = \dfrac{n_1 * N_2 * (N_1+N_2) * \log(n_1+n_2)}{2 * n_2}$

The four basic counts can also be used to compute other attributes such as programming time [73], number of bugs in a program [97] and understandability [188].

There are a number of reasons why Halstead's measures have been widely used [188]. Firstly, they are easy to calculate and do not require an in-depth analysis of programming features and control flow. Secondly, the measures can be applied to any language but yet are programming language sensitive. For instance, in a functional language or a 4GL a single token tends to carry more information than a similar token in a procedural language. And thirdly, there exists empirical evidence from both industry and academia that these measures can be used as good predictors of programming effort and number of bugs in a program.

Despite the above advantages, Halstead's measures have been criticised for several reasons:

- The cognitive psychology-based assumptions have been found to be erroneous [71].

- The experiments which were used to test the measures were badly designed [179] and statistically flawed [140]. Many of these were small-size experiments and used small sample sizes, which were unrepresentative of 'real' software systems.

- The counting rules involved in the design of the measures were not fully defined [179] and it is not clear what should be counted.

- There was failure to consider declarations and input/output statements as a unique operator for each unique label [248].

- The measures are code-based; it is assumed that 'software = programs' [140]. Although this may be true for some systems, others, especially those developed using modern software engineering techniques and tools, are likely to have automatic documentation support. The measures fail to capture the contribution that this documentation makes to the programming effort or program understanding.

- From a psychological point of view, the measures are inadequate on the grounds that they ignore the high-level structures (or chunks) that expert programmers use to understand programs [130].

12.5.3 Quality

In general terms, quality is defined as 'fitness for purpose' [141]. In other words, a quality product, be it a word processor or a flight control system, is one which does what the user expects it to do. This notion of quality does not only apply to a product, it can be extended to the maintenance process. A quality maintenance process is one which enables the maintainer to implement the desired change. Different measures can be used to characterise product and process quality

12.5.3.1 Product Quality

One way of measuring the quality of a software system is by keeping track of the number of change requests received from the users after the system becomes operational. This measure is computed by "dividing the number of unique change requests made by customers for the first year of field use of a given release, by the number of thousand lines of code for that release" [196 pp.69]. This measure only includes requests which pertain to faults detected by customers. The measure excludes feature enhancement change requests which are not contained in the software requirements specification. The number of change requests from users can serve as an indicator of customer satisfaction. It can also serve as an indicator of the amount of maintenance effort that may be required for the system.

The other measure of product quality is the number of faults that are detected after the software system becomes operational, usually after the first year of shipment. The same type of fault pointed out by more than one user is counted as a single fault. The number of users reporting the same fault may be used as a measure of the significance of the fault and therefore the priority that should be attached to fixing it.

12.5.3.2 Process Quality

This describes the degree to which the maintenance process being used is assisting personnel in satisfying change requests. Two measures of process quality are schedule and productivity [196].

The schedule is calculated as "the difference between the planned and actual work time to achieve the milestone of first customer delivery, divided by the planned work time" [196 p.72]. This measure is expressed as a percentage. A negative number signifies a slip and a positive number signifies early delivery.

The productivity is computed by dividing the number of lines of code that have been added or modified by the effort in staff days required to make the addition or modification. Effort is the total time from analysing the change requests to a successful implementation of the change.

12.5.4 Understandability

Program understandability is the ease with which the program can be understood, that is, the ability to determine what a program does and how it works by reading its source code and accompanying documentation. This attribute depends not just on the program source code, but also on other external factors such as the available documentation, the maintenance process and maintenance personnel. Some of the measures that can be used as an estimate of understandability are complexity, quality of documentation, consistency and conciseness.

Understandability usually has an inverse relation to complexity; as the complexity of a program increases, the understandability tends to decrease. From this perspective, understandability can be computed indirectly from McCabe's cyclomatic complexity and Halstead's program effort measure. Understandability can also be estimated from subjective ratings of the quality of documentation, consistency of programming style and the conciseness of the program text.

12.5.5 Maintainability

Software maintainability is "the ease with which the software can be understood, corrected, adapted, and/or enhanced" [229]. Maintainability is an external attribute since its computation requires knowledge from the software product as well as external factors such as the maintenance process and the maintenance personnel. An example of a maintainability measure that depends on an external factor is the Mean Time To Repair (MTTR): the mean time required to effect a change [95]. Depending on the circumstances, the calculation of MTTR may require information on the problem recognition time, administrative delay time, maintenance tools collection time, problem analysis time, change specification time and change time.

Maintainability can also be perceived as an internal attribute if it is derived solely from the software system. Several internal attributes of program source code can impact on maintainability, for example modularity. Thus, measures for these other internal attributes would need to be obtained in order to compute maintainability. Unfortunately, there is yet to be an exact model for determining maintainability. At present, measures such as complexity and readability [118] are used as indicators or predictors of maintainability.

12.5.6 Cost Estimation

The cost of a maintenance project is the resources – personnel, machines, time and money – expended on effecting change. One way of estimating the cost of a maintenance task is from historical data collected for a similar task. The major difficulty with this approach to cost estimation is that there may be new variables impacting upon the current task which were not considered in the past. However, the more that is collected the more accurate will be the estimate.

A second way of estimating cost is through mathematical models. One of these was Boehm's COCOMO model adapted for maintenance [36]. The updated COCOMO II [37] model, instead of being based on a single process model such as the waterfall model, has been interpreted to cover the waterfall model, MBASE/RUP (Model-Based Architecting and Software Engineering / Rational Unified Process), and incremental development. According to Boehm, the cost of maintenance is affected by attributes of factors called cost drivers. Examples of cost drivers are database size, program complexity, use of modern programming practices and applications experience of the maintenance personnel.

A third measure of cost is time in person-months required to modify a program.

12.6 Guidelines for Selecting Maintenance Measures

As already indicated, the main purpose of maintenance activities is to ensure that a software system can be easily modified, adapted and enhanced to accommodate changes. There are no hard and fast rules as to how these objectives can be achieved through the use of maintenance measures. There are, however, some guidelines that can be used in selecting suitable maintenance measures. These guidelines include well-defined objectives, fitness for purpose, ease of use, low implementation cost and sensitivity.

- *Clearly defined objectives:* Prior to deciding on the use of a measurement for maintenance-related purposes, it is essential to define clearly and unambiguously what objectives need to be achieved. These objectives will determine the measures to be used and the data to be collected.

- *Personnel involvement:* The purpose of measurement in an organisation needs to be made clear to those involved in the programme. And the measures obtained should be used for that purpose and nothing else. For instance, it needs to be made clear whether the measurement is to improve productivity, to set and monitor targets, etc. Without such clear expression of the purpose of measurement, personnel may feel that the measures will be used for punitive purposes and this can impede the programme.

- *Ease of use:* The measures that are finally selected to be used need to be easy to use, take not too much time to administer, be unobtrusive, and possibly subject to automation. As indicated earlier in this chapter, one of the reasons why source code-based measures are very popular is because they can be easily automated and collected in an unobtrusive way.

   Exercise 12.1 Develop two versions of a program of manageable size: one version in a procedural language and the other version in a functional language of your choice. (Note: manageable size will greatly depend on your level of expertise, but should be at least 30 LOC.)

   - For each version of the program calculate the complexity using McCabe's and Halstead's complexity measures;
   - Compare the two complexity values obtained above. Comment on your result.

Exercise 12.2 Two pharmaceutical companies have been merged following a take-over. As a result, their information systems for storing and managing information on drugs, customer names and addresses, and outstanding orders for products have to be merged. In one of the companies, the systems are written in C and a mixture of other databases and they run on a mainframe. The other company has programs which are all written in Cobol running on a mainframe as well. As a software measures consultant, what advice would you give to the company?

12.7 Summary

The main points that have been covered in this chapter are:

- Software measurement is the process of objectively and empirically quantifying an attribute of a software system and the process connected with its development, use, maintenance and evolution. A software measure is the result of measurement; it characterises the property of interest for a class of entities. Software metric is commonly used as a synonym for software measure although its use in this way has been criticised.

- Measures can assist maintainers to evaluate methods, tools and programs, to control the maintenance process, to assess the software system and maintenance process, to improve quality and productivity and to make predictions about various aspects of the software system and the maintenance process.

- There are several measures that maintainers can use, but some of the most commonly used ones are McCabe's cyclomatic complexity, Halstead's measures, schedule, person-months, Boehm's COCOMO models and MTTR.

- The main limitation of the above measures is their reliance on program source code alone despite the impact of several external factors on maintainability.

- Some of the guidelines for selecting a measure are ease of use, low cost of implementation and sensitivity to as many factors as possible.

The topics that have been examined so far have covered the process, the mechanisms and the management of software maintenance. Building upon these ideas, we can now look at how maintainability can be built into software systems.

PART IV: Building Better Systems

Overview

Given the problems of the maintenance crisis, it is important to learn the lessons of the past and to build new systems that will avoid past problems. This section of the book looks at how to build maintainability into systems and what tools are available to help both the developer and the maintainer to provide better and more reliable systems.

- **Building and Sustaining Maintainability**

If there is one thing we have learnt as the disciplines of Computer Science, Software Engineering and Software Maintenance have developed, it is that software systems evolve. A program only ever ceases to evolve when it is no longer used.

Given that evolution is an integral part of software systems, we need no longer waste time in the unattainable ideal of the "finished system", but can instead aim for the program that can change without loss of quality. Experience has shown what sorts of things compromise the integrity of a program – quick fixes causing unforeseen ripple effects, inadequate resources to address the problem of quick fixes, badly written or misunderstood code, inadequate resources, out of date documentation and so on.

In all areas we can look at both prevention and cure, but we must be realistic. We could say that resources *must* be available to allow all changes to be implemented via a more sophisticated model than quick-fix, but that doesn't address the case where quick-fix is the only option. The live system just fell on its face and it needs to be up and running again right now! There will always be times where change leads to loss of quality. In recognising this, we can look at ensuring the loss of quality is temporary. We can identify areas of potential problem and put safeguards in place. Code that is initially developed in accordance with best practice, is less susceptible to the problems of the quick fix, and such problems as occur can more easily be retrieved. The key is to take maintainability into account every step along the way.

- **Software Maintenance Tools**

We have moved far beyond the stage of maintaining systems manually. The activities of software maintenance need to be automated. We need tools to help upgrade and enhance systems and to find and correct errors.

The development and use of effective tools and diagnostics facilitates the whole maintenance process. It allows the processes to be better structured and organised. Feedback from the use of automated maintenance processes and support tools helps in the development of the field and provides the evidence needed to guide future progress.

Software maintenance tools are themselves software systems that evolve and need to be maintained.

Discussion Points

These points are intended to stimulate thinking and discussion on fundamental issues in software maintenance. The issues raised are explored in the chapters of this section, but it is a beneficial to think around these areas and try to draw conclusions yourself, before looking for answers in the text.

- **The "Best" Paradigm**

A small-to-medium sized software house runs a variety of different projects – commercial, government funded, research and development – and works in collaboration with a number of different bodies. These include commercial enterprises who essentially pay for the development of new products, or for specific features within existing products; government departments who pay for a job to be done, but operate a hands-off approach to the details of the work; research projects where the software house works in close collaboration with other software houses, academic institutions and users in developing new ideas and products.

To date, the software house operates on a single hardware platform, and uses a single programming language for software development. This situation will have to change. The company cannot remain at the forefront of the research and development world if its working practices are out of date. Government contracts will increasingly be calling for specific platforms and standards, and the commercial customers will expect a move forward.

This latter market is the one with the least incentive to change. The customers are happy with products they know. These products interface well with other products and the older systems they still use. These people are looking neither for upheaval nor to be pioneers ironing out the teething problems of newer technologies. Nonetheless, the world is moving on and already new customers are becoming harder to find.

What issues must the software house address and how should it go about it? Consider all factors that might be relevant, including the following:-

- Time: how long will it take to introduce new platforms?
- The client base: how should the various types of client be dealt with – the same or differently?
- Cost: what will need to be costed?
- Retraining: how long will it take to retrain staff and how should this be factored in?

Bear in mind that a small company cannot "lose" all its staff to lengthy retraining. It does not have the reserves to be able to put its current projects on hold.

- **The Best Tools for the Job**

You are about to embark upon a large software maintenance project on a system that has been in use for many years. The aims are to provide a more efficient system with the extra flexibility of running on a variety of hardware platforms, better security and future-proofing of the data processed by the system. No data must be corrupted or lost, either data that has been processed by the old version of the system or future data that will be processed by the new version. The system has a user base including people whose databases hold 30 years worth of data. There is a legal requirement to hold this data for a minimum of 100 years, so the system must take account of future upgrades of the sort not yet even thought about. The data is sensitive and its confidentiality must be assured, whilst allowing authorised users timely access.

List at least six software maintenance tools that your maintenance team might use. Include some you are familiar with, and some you are not. Assess these tools and try to make a judgement on how useful they could be and how best you might deploy them. In particular, look at each tool's effectiveness in terms of this specific project. Look at the issue of the project team's familiarity with each tool and why this might be an issue. How new on the market is each tool? Why might this be an issue?

13

Building and Sustaining Maintainability

"During software development, we regularly uncover errors, new requirements, or the results of earlier miscommunication... Furthermore, after baselining the design and delivering the product, even more new requirements will appear. All this means that you must select architectures, components, and specification techniques to accommodate major and incessant change."

Davis ([75], p.87)

This chapter aims to

1. Explain the need to build and sustain maintainable software systems.

2. Explain the role of impact analysis in maintainability.

3. Explain the role that technologies such as fourth-generation languages and object-oriented paradigms can play in achieving maintainability.

4. Discuss the key features of fourth-generation languages and how they affect maintenance.

5. Describe the key features of object-oriented paradigms and their effect on maintenance.

13.1 Introduction

The failure to use paradigms that enable software engineers to build and sustain maintainable software products has contributed in part to the software maintenance crisis and its associated cost [210]. The nature of orthodox software development and maintenance methods makes it difficult to accommodate the changing needs of users of these products [113]. In response to the need to develop and maintain, in a timely and economical fashion, software systems that meet users' requirements and are resilient to change and adaptation, various ideas have been advocated over the years e.g. the use of fourth-generation languages and object-oriented paradigms [156, 278, 280, 296]. The results of a survey in the mid 1990's of approximately 250 of the UK's largest investors in software systems indicated that object-oriented technology was becoming a mainstream technology [287] and that its potential to increase maintainability was one of the key driving forces behind this. Another trend which has had an impact upon the long-term maintainability of software systems is the adoption of quality assurance procedures. The number of software companies adopting the ISO 9000 quality standards series has increased rapidly since the early 1990's [141].

In this chapter, quality assurance issues and the way they affect maintainability are examined. Fourth-generation languages and object-oriented paradigms are discussed, concentrating on their key characteristics and how they impact upon maintainability.

13.2 Definitions

High level language – a computer programming language that is similar to a natural language and that requires each statement to be translated or interpreted into machine language prior to execution.

Impact analysis – the determination of the major effects of a proposed project or change.

Object oriented programming – computer programming in which code and data pertaining to a single entity (object) are encapsulated, and communicate with the rest of the system via messages.

Quality assurance – the systematic monitoring and evaluation of aspects of a project, service or facility to ensure that necessary standards of excellence are being met.

13.3 Impact Analysis

Managing change is fundamental to software maintainability. A key part of the management of change is determining what the ramifications and implications of the change will be.

We have already seen that program comprehension is one of the most expensive parts of software evolution. A key aspect in understanding the system is determining the impact of the changes that are proposed. This is impact analysis.

An impact analysis looks at questions such as which system will be affected by a change, where do the changes need to be made, how much code needs to be modified. Effective impact analysis is a vital element in retaining an augmenting the maintainability of a system.

13.3.1 Models and Strategies

Many different strategies can be deployed, and there are various techniques to model change and the impact of change. Choice of methodology is determined by the needs of a specific project, based upon the proposed change and the potential impacts.

Several formal models have been proposed (there is a useful overview in Bohner and Arnold [39 ch.6], looking for example at predicting the locations and size of a change [104, 106] or analysing dependencies in the software [135, 183].

We can look at the impact of change at different levels, from the higher level abstract components of a system, down to the detail which of which code statements are affected in a particular module.

Traditional approaches to impact analysis concentrate on analysis of source code e.g. using program slicing techniques or dependence graphs. Program slicing is a key tool to aid impact analysis (see chapter 14) especially in procedural and object-oriented programs [39 ch.4]. However, as we've seen in earlier chapters, software is not just programs, and software change affects more than just the source code.

Re-use helps because it tends to lead to better documentation of how components are changed and what other components might be affected.

Approaches that take a wider view of a software system have been developed. Han [123] for example, describes an approach that looks at change in design and implementation documents, but does not consider certain aspects such as changes in the scope of identifiers. Other approaches estimate the impact of code change from various standpoints e.g. the functional paradigm [154 p.5, 197 p.5].

13.3.2 Impact Analysis in Creating Maintainable Systems

Good example of the key importance of impact analysis in modifying software systems was the tackling of the Year 2000 problem [271], identifying all systems and subsystems that would not be able to cope with the changeover from 1999 to 2000.

Techniques developed to facilitate impact analysis allow greater efficiency and accuracy in assessing the impact and risks of making a change, thus decreasing the chances of inappropriate changes being embarked upon. Impact analysis is key in planning and managing software change and has the effect of making the resultant changed systems better and more maintainable.

13.4 Quality Assurance

Quality is widely defined as 'fitness for purpose' and this encompasses most of what many people mean when they talk about quality. However, in order to discuss quality in relation to a software product and the important role that quality has to play in building and sustaining maintainability, this definition must be widened. A useful definition is given by Ince in [141] in terms of quality factors. He cites correctness and maintainability as the two most important quality factors that a system can possess. The discussion here is of building maintainability into a system and, as such, maintainability will not be looked at as a quality factor by itself but rather as something which is affected by the other quality factors – fitness for purpose, correctness, portability, testability, usability, reliability, efficiency, integrity, reusability and interoperability.

Another important issue which impacts upon the quality of a system is the appropriate use of standards. There are in existence standards for many aspects of the software change process, for example documentation standards. There are also quality standards specifically adapted to the software process, for example the UK's TICKIT scheme which relates quality issues directly to software production. There are also standards, in existence and under development, specifically for software maintenance, for example the IEEE (STD) 1219-1993 – Standard for Software Maintenance. Use of software maintenance standards is not yet as widespread as the use of general quality standards but the adoption of such standards is becoming more widespread.

13.4.1 Fitness for Purpose

Fitness for purpose – does the product do the job it was intended to do – is an obvious criterion by which to measure quality. In order to see what it means in terms of the maintainability of a system it is necessary to look at how it is measured. The key to enabling measurement of fitness for purpose is the requirements analysis. It is this which gives the detail of the purpose of the system. In measuring fitness for purpose, we are measuring against the requirements: does the system meet its requirements? If this question cannot be answered – if, for example, there is no formal record of the requirements, or the requirements are couched in nebulous terms – there is no reliable measure of quality through fitness for purpose. Thus the formal statement of requirements is very important in the building of a quality system. It must be taken into account at the time the requirements are drawn up that the system will be measured against them.

Requirements should be hard. For example, the requirement that a system should respond quickly is a soft requirement and can only be measured subjectively, whereas the requirement that the system should respond within 3 seconds is a hard requirement and can be measured objectively.

How is maintainability affected? Without formal, hard requirements, change is hard to evaluate, the effects of change are hard to analyse and the nature of the change is not always easy to identify. Suppose that a user requests that a certain feature be 'speeded up'. Against a vague original requirement that a particular feature be performed 'not too slowly', it is difficult to determine the best course.

The obvious thing may be to attempt a more efficient rewrite of the relevant algorithm. Against a hard requirement such as 'response time under 3 seconds for a Pentium IV processor', it is easier to analyse the situation. Perhaps there is nothing further to be gained from any code amendment, and the solution is for the user to upgrade to a faster processor. If this is obvious from the outset, much time can be saved; modification is effected quickly without any waste of resources on unfeasible solutions – the system is more maintainable.

13.4.2 Correctness

There is as yet no way of proving a system to be correct. Nonetheless, there is much that can be done towards decreasing the level of errors in a system. Chapter 5 describes some system life-cycle models and the advantage of structured system development and maintenance. A reduction in the number of errors is one of the advantages. Building correctness into a system has the obvious advantage that less time will be spent on corrective maintenance. A maintenance-conscious life-cycle model will help maintain the correctness of a system. The effect of an appropriate model upon sustaining the maintainability of a system is illustrated by the example in Chapter 5 where maintainability at the ACME Health Clinic was built **out** of the system by use of an inappropriate model.

13.4.3 Portability

Portability encompasses many things, for example moves between

- hardware platforms, for example porting a system from a VAX to a PC;
- operating systems, for example from Windows to LINUX to widen a market, from VAX/VMS to Windows when an organisation moves from a VAX base to a PC base;
- programming languages, for example upgrading a system from DOS-based to Windows-based by rewriting in a different language or rewriting a system to adhere to a new in-house standard, for example Fortran 77 to ANSI C;

- countries, for example an organisation may wish to widen its market for a product from the UK to Europe. The product would need to be available in all European languages.

Building for portability will enhance maintainability by easing moves between platforms, languages and so on. The building of portability into a system means the avoidance of features which tie a software system to a particular platform or language. Adhering to standards can help portability as can appropriate decisions regarding what should be hard-coded and what should not. For example, adapting a system from single language to multilingual is far easier if the parts which must change are not embedded in the code but are read in, perhaps from multilingual term sets. Upgrading such a system may be just a case of providing the appropriate term set.

13.4.4 Testability

A system that is easy to test is also easier to change effectively because it is easier to test the changes made. It does not automatically follow that a system that is hard to test will be harder to change *per se* but if the system cannot be tested effectively, it is hard to engender confidence that modifications have been carried out successfully. A good requirements specification is a necessity in enhancing testability. For the system to be testable, it is a prerequisite to know what is to be tested, how it should be tested and what the results of previous tests were. Following from this is the issue of keeping up-to-date documentation. If there is a change in requirements or a change in any test procedure, documentation is essential to maintain the testability of the system. This illustrates that these factors cannot be considered in isolation. They will always interact.

13.4.5 Usability

If a system for any reason is not used, it may as well not exist. Maintenance is only an issue for a system that is used and that evolves with use.

13.4.5.1 Case Study – Usability

An interesting example is furnished by a project carried out at the research institute of the ACME Health Clinic. Under investigation was the electronic warning system in the Intensive Therapy Unit of a nearby general hospital. The purpose of the system was to warn medical staff of

> untoward changes in patients' conditions. The system was fairly simple in concept – various vital signs were monitored, for example blood pressure, and if one of these should fall outside a given range an alarm was sounded. The problem with the system was its simplicity. A normal blood pressure range varies from patient to patient and often cannot be used in isolation as an indication of a problem. Other factors, such as current medication, patient's age and condition and so on are also important. It was vital that the system didn't miss any untoward change and it was thus set to trigger an alarm if there was any possibility of a problem. This inevitably led to a large number of false alarms and this ultimately made the system unusable. The staff spent more time dealing with false alarms than was saved through not having to carry out routine monitoring. When the ACME research institute began its investigations the electronic system, though still in place, was never turned on.
>
> An experimental neural net system was installed. This took as its baseline parameters the normal ranges of the original system. When an alarm was sounded by the system, the medical staff gave feedback as to whether or not it had sounded appropriately From this feedback, the system learnt what constituted a problem situation for a particular patient and consequently gave fewer false alarms. The system had to be taught for each new patient. It began in a state that was identical to the old system and became more and more efficient the longer it monitored a patient.

The basic rule on usability is simple. If a system is not used, it is useless. It does not matter how good it is at doing its job or how well engineered it is; if for any reason, the users cannot, or will not, use it, it is no more use than if it does not exist at all, like the ITU system that was never turned on.

13.4.6 Reliability

Varying degrees of importance can be attached to reliability, depending upon the application. Building in a high degree of reliability can be costly and is not always necessary. The reliability of an air traffic control system, for instance, must be greater than for a word processing package. Reliability is closely allied to trust. If a customer has no trust in a system, he or she will not use it.

It is interesting to note in the example in the above case study, that the neural net ITU system never got beyond the stage of a trial research system because the staff did not trust it. The reason for this lack of trust was not that the system had ever shown itself to be unreliable, quite the reverse, but that the state of the art concerning neural net technology at the time was such that the means by which the system learnt to monitor the patients' vital signs could not be fully explained.

13.4.7 Efficiency

The efficiency of a system, how it makes use of a computer's resources, is not always easy to quantify. A requirements specification will often specify speed and storage requirements and response times, but there is often an implicit assumption that a system will make 'the most efficient' use of the available resources. In terms of maintainability there is a need to make these assumptions explicit. A request for a modification to make a particular feature 'faster' or 'better' is easier to address when it can be matched to a hard requirement.

13.4.8 Integrity

The integrity of a system can be interpreted in two ways:

1. Is the system safe from unauthorised access?
2. Can system integrity be guaranteed from a configuration management point of view? Has the system been built from a consistent and reproducible set of modules?

The importance of the latter has been covered in Chapter 11. The former is what is referred to in the ISO 9000 series of Quality Standards where integrity is described in terms of a system's ability to prevent unauthorised access. A desirable level of integrity in this sense varies widely from system to system. Some systems will include provision for levels of access in requirements specifications and some will not. In most systems, even where unauthorised access is not a major issue, there will usually be an assumption that the system should be safe from unauthorised access.

An important point regarding maintainability is that the requirement is made explicit even in cases where it is not immediately perceived to be a vital issue.

Integrity in the sense of a consistent and reproducible configuration is vital to maintainability. Without it, reproducing a system becomes a matter of guesswork and the implementation of change a very hit or miss affair.

13.4.9 Reusability

Reusability is a factor that is absolutely central to the maintainability of a system. Its importance is such that an entire chapter has been given over to it in this book (Chapter 8). This section will not repeat what has been said in Chapter 8, but the reader is referred back to this chapter for the details of reuse and reusability. A point to note is that reusability as a quality factor is not of direct interest to a customer. Although the reusability of a system is likely to have an advantageous effect upon future systems and enhancements, a customer's direct interest is in using a system rather than any future reuse of its component parts.

13.4.10 Interoperability

The ability of a system to interact with other systems is a very important factor. People want to be able to move data between applications without loss. There was a time when it was all but impossible to move a document between word processors without, at the very least, losing all formatting information. There is a commercial advantage to keeping systems segregated. If data can be switched easily from one package to another, a customer can move easily between packages whereas, if moving to a different package involves loss of data, a customer can be effectively tied to a package. In the early days of the software industry, this scenario was widespread. Even nowadays there are areas, for example healthcare computing, where healthcare facilities are tied to old and inefficient systems because to change would involve the loss of significant data accumulated over decades. The trend, however, is towards interoperability and there is little doubt that software suppliers, certainly of health care systems, will soon have to comply with specific requirements in this area. Additionally, the software world is such that market advantage of isolated systems is dwindling.

> **Exercise 13.1** How would you go about persuading a customer, who is having a new system developed, to budget for reusability and testability?

Building and Sustaining Maintainability   279

This section has briefly discussed quality factors and their impact upon maintainability. The following sections look in more detail at some specific technologies and the way that these impact upon maintainability.

13.5 Fourth-Generation Languages

In the early days of computing, programming was undertaken mainly by professional programmers. As prices fell and personal computers became more widely available in a broad range of working environments, end-users, who often were not professional programmers, wanted to use the computers to perform tasks such as storing and manipulating data, or even to develop their own applications without necessarily needing the support of professional programmers. Conventional programming languages were an option, but required significant investment of time and effort to learn. The tools to enable users to achieve these objectives were **fourth-generation languages** (4GLs).

The use of the term 'fourth-generation languages' stemmed from the classification of programming languages according to their generations. The use of **first-generation languages** entails programming computers using binary notation. These languages require a good understanding of low-level details of the machine such as physical storage locations and registers. Programs written using these languages are very dependent on the specific machine for which they are written. An example is machine code.

Second-generation languages were an improvement of the first-generation ones. Instead of specifying the physical location in the computer, symbolic addresses are used to designate locations in memory. Second-generation languages are slightly less machine dependent. An example is symbolic assembler.

Third-generation languages, also known as high-level languages, are more independent of the machine than second-generation languages and as such their use does not require knowledge of the machine instruction set. Thus, programs can be easily ported to different machines. Also, third-generation languages are generally standardised and procedural in nature – their use requires adherence to some rules and regulations. These languages are often used to solve scientific or commercial problems. Examples are Pascal, Cobol, Ada and Modula-2.

Note that C is often put into this category, but it is in fact nearer to an assembly language. Although it is much easier to program using these high-level languages in comparison with their predecessors, they still present several difficulties which include:

- Writing and debugging programs is a significantly slow, difficult and expensive process. Often these difficulties contribute to late delivery of software products.

- Many of them can only be used effectively by professional programmers. If there is a dearth of the relevant professionals, projects will be significantly slowed.

- The implementation of changes to complex software systems is slow, difficult and hence can greatly increase maintenance costs.

- Several lines of code need to be written to solve a relatively small problem, thereby impeding programmer productivity.

In response to the above problems, 4GLs were created. In other words, the advent of 4GLs was seen as a way of reducing dependence on professional programmers and giving users the power to obtain fast results to support their day-to-day operation without the need for extensive programming.

Martin [186] provides a taxonomy of 4GLs which consists of simple query languages, complex query and update languages, report generators, graphics languages, decision-support languages, application generators, specification languages, very-high-level programming languages, parameterised application packages and application languages. There is a wide variety of commercially available 4GLs. Martin [186] also provides a comprehensive coverage of these tools. Some of the most commonly used ones include SQL, Oracle, Ingres, and FOCUS.

SQL (or Structured Query Language), as the name signifies, is a query language that is used in conjunction with a database and allows the user to obtain various types of information from the database. For instance, the command

```
LIST PATIENT_NO  AGE FOR AGE < 10 TO PRINT
```

accesses a database of patient records and prints the patient number and age of each patient who is less than 10 years old.

Oracle and Ingres are both examples of decision-support languages. They permit users to build databases and manipulate data in order to obtain decision-support information. These tools are commonly used for business-oriented problems such as analysis of financial matters and for making investment projections.

In principle, we can have these different categories of 4GLs. In practice however, the distinction is not so clear-cut; some packages combine facilities offered by more than one of these strands of 4GL. An example of such a package is FOCUS. It provides a wide spectrum of facilities such as report generation, database query, screen generation, graphics and financial modelling and also enables generation of applications.

Some 4GLs are described as non-procedural languages because they allow the user to specify 'what' the application is to do but not in detail 'how' this is to be achieved. Examples of non-procedural languages include application generators, database query languages and form designers. In contrast to non-procedural languages are procedural languages which require that the user specifies how each action is to be accomplished. Examples of procedural languages include Pascal, Modula-2, Cobol, and C. Certain 4GLs, however, sometimes combine the characteristics of both non-procedural and procedural languages.

13.5.1 Properties of Fourth-Generation Languages

Although 4GLs have different characteristics depending on factors such as their functionality, operational environment and target users, there are some properties which are common to many of them. Martin and McClure [186, 188] in a survey carried out in the early 1980's provided an extensive list of these characteristics. It must however be noted that further studies and advances led to the reappraisal of some of these.

- *They are easy to use.* This is undoubtedly true in relation to 1980's alternatives, but a less significant characteristic now.

- *They can be employed by non-professional programmers to obtain results.* True of course, but what was heralded as a great advantage turned out to be a double-edged sword (see section on weakness of 4GLs).

- *They use a database management system directly.*

- *They require an order of magnitude fewer instructions than other conventional languages such as Cobol.*
- *Where possible, they use non-procedural code.*
- *Where possible, intelligent default assumptions about what the user wants are made.*
- *They are designed for on-line operations.*
- *They encourage or enforce structured code.* This has proved true only to a point for early 4GLs. Maintenance programmers struggling with badly written 4GL code can testify to reams of ill-structured code. However, in relation to early alternatives, the statement holds.
- *They make it easy to understand someone else's code.* Once again, this characteristic and the next one were of greater significance when compared to 1980's alternatives.
- *They are designed for easy debugging.*
- *Non-technical users can learn to use a subset of the language after a two-day training course.*
- *They allow results to be obtained in an order of magnitude less time than with Cobol or PLII.* It is not clear that this characteristic is backed up by rigorous empirical study.
- *Where possible, documentation is automated.*

13.5.2 Impact on Maintenance

By virtue of the above characteristics, the use of 4GLs to develop and maintain applications impacts on software maintenance in many ways.

13.5.2.1 Increased Productivity

One of the major problems with applications developed with third-generation languages such as Cobol and Fortran is the time required to effect change. In organisations that depend on the effective operation of their software systems, delays in implementing change can be disruptive and costly. One of the strengths of 4GLs is that they enable more rapid implementation of change, thereby increasing productivity. For instance, adding a sorting procedure for a database may require in excess of 50 lines of a third-generation language in comparison with one line of 4GL code.

13.5.2.2 Reduction in Cost

Due to the reduction in time required to develop and maintain applications using 4GLs, they tend to cost less than conventional application development. Major enhancements can be undertaken in hours, unlike traditional programming language applications which may take several weeks or months.

13.5.2.3 Ease of Understanding

As discussed in Chapter 6, prior to modifying other people's programs, it is essential to understand them. A good 4GL facilitates this. In an industry where there is a shortage of qualified staff and a high turnover of maintenance personnel, the desire to shorten comprehension time is one of the driving forces behind 4GLs [178].

13.5.2.4 Automatic Documentation

In many 4GL-oriented applications, a large proportion of the documentation is generated automatically. Considering the significant role that documentation plays in maintenance of other people's programs, this feature can ease considerably the job of maintenance personnel.

13.5.2.5 Reduction in Workload

One of the major problems contributing to the software crisis, where demand for software systems exceeds supply, has been the shortage of professional programmers. The user-friendly and easy to learn nature of many 4GLs allowed end-users to implement modifications with little or no assistance, thereby reducing the workload for the maintenance personnel.

13.5.3 Weaknesses of Fourth-Generation Languages

In spite of the above potential benefits to maintenance, these languages do have weaknesses which include the following.

13.5.3.1 Application-Specific

The very fact that many of these languages are targeted at specific application domains makes it difficult to use them for applications other than those for which they were originally designed. This can also make it uneconomical or even impossible to enhance the functionality of an application because the language originally used to develop it is not powerful enough, unlike third-generation languages which can support a wider spectrum of applications.

13.5.3.2 Proprietary

Many 4GLs are not compatible; that is, they are proprietary and are not 'open languages' [178]. Once a 4GL system is purchased from a vendor, the organisation concerned cannot easily migrate to other similar systems or reuse code from other environments without huge cost implications, thereby impinging on the long-term evolution of the system.

13.5.3.3 Hyped Ease of Use

There have been a lot of claims in the literature that 4GLs are designed for non-professional programmers. However, not only are some programming constructs out of the reach of non-computer-literate users, a 4GL itself is no substitute for a good grounding in software engineering theory [82]. Thus, 'ease of use' may actually translate to unmaintainable code.

13.5.3.4 Poor Design

The ease of use issue means that systems can be developed by people with no expertise or grounding in software engineering, or by people with no thorough understanding of the business problem being solved. This can lead to badly designed and implemented systems with little or no documentation [82]. As such, the systems soon become unmaintainable.

4GLs have the potential to speed up productivity and reduce cost, but as Linthicum explains,

> *"... these tools lock you into a vendor, not a standard. 4GLs don't provide the same degree of flexibility or performance as 3GLs... Full-featured object-oriented programming languages and development environments like C++ may be the best alternative to the weaknesses of 4GLs."*
>
> Linthicum ([178], p.42)

13.6 Object-Oriented Paradigms

Early procedural programming is analogous to the 'waterfall' model. It developed in much the same way. It was appropriate to early software development contexts.

Originally, computers were used to solve well-defined, mathematically based problems. The idea of following a sequence of instructions was appropriate and relevant. Early programs written in machine code or assembler were the 'code-and-fix' and 'quick-fix' of programming languages. Simple sequences of instructions were fine for simple and clearly defined problems.

As the problems to be addressed became more complex, procedural languages and programming techniques became more sophisticated to deal with them. Techniques of structured systems analysis and design were developed, but essentially the underlying philosophy of a computer program being a sequence of instructions to be followed, remained the same. A comparison can be made with the waterfall and other similar development and maintenance models. These are more sophisticated versions of code-and-fix and quick-fix, but not dissimilar in essence, and still with fundamental shortcomings.

Nowadays, systems that are being computerised are far too complex to be captured by sequences of instructions. There are no defined start and end points. Where, for example, does the "program" that is the world Telecom system start and end? The concept does not make sense.

The object-oriented paradigm was developed to handle the design, development and maintenance of industrial-strength software [42]. A major characteristic of these systems is that they are inherently complex [42, 169 ch.12]. Such systems, e.g. air traffic control systems, airline ticket reservation systems and spacecraft control systems, are large and dynamic networks of interacting systems. These interacting systems themselves are made up of smaller systems and so on until at some level we eventually find familiar small systems that can be modelled procedurally. Thus procedural programming fits into object-orientation in the way that code-and-fix and quick-fix remain relevant to development and maintenance.

In this context, the system to be programmed becomes a series of elements, each of which is a self-contained system.

13.6.1 Decomposition to Aid Comprehension

The level of complexity of industrial-strength software systems makes it impossible for a single individual to understand the entire system all at once; there is a limit to how much information the human brain can handle and process at any given time [194]. The use of decomposition during the development of these systems was hailed as one of the first effective means of addressing the issue of complexity [42, 215]. This is based on the premise that in order to understand a system, we only need to comprehend some of its constituents at any one time rather than the whole system. Decomposing a system allows the production of these constituents. There are two ways in which a system can be decomposed: algorithmic decomposition and object-oriented decomposition [42].

Algorithmic decomposition was one of the most popular approaches used by software engineers and usually came under the guise of 'top-down structured design'. Here, the system is perceived as a process – or a collection of **algorithms** – and during decomposition, the process is broken down into sub-processes each of which in turn is represented as procedures, functions or modules depending on the programming language. For instance, the design (or algorithmic decomposition) of a spelling checker system yields the output given in Figure 13.1 [255].

This approach to software development and maintenance has a number of weaknesses. Firstly the output from each phase of the life-cycle is represented in a different form or language [266]. For instance, the design of a system can be represented graphically using structures such as data flow diagrams and structure charts whereas the implementation is in textual form (using a suitable programming language). Secondly, issues of abstraction and information hiding are not necessarily dealt with properly [42].

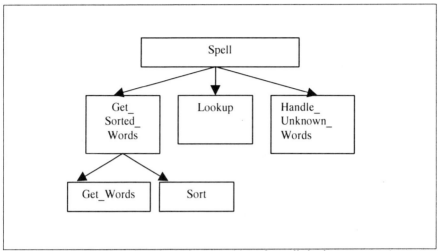

Figure 13.1 Algorithmic decomposition of a spell checker system

Object-oriented decomposition is the approach in which the system is viewed as a collection of objects that interact to perform a higher-level function. Each object exhibits unique behaviour usually characterised by the operations that it performs, and those that other objects perform on it. The objects communicate with each other through **message-passing**; that is, sending instructions on the service that is required. Object-oriented decomposition involves abstracting these objects and operations from the problem domain. An object-oriented decomposition equivalent of the spelling checker system in Figure 13.1 is given in Figure 13.2. In this example, the object, **SpellingChecker**, first issues a message, **GetWords**, to another object, **Document**, requesting words. After receiving the words, SpellingChecker then instructs another object, **Dictionary**, to check the spelling of the words. This is achieved by passing the message, **Lookup**.

The object-oriented paradigm is based on the view that the real world consists of sets of objects such as cars, cats, desk, tables etc. These objects have attributes which describe some aspects of the object; for example, a car has wheels, tyres, windscreens, etc. They can also perform **operations** and operations can be performed on them by other objects. Objects that have a group of similar attributes are considered to belong to a **class** and each of the objects is an **instance** of that class.

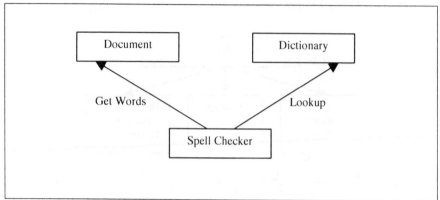

Figure 13.2 Object orientation of a spell checker system

Each object in a class **inherits** the attributes of that class. This process is known as inheritance. Suppose that we have a class called **UniversityEmployees** with attributes such as **EmployeeName** and **Salary**. Each instance of the class UniversityEmployees, for example professors, lecturers, research assistants and secretaries, inherits the attributes EmployeeName and Salary.

In an object-oriented system containing code libraries, the process of hiding the implementation details of an object and its associated operations behind a well-defined interface is known as **encapsulation**. The concept of encapsulation is similar to the notion of using definition and implementation modules in Modula-2 to separate the program interface from implementation details. Encapsulation is a particularly important concept for maintainability. It allows objects inherently to be units of reusable code, which have the benefits of component reuse: increased productivity and software quality and ease of code migration (Chapter 8). Additionally, systems built from these objects are extensible; the functionality of such systems can be increased through inheritance [113, 114].

13.6.2 Impact on Maintenance

Advocates of the object-oriented paradigm argue that one of its main advantages is that there is a common view of what happens in the real world and how this is implemented in the software, and as such, the transformation from the analysis phase to the implementation phase is much clearer and less error prone [266].

Booch [42, 41] has also pointed out a number of advantages of an object-oriented view of software development over orthodox methods such as top-down structured design or data-driven design:

- It yields smaller systems due to the reuse of common mechanisms.
- It facilitates the production of systems that are resilient to change and hence easily evolvable considering that its design is based on a stable intermediate form. The potential of object orientation to increase maintainability is a contributory factor to its popularity [287].
- The risks associated with complex systems are reduced because object-oriented systems are built to evolve incrementally from smaller components that have been shown to satisfy the requirements.
- Products from object-oriented decomposition can be stored in libraries and reused [25]. As discussed in Chapter 8 this has the advantage of expediting personnel productivity, high quality software and a reduction in cost.

Despite the benefits of deploying object-oriented techniques, their application is not universal. It takes time to bring a new paradigm on stream. There is a large body of code in existence requiring maintenance. Thus, even if object-orientation becomes the accepted paradigm for software development, the need for expertise in non object-oriented techniques will persist for a very long time. It is not necessarily appropriate or cost effective to convert existing systems.

Education and training is another issue. In the mid 1990's, there was an insufficient level of object-orientation education and training [156]; a large proportion of mainstream programmers had little or no educational background in object-oriented techniques. It can be prohibitively expensive for industry to retrain its personnel. In a large survey on object-oriented issues, conducted in the UK, investment in personnel was found to cost at least 10 times that in hardware or software [287]. For an appropriately trained body of experts to come up through the ranks of the colleges and universities takes time. Training the trainers adds to this. A strategic decision to swap to an object-oriented language in a mainstream Computer Science course, if not backed up by staff resources, can lead to object-oriented languages being taught using procedural programming techniques and philosophies.

The problems of which language to use [114] bedevil any advance of this type. There are risks in choosing one language over another before the foundation work on the underlying paradigm is settled.

13.6.3 Migration to Object-Oriented Platforms

As a result of the benefits of object-oriented technology there has been a tendency to migrate existing systems based on traditional paradigms by using object-oriented techniques and languages. In this section, the approaches and personnel issues concerned with this migration are discussed.

13.6.4 Approaches

Migration to object-oriented platforms can be approached in a number of ways. The first is to rewrite the whole system. In other words, throw away the current system and start from scratch, but develop the new system from an object-oriented perspective. This may be an option for small systems of a few thousand lines of code. For many large systems – usually hundreds of thousands or several million lines of code – that represent a significant part of the assets of the organisations that own them, a better approach is required.

The second approach to migration, especially appropriate in the early days of moves to object-oriented systems, was to use object-oriented analysis as a 'springboard'; that is, perform object-oriented analysis of the existing system and implement it using a mainstream but non-object-oriented language such as Cobol or C and then migrate to a suitable object-oriented language at some later time [113]. A prototype could be used to validate the specification with the user. The key advantage of this approach was that it avoided the risk of choosing an object-oriented programming language that would prove a bad choice as object-oriented languages themselves evolved.

The third, and possibly the approach preferred by most organisations, is that which permits organisations to reap the benefits that object orientation offers as well as securing the investment that has been made in their existing systems. This objective can be achieved through techniques such as abstraction engineering [218] and object wrapping [113, 218]. The process of **abstraction engineering** involves taking the existing non-object system and modelling it as a set of objects and operations. This enables the identification of key reusable components which themselves can be assembled to form new objects that can be used for both perfective and preventive maintenance of the existing system as well as the development of new systems. For example, there may be a need to enhance a patients' appointment system, embodied within a much larger hospital information system, so that other specialist standalone packages can be integrated into the appointment system. Rather than develop a new system, the appointment system can be isolated and encapsulated in the form of objects that can be used in other systems.

After identifying objects through abstraction engineering, programs which allow the objects to be accessed in a formal and controlled fashion are developed through a process known as **object wrapping**. These programs are called **wrappers**. The wrappers serve as interfaces to these objects and are what any prospective user of the object will be presented with. The wrapped objects can then be implemented in one or more object-oriented programming languages. The main advantage of object wrapping is that after an object has been wrapped, it can be reused in several other systems as if it was developed from scratch.

13.6.5 Retraining Personnel

The key issues that preoccupy the software community in relation to this change process are usually technical and managerial in nature. An area that has been neglected is the **retraining** of personnel – analysts, designers and programmers – already involved in mainstream technologies or programming languages, such as structured programming and Cobol [156]. Such retraining is essential since it can be used to capitalise on the existing knowledge base that the personnel have acquired by virtue of their experience.

Undoubtedly the retraining process is not only an expensive activity [287] but also a difficult task.

"There is nothing more difficult to arrange, more doubtful of success, and more dangerous to carry through than initiating changes"

Machiavelli (quoted in [114], pp. 20-2)

Nonetheless, the transition to a new technology need not necessarily be perceived as revolutionary but rather as an evolutionary process. It is important to select and apply training techniques that bridge the gap between the old and new technologies. That is, make explicit the links between familiar concepts in the old technology and corresponding concepts in the new technology.

Krupinski and Vlamis [156] provide suggestions on the techniques that can be used to assist Cobol programmers become proficient in object-oriented programming. For example, they link the process of hiding implementation details behind a well-defined interface in traditional programming languages to the concept of encapsulation in object-oriented languages. Another method, 'Objects 9000', being used to facilitate conversion to the object-oriented paradigm, involves introducing object-orientation in connection with ISO 9000 quality standards [87].

Although little attention has been paid to the retraining of personnel in connection with the migration of legacy systems, there are examples in which these systems have been reengineered successfully using object-oriented techniques. In the next section some of these examples are discussed.

13.7 Object-Oriented Techniques in Software Maintenance

The application of object oriented techniques is more common in the development of new systems than in the maintenance of existing systems. There are, however, examples in which these techniques have been applied successfully in the reengineering of software systems. In this section we will look at three such systems. The experiences from these ventures by the organisations concerned are also discussed.

13.7.1 Case Study – Mobile2OOO

Mobile2OOO, a Customer Account Management and Billing System, developed by American Management Systems, Inc. (AMS), is a customer account management and billing system used within the cellular telephone industry [278]. The mainframe-based system consists of about 200 on-line and 600 batch/report programs all of which constitute around 2.2 million lines of Cobol code. As a result of the potential of object-oriented technology to broaden its functionality and to increase its ease of use, Mobile2OOO was reengineered using object-oriented and Graphical User Interface (GUI) techniques. The ultimate goal was to develop a version of Mobile2OOO called 'Mobile2OOO GUI' which is based on a client/server architecture[17]. The client is an Intel-based PC running OS/2. The server can be an OS/2-based server or an IBM mainframe.

During implementation, the Mobile2OOO system was first analysed objectively, bringing out its strengths and weaknesses, through reverse engineering. The specific goals for reimplementing the system using object-oriented technology were then identified. The desired functionality was implemented using Smalltalk/V with ENVY as the configuration manager and WindowBuilderPro as the user interface design tool. Local data was stored as persistent objects and in SQL tables. With the aid of Communications Manager for OS/2, the workstation – acting as a client – communicates in a peer-to-peer fashion with the server.

The experiences from the project were threefold. It showed firstly, that during reengineering, it is important to develop a methodology which combines what has been successful in the past with those processes and procedures unique to object technology. Secondly, developers need to be offered training in the object-oriented paradigm using the technologies that will be deployed to reengineer the legacy system in question. And thirdly, there is a need for constant iteration to extend and improve the desired functionality.

13.7.2 Case Study – Insight II

Insight II is an interactive molecular modelling system jointly developed by the Monsanto Corporation and the University of California, San

---

[17] In a client/server architecture, a software system known as a 'server' performs operations requested by other systems, known as 'clients' [257].

Francisco, originally for modelling protein [205]. This system, which was developed around 1984 based on a procedural development paradigm, is a workstation-based graphical application primarily used by research chemists for visualisation, simulation and analysis of molecules and also as a tool for basic research and pharmaceutical development.

As Insight II increased in size – reaching 120,000 lines of C code in 1988 – to accommodate new functionality such as molecular modelling subsystems for synthetic polymers and inorganic catalysts, there was increasing difficulty in maintaining its reliability. Another problem with Insight II was its inability to support an open architecture that would allow users to create their own applications within a well-defined framework.

In response to these problems, a new application framework had to be developed. Due to its potential to offer solutions to the problems of extensibility, efficiency and reliability, the object-oriented paradigm was chosen for this task. It was also chosen because of its support for encapsulation and consistency, two essential characteristics for an open architecture.

Instead of completely rewriting the existing system, an evolutionary approach to developing the architecture was chosen. A class library that reimplements Insight II was developed while ensuring that the old applications and their core – architecture – were still working. The code of the old system was encapsulated with a 'jacket' – or wrapper – that gives the appearance of an object oriented system, called 'Chembench'. The old applications were then migrated, in a piecemeal fashion, to the new object-oriented interfaces. The main advantages of this approach were that the substantial investment made in the existing system was not wasted and there was an opportunity to build on past successes. One disadvantage of this approach, however, was that the jacket was constrained by some limitations in the old system.

A number of lessons were learned from the migration of Insight II to an object-oriented platform. Firstly, the maintainability and extensibility of the new system was substantially improved. This is apparent in the increased rate of adding functionality and the decreased rate of reported errors. Secondly, major extensions of the system have been undertaken while maintaining reliability. Prior to the migration, such extensions were either abandoned or could only have been undertaken at the risk of disastrous long-term consequences. Thirdly, the use of jackets and the piecemeal approach to migration allowed the existing system to run alongside the entire process. And finally, the migration successfully led to an open architecture that offered sufficient encapsulation and interface consistency, thus making it easy for users to use it as a basis for their own applications.

Despite the success of this project, problems were encountered. One was the inability to modify some classes because migration to Chembench was incomplete. Another problem was the difficulties encountered due to the use of C instead of C++; one of the host platforms for Chembench did not have C++ available and some of the personnel involved had no C++ expertise.

13.7.3 Case Study – Image Filing System

Due to the need for a software development methodology which could simplify the maintenance and modification of a large software system, the object-oriented paradigm was chosen by a group of researchers in a major multinational corporation [296]. The paradigm was chosen on the grounds that it provides a stable architecture and a modifiable software system. A two-phase project to investigate the applicability and usefulness of using object-oriented techniques to develop large-scale software systems was set up.

During the first stage of the project, a year was spent analysing, designing, and developing a prototype for an existing image filing system using Coad's Object-Oriented Analysis and Object-Oriented Design and C++. This system – constituting several million lines of code – consisted of two layers. The upper layer made up of three subsystems: image definition, image entry and image retrieval; the lower layer consisting of two subsystems: a user interface and a database. The result of this phase indicated that the use of object-oriented techniques could be applied to develop large-scale software systems.

The second phase of the project involved evaluation of the effectiveness of object-oriented techniques. The approach used was to apply Hatley's Real-Time Structured Analysis (RSA) and Rumbaugh's Object Modeling Technique (OMT) to the same subsystem of the image filing system – the image retrieval subsystem in this case – and evaluate their analysis processes and the corresponding results. Three criteria were used to carry out the evaluation: separation of role between analysis and design; ease of proceeding to the analysis process; and ease of understanding the results of analysis.

The results from the second phase of this project are threefold. Firstly, analysts applying RSA tend to introduce more design decisions earlier in the analysis than when using OMT. This gives rise to an inflexible specification that depends on the design decisions. Secondly, the analysis process of RSA is less straightforward and more time-consuming than that of OMT. Also, due to the hierarchical structure of functional models and the tight coupling between the functional model and dynamic model of a system in RSA, a small change can have extensive effects. On the other hand, when using OMT, a modification to a dynamic model or functional model does not affect the object model[18]. This is because the details of the dynamic model and functional model are encapsulated by the object concerned. Thirdly, the analysis results of RSA are easier to understand than those of OMT.

As a general conclusion, "RSA is useful for analysts whose purpose is to specify the analysis results for customers and designers, while OMT is useful for analysts whose purpose is to analyse an unfamiliar problem for their own sake" [296 p.43].

Exercise 13.2 Below is a problem statement from a client who wants an information system for students' examination marks:

> *Due to an increase in the number of students, an information system for managing students' examination marks is needed. Using the system, each lecturer should be able to store students' examination marks. A lecturer should also be able to modify the marks (for his or her course only) and make enquiries about the names and grades of all students who attain a certain score, for instance 75% or more, for each module.*

- Develop the above system using a third-generation language such as Modula-2 or Ada and also develop the same system

---

[18] Provided the modification does not affect messages to and from the object.

using a suitable 4GL. Compare the comprehensibility and maintainability of the two systems.

- Modify both systems to allow tutors and students also to make enquiries. Tutors should only be allowed to view the marks of their tutees and students should only be allowed to view their own marks. Comment on the time and ease of effecting this change for both systems.

13.8 Summary

The key points that have been covered in this chapter are:

- It is essential to build maintainability into software systems, but it is even more important to sustain maintainability while the systems evolve.

- Comprehensive impact analysis as an integral part of implementing system change is key in building and sustaining maintainability in systems.

- Technologies such as 4GLs and object-oriented paradigms aim to achieve this objective.

- Using 4GLs to develop applications can lead to easily understood code, increased productivity automatic documentation and reduced maintenance cost. However, 4GLs are not the cure-all solution they have sometimes been hyped up to be. Problems can arise through the development of systems by people who do not have the appropriate foundation knowledge in software engineering or maintenance.

- Object-oriented paradigms give rise to systems that are resilient to change since design is based on a stable intermediate form. However, it is important to note that despite the increasing popularity of object-oriented techniques, it is still early days for object-oriented development of large complex systems.

In this chapter, the effects of using 4GLs, object-oriented techniques, quality assurance procedures and standards on the maintainability of software systems have been discussed. Also, some case studies illustrating the applicability of these techniques in large-scale industrial systems have been examined. To increase the productivity and efficiency with which some of these techniques and procedures can be applied, it is important to work with suitable tools. In the next chapter, some of these tools are described.

14

Maintenance Tools

A tool is only as good as its user

This chapter aims to

1. Discuss a number of criteria that can be used as guidelines to choosing tools.

2. Outline some general categories of the most commonly used maintenance tools.

3. Describe the key features of tools that can be used to support tasks such as program comprehension, reverse engineering, configuration management, debugging, testing and documentation.

4. Explain how the above features enable the software maintainer to understand and to modify software systems.

14.1 Introduction

There may be no 'silver bullets' for maintenance problems, but the use of tools to support the software maintainer can significantly simplify the task, increase efficiency and productivity, and support the evolution of the entire software system.

In this chapter, some general criteria for selecting tools are discussed. Also, a survey of the key features of commonly used software maintenance tools is presented. The criteria and features given can be used as guidelines for evaluating the suitability of a prospective tool – assisting the user to make an informed choice. It is not the aim of this chapter to provide a comprehensive list of specific products and their vendors (see, for example, [300] for such information).

14.2 Definitions

Tool – implement or device used to carry out functions automatically or manually.

Software maintenance tool – an artefact used to carry out automatically a function relevant to software change.

14.3 Criteria for Selecting Tools

There are several vendors developing and marketing a wide variety of tools that claim to support software maintenance. Some of them apparently serve the same purpose, but in practice differ in cost and in many other respects. Bearing this in mind and prior to acquiring a tool for software maintenance work, there are a number of factors that should be taken into consideration:

- *Capability:* This is one of the most important criteria to consider when evaluating a tool. The tool must be capable of supporting the task to be performed. When a technique or method is to be supported by a tool, it is necessary to ensure first that it works without a tool; that is, by hand. As Davis points out, "if a technique doesn't work without automation, it won't work with automation" [75, 34].

- *Features:* After having decided that the technique or method can benefit from automated support, the features expected of any potential tool need to be considered. As a simple example, a useful word processor will need to provide not just an editor, but also other features such as a spelling checker, thesaurus, drawing and search facilities. Similarly in maintenance, particular features may be required of a tool. The importance of each of these features should be rated and the tool selected accordingly.

- *Cost and benefits:* The cost of introducing a tool needs to be weighed against the benefits. The benefits that the tool brings need to be evaluated in terms of indicators such as product quality, productivity, responsiveness, cost reduction, and extent of overlap or dichotomy between different groups with respect to their way of doing things [170].

- *Platform:* The platform refers to the specific hardware and software environments on which the tool runs. Examples include: IBM mainframe and mini platforms such as MVS and AS/400 respectively; PC-based operating systems such as Macintosh OS, MS-DOS and Windows; and LINUX and UNIX variants. The platform where the tool is to be mounted needs to be considered.

- *Programming language:* This refers to the language that will be used to write the source code. Examples include Java, Ada, C, C++, Cobol, Fortran, Modula-2, Lisp and Prolog. To be on the safe side, it is important to obtain a tool that supports a language that is already (or is likely to become) an industry standard. This is particularly important in situations where there is migration to a new paradigm, for example migration to object-oriented development.

- *Ease of use:* The ease with which users can get to grips with the tool determines, to some extent, its acceptability. Usually, a tool that has a similar 'feel' to the tools that users are already familiar with tends to be accepted more easily than one which is radically different. For example, introducing a command-driven tool into a menu-driven environment will cause more problems for the users than a menu-driven tool.

- *Openness of architecture:* The ability to integrate a tool with others from different vendors plays a major role in its extensibility and flexibility. This is particularly important in situations where the desired tool needs to run in conjunction with existing tools. Another reason for selecting a tool with an open architecture is that in very complex maintenance problems a single product from one vendor may not be capable of performing all the required tasks. For instance, many CASE tools provide support for code analysis but lack the capability of extracting business rules from the code [185]. In such cases there is a need to purchase additional tools from other vendors to supplement the existing ones and it is important that they can be integrated. In short, avoid proprietary tools if you can.

- *Stability of vendor:* It is important to consider the reputation of the vendor before acquiring a tool. Due to high competition in the computing industry, a company who cannot keep up with the competition may disappear from the scene and leave its users with no support. As such, it is essential to look into the background of any company being considered as a supplier of a tool. If the tool is one with an open architecture then this factor may not be so important.

- *Organisational culture:* Organisations usually have a particular way in which they operate; a working culture and work patterns. In order to increase the chances of the tool being accepted by the target users, it is essential to take such culture and work patterns into consideration [170].

14.4 Taxonomy of Tools

In principle, it is possible to distinguish between classes of software maintenance tools, usually based on the task that they support. For instance, visualisation tools support program comprehension. In practice, however, it is difficult to have such fine-grained distinction primarily due to the diversified and interrelated nature of software maintenance activities. For example, some debuggers – used for correcting errors in programs – also offer visualisation facilities.

In this section an attempt is made to classify maintenance tools based on the specific tasks that they support. In cases where a tool supports more than one task, this will be pointed out in the discussion. The categories of tasks for which tools will be discussed are:

- Program understanding and reverse engineering
- Testing
- Configuration management
- Documentation and measurement.

14.5 Tools for Comprehension and Reverse Engineering

Program understanding and reverse engineering have been combined because they are strongly linked. Program understanding involves having a general knowledge of **what** a program does and how it relates to its environment; identifying **where** in the system changes are to be effected; and knowing **how** the different components to be modified work. Reverse engineering goes a step further by enabling analysis and different representations of the system to promote that understanding.

As a result of the large amount of time used to study and understand programs [69, 214], tools that promote understanding play a major role in the implementation of change. Tools for reverse engineering and related tasks such as redocumentation, design recovery, specification recovery and reengineering also achieve the same goal. The majority of tools in this category are visualisation tools, that is, tools that assist the programmer to form a mental model of the system under examination by virtue of the visual impact they create. Examples of program understanding and reverse engineering tools include the program slicer, static analyser, dynamic analyser and cross-referencer.

14.5.1 Program Slicer

One of the major problems with software maintenance is coping with the size of the program source code. It is important that a programmer can select and view only those parts of the program that are affected by a proposed change without being distracted by the irrelevant parts. One technique that helps with this problem is known as slicing – a mechanical process of marking all sections of a program text that may influence the value of a variable at a given point in the program [285]. The tool used to support slicing is known as a **program slicer** [105]. The program slicer also displays data links and related characteristics to enable the programmer to track the effect of changes.

14.5.2 Static Analyser

In an attempt to understand a program, there is usually a need to obtain information about different aspects of the program such as modules, procedures, variables, data elements, objects and classes, and class hierarchy. A **static analyser** allows derivation of this information through careful and deep examination of the program text. Some authors also refer to this type of tool as a 'browser' [206]. Generally, a static analyser:

- allows general viewing of the program text – serves as a **browser**;
- generates summaries of contents and usage of selected elements in the program text such as variables or objects.

14.5.3 Dynamic Analyser

When studying a software system with the aim of changing it, simply examining the program text – static analysis – may not provide all the necessary information. Thus, there is a need to control and analyse various aspects of the program when it is executing. A tool that can be used to support this process is known as a **dynamic analyser**. Generally, the dynamic analyser allows a maintainer to trace the execution path of the system while it is running – it acts as a tracer. This permits the maintainer to determine the paths that will be affected by a change and those through which a change must be made.

14.5.4 Data Flow Analyser

A **data flow analyser** is a static analysis tool that allows the maintainer to track all possible data flow and control flow paths in the program and also to backtrack [275]. This is particularly important when there is a need for impact analysis: studying the effect of a change on other parts of the system. By tracking the flow of data and control, the maintainer can obtain information such as where a variable obtained its value and which parts of the program are affected by the modification of the variable.

Generally, a data flow analyser also:

- allows analysis of program text to promote understanding of the underlying logic of the program;
- assists in showing the relationship between the different components of the system;
- provides pretty-printers that allow the user to select and display different views of the system.

14.5.5 Cross-Referencer

The **cross-referencer** is a tool that generates an index of the usage of a given program entity. For example, it can produce information on the declarations of a variable and all the sections in the program in which it has been set and used. During the implementation of a change, the information this tool generates helps the maintainer to focus and localise attention on those parts of the program that are affected by the change.

14.5.6 Dependency Analyser

A **dependency analyser** helps the maintainer to analyse and understand the interrelationships between entities in a program. This tool is particularly useful in situations where logically related entities, such as variables, may be physically far apart in the program. Generally, a dependency analyser:

- can provide capabilities that allow a maintainer to set up and query a database of the dependencies in a program. Information on dependencies can also be used to determine the effect of a change and to identify redundant relationships between entities [290];
- provides a graphical representation of the dependencies in a program where the node in the graph represents a program entity and an arc represents the dependency between entities.

14.5.7 Transformation Tool

A **transformation tool** converts programs between different forms of representations, usually between text and graphics; for example, transforming code to visual form and vice versa [233]. Because of the impact that visual representations can have on comprehension, the use of a transformation tool can help the maintainer view and understand the system in a way that would not be possible with, for example, just the textual representation. The tool usually comes with a browser and editor, which are used to edit the program in any of its representations.

14.6 Tools to Support Testing

Testing is one of the most expensive and demanding tasks in software development and maintenance and can benefit greatly from automated support.

14.6.1 Simulator

Using a test **simulator**, a controlled environment is set up for the testing to take place. The system to be tested is simulated in this environment and the appropriate set of tests carried out. The set-up and components of the environment will depend on the type of application being tested. For instance, a simulator for a real-time system needs to provide a priority-based, event-driven, multitasking environment together with interprocess communication through message queues and shared memory [291].

The key advantage of this approach to testing is that it allows the maintainer access to a richer set of tools than may otherwise be available. The other advantage is that the maintainer can try out the effect of a change before implementing the change on the actual operational system. The disadvantage is that the results and observations may be misleading since some of the constraints in the real environment may not be reflected in the controlled environment.

14.6.2 Test Case Generator

Sets of test data used to test the functionality of the system undergoing modification are produced. The test data can be obtained from the system as well as data files. The tool that assists in generating test data is called a **test data generator** [225]. The tool usually requires definition of the criteria for generating the test cases.

14.6.3 Test Paths Generator

Prior to undertaking integration and unit testing, it is important to know all the potential data flow and control flow paths that may have been affected by a change. This information enables the maintainer to carry out the appropriate set of tests to ensure that a change has achieved the desired effect. **Test path generators** can be used for this purpose [189]. Sometimes, the combination of potential test paths can be so large that some criteria must be introduced for selecting the most important paths.

14.7 Tools to Support Configuration Management

Effective configuration management is not possible without the aid of some kind of automated support tools in most maintenance environments [181]. Keeping track of the objects produced during modification to a software system is not a trivial task. There may be thousands of files – source files, binary files – and an enormous amount of associated documentation. Add to this the fact that much software maintenance is carried out in a distributed network environment, perhaps with a mix of hardware platforms, and the magnitude of the problem becomes apparent.

Configuration management and version control support tools act as a repository for the objects that make up a software system. A specific configuration is created by taking objects – usually particular versions of source files – out of a central repository and putting them into a private work area. Examples of classic tools in this area are Source Code Control System and Revision Control System (RCS). Other, more sophisticated tools have been developed on top of these, for example Open Development Environment (ODE) is a system built on RCS with a view to tackling the specific problems of a parallel development environment.

It is outside the scope of this book to look in detail at a comprehensive list of configuration management support tools but a brief overview of a classic support tool, Source Code Control System, will be given.

14.7.1 Source Code Control System

Source Code Control System (SCCS) consists of various utility programs usually accessed by a front end such as the *sccs* UNIX command. An associated SCCS history file may be created for each file and the SCCS programs will be applied to the relevant history files such that versions can be tracked and programmers can keep track of which files have been changed and when.

Creation of a history file for a source code file on a UNIX platform would involve the following steps:

- Renaming the original source code file in the current directory.
- Creating the history file in the SCCS subdirectory.
- Performing an 'sccs get' on the renamed source code file to retrieve a read-only copy of the initial version.

SCCS can be used to perform various actions on versioned files. For example, a working copy of a file that has been checked out for editing may be compared with a version from the SCCS history. A file that has been checked out for editing will be locked so that no one else can edit that version. SCCS will also produce administrative information such as listing all the files currently being edited and will include information on the specific version being edited and the person doing the editing.

14.7.2 Other Utilities

There are many utilities that can be used to keep track of files and filestores. SCCS is one of the more sophisticated. Many of the familiar programs and utilities have their part to play. For example, *ls* and *dir* commands, and file manager tools give information on files and directory structure. *Find* tools and the *grep* command allow searches for specific patterns within files. Similar utilities exist on all platforms. The important thing is to be aware that such tools exist and to take advantage of whichever are the most appropriate in a particular situation.

14.8 Other Tasks

14.8.1 Documentation

As stressed throughout this book, the importance of documentation for software maintenance cannot be overemphasised. Its importance is reflected in the observation that lack of documentation is considered to be one of the major problems that software maintainers face [77, 176]. There is a wide variety of documentation tools which include hypertext-based tools [107], data flow and control chart generators, requirements tracers, and CASE tools.

14.8.2 Complexity Assessment

Usually in maintenance projects, it is essential to assess the complexity of a system before effecting any change to it. A **complexity quantifier** is a tool used to measure the complexity of a program. Such complexity measures are usually based on factors such as the underlying algorithm of a program or its structure. Tools that automatically generate, for example, McCabe's cyclomatic number can be used to pinpoint where the software is too complex to be reliable and to quantify the number of tests needed [189].

> **Exercise 14.1** Investigate the Source Code Control System available on your system and explain how you would use it as part of a large software project.
>
> **Exercise 14.2** A major University has a large computer system used for storing and managing information about all its students and staff. The system: (i) is 25 years old; (ii) was developed using structured programming

techniques in Cobol communicating with relational databases; (iii) is running on an IBM mainframe; and (iv) has over 500,000 lines of code.

The system has undergone several modifications, both planned and quick fixes, and has become too expensive to maintain. In the light of these difficulties, the University wants to take advantage of the benefits of object-oriented development but without discarding its current system. Unfortunately, over 90% of the staff who maintain the system are new and are not familiar with its implementation.

- Identify the major tasks that need to be performed by the software maintenance personnel.
- For each of these tasks, identify a suitable type of tool (or sets of tools) to assist the maintainers.
- Using the information contained in an appropriate guide (e.g. Zvegintzov [300]) and elsewhere, make recommendations on the most suitable commercial tools.

There is a wide variety of tools available to software maintainers. Examples that have not been covered in this chapter, mainly because they have been documented extensively elsewhere, are debuggers, editors (including syntax-sensitive editors), and programming languages [108, 300].

14.9 Summary

The key points that have been covered in this chapter are:

- There are several criteria for selecting a suitable maintenance tool. Criteria include capability features, cost and benefits, platform, programming language, ease of use, openness of architecture, stability of vendor and organisational culture.
- Some general categories of maintenance task that can benefit from automated support are program understanding, reverse engineering, configuration management, debugging and testing.
- There are several tools that support each of the above tasks, but they have some general features in common.

- There are a number of ways in which the above features enable the software maintainer to understand and modify software systems.

In this chapter various issues underpinning the selection and use of tools, and how they assist maintainers, have been discussed. The dynamic nature of activities within the software industry, especially with respect to paradigm shifts, presents great challenges to all members of the maintenance team. An overview of some of these challenges is given in the next section.

PART V: Looking to the Future

The aims of this book have been to facilitate understanding of
1. The context of maintenance: the fundamentals of software change, the maintenance framework, maintenance process models, the different types of maintenance activity, the problems facing maintenance organisations and some of the solutions to these problems.
2. What happens during maintenance: program comprehension, reverse engineering, software reuse, testing and the management of the process.
3. How to keep track of the maintenance process: overall and at a more detailed level.
4. How to build better systems: the use of support tools and the means by which maintainability may be built into software systems.

Overview

This final section of the book aims to reflect on the past and present of software maintenance as an academic discipline and as a 'trade' dating back to the late 1970's, highlighting some pertinent research issues. It also attempts to make a prognosis of the maintenance-related challenges that lie ahead within the software industry.

The Past and Present

Software maintenance as an academic subject and as an occupation has come a long way. In the early days, the wider issues of software maintenance were simply not understood. The fact that software systems evolved was not fully appreciated, let alone the implications of this continual need for change.

In academia historically, maintenance received far less attention than development of new systems [26]. This is evident in the comparatively small number of publications and active researchers in the area in the early days of the discipline. In industry, the situation was not much different; software maintenance was considered a second-class job, one that was dull and that entailed unexciting detective work [129]. This is evident in the less competitive wage levels and much poorer career prospects of software maintainers.

With time, software systems increasingly became an integral part of the fabric of many organisations, grew bigger and more complex, and their maintenance consumed a significant proportion - up to 70% - of the software life-cycle budget for these organisations [4, 35, 176]. In addition to these rising maintenance costs, the recession in the early 1990's led to severe cuts in budgets for the development of new systems [9]. The cuts meant not only an increased need to get more from existing systems but also the need to ensure that these systems were much more maintainable than was deemed necessary before. The systems became assets that needed to be protected [218].

The two factors of rising maintenance costs and a reduction in resources for development of new systems marked a turning point in the treatment and perception of software maintenance issues. Attention on software maintenance intensified. This can be seen in the increasing number of conferences, workshops, books, journals, organisations and special issues of mainstream journals dedicated specifically to software maintenance [300]. Also, there is evidence of maintenance-related issues being viewed in a more positive light than before by management [78]. A by-product of the increasing interest in software maintenance activities was an increased level of research activity.

Research Areas

The discipline of software maintenance has progressed rapidly from barely being recognised as a discipline in the middle of the 20th century, to spawning a plethora of journals, conferences and special interest groups at the start of the 21st. Work is on-going in all areas at all levels. Software maintenance, once the poor relation, looks likely to be a major driver of progress in the software industry into the future.

Classification

Classification is a classic aid to understanding, and classifying the elements of software maintenance helps towards a deeper understanding of the processes involved. Such classification is not as straightforward as it might appear. We have covered the topic to a degree within this text, but work on effective classification is on-going. A good starting point for an in-depth study of this area is Chapin *et al* [59] on types of software maintenance and evolution.

Software Experience Bases

Conradi *et al* propose the following research questions in [67]:

1. What kind of experience is most useful to developers?
2. How should experience be structured and classified?
3. Is a self-sufficient and self-organising software experience base a realistic goal?
4. Which environments are suited to software experience bases and which are not?

Software Reuse

Software reuse is an area of great potential benefit to the software industry. Many of the reasons it is not yet achieving its potential have not been fully explored – the management of the reuse process, the representation of information appropriate to reuse, the legal considerations and so on. These are all good starting points for research which would have the potential to lead to wide implementation of reuse strategies and thus be of great benefit to the software industry.

Support Tools

There is enormous scope for the development of automated support tools. Many such tools already exist but are not in widespread use and are not demonstrably benefiting the software industry. Why is this? Are the tools too specialised, too general, of no real use...?

The task of software maintenance is such a vital and complex one that it can no longer be done effectively without automated support.

The push towards interoperability provides the basis for a huge leap forward in this area.

Software Measurement

There is a great deal of work to be done in the area of measurement. Consider the following questions:

- What is the maintainability of this software module?
- What will be the maintainability of this system if we carry out this modification in this way as opposed to that way?

Imagine the potential benefits of being able to say 'This module has a maintenance factor of 6.7 and if incorporated in this way will produce a system with a maintenance factor of 2.4.'

The current situation is a long way from this, but perhaps one day a maintenance manager will be able to use a software support tool to pick a component from a reuse library according to quantifiable safety, reliability and maintainability criteria.

Program Comprehension

Teasley [265] provides thought-provoking insights into areas of programmer behaviour that are both very important and largely unexplored. She argues that any comprehension task is affected by three major elements:

1. Who is doing the comprehending?
2. What are they comprehending?
3. Why do they want to comprehend?

She claims that many studies on programmer behaviour have concentrated on WHO, but WHAT and WHY, questions fundamental to the key area of program comprehension, have largely been ignored.

Program comprehension, is an area that crosses discipline boundaries. This can be problematic in finding funding for basic research. Many funding bodies talk about the importance of multi-disciplinary research, but the mechanisms set up to approve specific project proposals tend to be biased against projects that do not sit firmly within one discipline.

The Software Maintenance Process

A significant step on from work on the Laws of Software Evolution first formulated in the 1960's (see chapter 3) has been the FEAST (Feedback, Evolution And Software Technology) projects. These investigated the role and impact of feedback in E-type systems and the software process. Detailed inspection of the results of the FEAST projects provides an excellent grounding for anyone wanting to research this area. See for example [171, 268].

As we have seen, software maintenance consumes a huge proportion of the total resource required to keep a system operational. There is much to be gained from improving the processes themselves and understanding how they interact. It has been recognised that the sharing of experience between software maintainers is necessary to improve the overall processes [63], but how this may best be brought about is still open to debate.

The Threesome Marriage

As important as the change of attitude towards software maintenance is an increased understanding of the interrelation between the three concepts that drive software maintenance issues, an area we term the 'threesome marriage'. These are software reengineering, software reuse and object-oriented techniques. Migration of systems, seen as a way of addressing maintenance problems, can be considered a form of **reengineering**; that is, reverse engineering to analyse and improve understanding of the system as it is, followed by the traditional forward engineering using a suitable paradigm or platform. That paradigm at present seems to be the **object-oriented** paradigm. The concept of viewing a system as a set of objects and operations during object-oriented development gives rise to objects and operations that can be reused, thereby promoting **software reuse**. This 'marriage' is important because the concepts not only impact strongly upon each other, but their understanding and application stand to play a major role in the current trend of migrating legacy systems to alternative platforms.

The Best of Both Worlds

Organisations may be willing to join the bandwagon of technologies such as object-oriented and client/server systems [287], but only if they can see a clear commercial payback. Many will not contemplate doing so at the expense of their existing systems. These systems represent major assets and are at the very heart of working culture. As a result, there is an urgent need to provide migration paths that enable organisations to get the best of both worlds; that is, cash in on the benefits of the best technology as well as retaining the value of their existing systems. To achieve this goal, adaptation of the new technologies to incorporate these systems is the way forward.

Software maintenance is maturing as a discipline. It has already provided tangible benefit to the software industry, and has the potential to provide enormous benefit to future generations of systems.

References

1. A. Abran, H. Nguyenkim. **Measurement of the maintenance process for a demand-based perspective**. Journal of Software Maintenance: Research and Practice, 5(2):63-90, June 1993.

2. G. Aharonian. **Social and economics problems with defense software reuse**. In Proceedings, Reuse in Practice Workshop. Software Engineering Institute Pittsburg, PA, July 11-13 1989.

3. P Aiken, A. Muntz, R. Richards. **DoD legacy systems: Reverse engineering data requirements**. Communications of the ACM, 37(5):26-41, May 1994.

4. G. Alkhatib. **The maintenance problem of application software: An empirical analysis**. Journal of Software Maintenance: Research and Practice, 1:83-104, 1992.

5. C. M. Allwood. **Novices on the computer: a review of the literature.** sInternational Journal of Man-Machine Studies, 25:633-58, 1986.

6. ANSI/IEEE. **IEEE Standard Glossary of Software Engineering Terminology** Technical Report 729, 1983.

7. G. Arango, I Baxter, P Freeman. **Maintenance and porting of software by design recovery**. In Proceedings, Conference on Software Maintenance, pages 42-9, Los Alamitos, California. IEEE Computer Press, 1985.

8. ARIANE 5, **Flight 501 Failure**, Report by the Inquiry Board, Chairman: Prof. J. L. Lions, Paris, 19 July 1996.

9. R. S. Arnold. **Software Reengineering: a quick history** Communications of the ACM, 37(5): 13-14, May 1994. This article traces the origin of software reengineering from the mid-1960's to mid-1990's practices and future expectations. It is also pointed out that the interest in maintenance in reengineering existing software systems stemmed from the apparent shortage of resources for development of new systems.

10 J D Arthur, R E Nance. **Verification and Validation without Independence: a recipe for failure**. Systems Research Centre, Virginia Polytechnic Institute and State University. 2001.

11 J. D. Arthur, K. T. Stevens. **Document quality indicators: A framework for assessing documentation adequacy**. Software Maintenance: Research and Practice. 4(3):129-42, 1992.

12 L. J. Arthur. **Software Evolution: The Software Maintenance Challenge**. John Wiley and Sons, New York, 1988.

13 R. M. Baecker, A. Marcus. **Human Factors and Typography for More Readable Programs**, Addison-Wesley Reading, MA, 1990. In this very good book, Baecker and Marcus discuss some important issues of program visualisation and give guidelines on how to present programs in an easily understood way.

14 F. T. Baker, H. Mills. **Chief Programmer teams**. IBM Systems Journal, 11(1):56-73, 1972.

15 V Basili, S. K. Abd-El-Hafiz. **Packaging Reusable Components: The Specification of Programs**. Technical Report UMIACS-TR-92-97, University of Maryland, College Park, MD 20742, September 1992.

16 V R. Basili. **Viewing software maintenance as reuse-oriented software development**. IEEE Software, 7:19-25, January 1990.

17 V R. Basili, D. H. Hutchens. **An empirical study of a syntactic complexity family**. IEEE Transactions on Software Engineering, SE-9:652-63, 1983.

18 V R. Basili, H. D. Mills. **Understanding and documenting programs**. IEEE Transactions on Software Engineering, 8:270-83, 1982.

19 V R. Basili, H. D. Rombach, J. Bailey, A. Delis, F. Farhat. **Ada reuse metrics**. In P A. Leslie, R. O. Chester, and M. F. Thoefanos, editors, Guidelines Document for Ada Reuse and Metrics (Draft), pages 11-29. Martin Marietta Energy Systems, Inc., Oak Ridge, Tenn., under contract to US Army, AIRMICS., March, 1989.

20 V R. Basili, H. D. Rombach, J. Bailey, B. G. Joo. **Software reuse: A framework**. In Proceedings of the Tenth Minnowbrook Workshop (1987, Software Reuse), Blue Mountain Lake, N.Y, July 1987.

21 V R Basili, G Caldiera, F Lanubile, F Shull. **Studies on Reading Techniques**. Report of the Experimental Software Engineering Group (ESEG), University of Maryland, USA. 1996.

22 B. Beizer **Software testing techniques** 2nd edition Van Nostrand Reinhold. New York. 1990.

23 L. A. Belady, M. M. Lehman. **Programming system dynamics or the metadynamics of systems in maintenance and growth**. In M. M. Lehman and L. A. Belady, editors, Program Evolution: Processes of Software Change, Chapter 5. Academic Press, London, 1985.

24 P Benedusi, A. Cimitile, U. De Carlini. **A reverse engineering methodology to reconstruct hierarchical data flow diagrams for software maintenance.** In Proceedings, IEEE Conference on Software Maintenance, page 180, Los Alamitos, CA, 1989. IEEE Computer Society, IEEE Computer Society Press. 1989.

25 D. W Bennett. **The Promise Of Reuse.** Object Magazine, 4(8):33-40, January, 1995.

26 K. Bennett, B. Cornelius, M. Munro, D. Robson. **Software maintenance.** In J. McDermid, editor, Software Engineer's Reference Book, Chapter 20, pages 20/1-20/18. Butterworth-Heinemann Ltd, Oxford, 1991.

27 K. H. Bennett, M P Ward. **Theory and practice of middle-out programming to support program understanding.** In Proceedings, IEEE Third Workshop on Program Comprehension, pages 168-175, Los Alamitos, California, November. IEEE Computer Society, IEEE Computer Society Press, 1994. Describes how a domain-specific programming approach called Middle-Out Programming can facilitate program understanding.

28 L. Bernstein. **Tidbits.** ACM SIGSOFT - Software Engineering Notes, 18(3):A-55, July 1993.

29 T. J. Biggerstaff. **Design recovery for maintenance and reuse.** Computer, 22(7):36-49, July 1989.

30 T. J. Biggerstaff, A J. Perlis. **Foreword.** IEEE Transactions on Software Engineering, SE-10(5):474-477, September 1984.

31 T J. Biggerstaff, A. J. Perlis. **Introduction.** In T. J. Biggerstaff and A. J. Perlis, editors, Software Reusability: Concepts and Models, volume 1, pages xv-xxv. ACM Press/Addison-Wesley New York, 1989.

32 T. J. Biggerstaff, C. Richter. **Reusability framework, assessment, and directions.** In T. J. Biggerstaff and A. J. Perlis, editors, Software Reusability: Concepts and Models, volume 1, Chapter 1, pages 1-17. ACM Press/Addison-Wesley, New York, 1989.

33 B. I. Blum. **The software process for medical applications.** In T. Timmers and B. I. Blum, editors, Software Engineering in Medical Informatics, pages 3-25, North-Holland. Elsevier Science Publishers B.V, 1991

34 B. I. Blum. **Resolving the software maintenance paradox.** Journal of Software Maintenance: Research and Practice, 7(1):3-26, January-February 1995.

35 B. W Boehm. **Software Engineering Economics.** Prentice-Hall, Inc., New Jersey, 1981. Chapter 30 of this book shows how the COCOMO model can be used to estimate the cost of maintenance work using different cost drivers.

36 B. W Boehm. **The economics of software maintenance.** In R. S. Arnold, editor, Proceedings, Workshop on Software Maintenance, pages 9-37, Silver Spring, MD. IEEE Computer Society Press, 1983. In this paper Boehm argues

that economic models and principles can help us: (i) improve maintenance productivity; (ii) understand the software maintenance process. The COCOMO model and Belady-Lehman laws of program evolution are used to illustrate these theses.

37 B B Boehm, E Clark, E Horowitz, C Westland, R Madachy, R Selby. **Cost Models for Future Software Life Cycle Processes: COCOMO 2.0.** Annals of Software Engineering. Special Volume of Software Process and Product Measurement. J D Arthur & S M Henry Eds. J C Baltzer AG Science Publishers, The Netherlands. 1:45-60. 1995.

38 D. A. Boehm-Davis, R. W Holt, Alan C. Schultz. **The role of program structure in software maintenance.** International Journal of Man-Machine Studies, 36:21-63, 1992.

39 S Bohner, R Arnold. **Software change impact analysis.** IEEE Computer Society Press. 1996

40 C. Boldyreff, J. Zhang. **From recursion extraction to automated commenting.** In P A. V Hall, editor, Software Reuse and Reverse Engineering in Practice, Chapter 12, pages 253-270. Chapman and Hall, London, 1992.

41 G. Booch. **The five habits of successful object-oriented projects.** Object Magazine, 4(4):80, 78-79, July-August, 1994.

42 G. Booch. **Object-Oriented Analysis and Design with Applications**, 2nd edition. The Benjamin/Cummings Publishing Company, Inc., Redwood City, California, 1994. An excellent book on the conceptual issues and applications of the object oriented paradigm. In many of the chapters, Booch examines how different principles of object-oriented analysis and design impacts on maintenance and evolution of different applications.

43 F. Bott, M. Ratcliffe. **Reuse and design.** In P A V Hall, editor, Software Reuse and Reverse Engineering in Practice, Chapter 2, pages 35-51. Chapman and Hall, London, 1992.

44 L Bottaci, **Efficient Strategies for Selective Mutation Testing**, Goldsmiths Seminar series 1999/2000. 14th March 2000.

45 D. Boundy. **Software cancer: The seven early warning signs.** ACM SIGSOFT Software Engineering Notes, 18(2):19, April 1992.

46 L Briand, Y Kim, W Melo, C Seaman & V Basili. **Q-MOPP: Qualitative evaluation of Maintenance Organisations, processes and Products.** Journal of Software Maintenance. 10(4):249-278. 1998.

47 F. P Brooks. **No silver bullet – essence and accidents of software engineering.** IEEE Computer, 20(4):10-20, April 1987.

48 R. Brooks. **Towards a theory of the comprehension of computer programs.** International Journal of Man-Machine Studies, 18(6):543-54, June 1983.

49 P Brown. **Integrated hypertext and program understanding tools.** IBM Systems Journal, 30(3):363-92, 1991.

50 F Calzorari, P Tonelli & A Antoniol. **Dynamic Model for Maintenance and Testing Effort**. In proceedings International Conference on Software Maintenance, ICSM98. pp104-112 1998.

51 D A Camplin & G Keller. **Quality, Safety & the Medical Devices Directives**. Working Paper for EU Telematics Framework IV Project Image Guided Orthopaedic Surgery II. January 1998.

52 D. Catton. **Converting sequential applications for parallel execution with Strand88 harness**. In P A. V Hall, editor, Software Reuse and Reverse Engineering Practice, Chapter 18, pages 387-413. Chapman and Hall, London, 1992. Describes a system, STRAND88, which provides a migration path from sequential to parallel processing hence offering many organisations an opportunity of reaping the benefits of parallel hardware without having to replace their existing sequential applications.

53 CEN document: **CR 14300 2002 Health Informatics – Interoperability of healthcare multimedia report systems**, (further information available at the CEN website http://www.centc251.org/) 2002.

54 CEN document: **ENV 1613 1995 Medical Informatics - Messages for exchange of laboratory information I**, (further information available at the CEN website http://www.centc251.org/) 1995.

55 CEN document: **ENV 1828 1995. Medical Informatics - Structure for classification and coding of surgical procedures,** (further information available at the CEN website http://www.centc251.org/) 1995.

56 CEN document: **ENV 1614 1995 Healthcare Informatics – Structure for nomenclature, classification and coding of properties in clinical laboratory sciences II**, (further information available at the CEN website http://www.centc251.org/) 1995.

57 N. Chapin. **Supervisory attitudes towards software maintenance.** In Proceedings of the 1986 National Computer Conference. pages 61-8, AFIPS Press, 1986.

58 N. Chapin. **The job of software maintenance**. In Proceedings of Conference on Software Maintenance, pages 4-12, Washington D.C., IEEE Computer Society Press, 21-24, September 1987.

59 N Chapin, J E Hale, K Khan, J F Ramil, W Tan **Types of Software Maintenance and Evolution** ICSM 2000 11-13 Oct 2000 San Jose CA (revised version: Journal of software maintenance and evolution: research and practice. 13(1):3-30 2001.

60 E. J. Chikofsky, J. H. Cross Jr. **Reverse engineering and design recovery: A taxonomy**. IEEE Software, 7:13-17, January 1990.

61 S. C. Choi, W Scacchi. **Extracting and restructuring the design of large systems**. IEEE Software, 7:66-71, January 1990. Describes an approach that can be used to extract and restructure system designs. This approach involves

first mapping the resource-exchange among modules, then deriving a hierarchical design description using a system-restructuring algorithm.

62 C. K. S. Chong Hok Yuen, **Phenomenology of Program Maintenance and Evolution**, PhD Thesis, Dept of Computing, Imperial College, UK. 1981.

63 F Coallier, A Graydon, & M Ficcici (originators of concept on which model is based), **The Trillium Model**. Available as e-document at http://www2.umassd.edu/swpi/BellCanada/trillium-html/trillium.html 1995.

64 A. Colbrook, C. Smythe, A. Darlison. **Data abstraction in a software re-engineering reference model**. In Proceedings, IEEE Conference on Software Maintenance, pages 2-11, Los Alamitos, CA, 1990. IEEE Computer Society, IEEE Computer Society Press. Argues that there is a need for a software reengineering framework which supports abstraction during reverse engineering. An 8-layer Source Code Re-engineering Reference Model (SCORE/RM) is proposed to that effect.

65 D. Comer, M. Halstead. **A simple experimentation in top-down design**. IEEE Transactions on Software Engineering, SE-S (2):105-9, March 1979.

66 T. N. Commer Jr, I. R. Comer, D. J. Rodjak. **Developing reusable software for military systems - Why it is needed and why it isn't working**. ACM SIGSOFT Software Engineering Notes, 15(3):33-8, July 1990.

67 R Conradi, M Lindvall, C Seaman. **Success Factors for Software Experience Bases: what we need to learn from other disciplines.** In proc. ICSE'2000 workshop on Beg, borrow or steal: using multidisciplinary approaches in empirical software engineering research. Limerick, Ireland. 2000.

68 OMG CORBAmed DTF. **Person Identification Service (PIDS)**. OMG TC Document corbamed/98-02-29. 1998.

69 T. A. Corbi. **Program understanding: Challenge for the 1990s**. IBM Systems Journal, 28(2):294-306, 1989. Discusses the importance of program comprehension in maintenance and makes a case for developing tools that assist programmers in understanding existing code.

70 B. J. Cornelius, M. Munro, D. J. Robson. **An approach to software maintenance education**. Software Engineering Journal, 4(4):233-40, July 1988.

71 N. Coulter. **Software science and cognitive psychology** IEEE Transactions on Software Engineering, SE-9(2):166-171, 1983.

72 J. H. Cross, E. J. Chikofsky, C. H. May Jr. **Reverse engineering**. In M. C. Yovits, editor, Advances in Computers, pages 199-254. Academic Press, London, 1992.

73 B. Curtis, S. B. Sheppard, P Milliman, M. A. Borst, T. Love. **Measuring the psychological complexity of software maintenance tasks with the Halstead and McCabe metrics**. IEEE Transactions on Software Engineering, 5:96-104, 1979.

74   P. H. Damsté, Utrecht Netherlands, **Concentric Man : Human systems of communication, adaptation and defence**. e-book: published at, and downloadable from http://home-1.worldonline.nl/~knmg0234/ 1999.

75   A. M. Davis. **201 Principles of Software Development,** McGraw-Hill, Inc., New York, 1995.

76   J. S. Dean, B. P McCune. **An informal study of maintenance problems.** In R. S. Arnold, editor, Proceedings, Workshop on Software Maintenance, pages 137-9, Silver Spring, MD. IEEE Computer Society Press, 1983.

77   S. Dekleva. **Delphi study of software maintenance problems.** In Proceedings, Conference on Software Maintenance. pages 10-17, Orlando, Florida, November, 1992. IEEE, IEEE Computer Society Press.

78   S. M. Dekleva. **Software maintenance: 1990 status.** Journal of Software Maintenance: Research and Practice, 4:233-47, 1992.

79   T. DeMarco. **Controlling Software Projects: Management, Measurement and Estimation.** Yourdon Press, New Jersey, 1982.

80   F. Detienne. **Psychology of Programming,** Chapter 3.1, pages 205-22. Academic Press, London, 1990.

81   R. Dewar, A. Grand, Y Liu, E. Schonberg, J. T. Schwartz. **Programming by refinement, as exemplified by the SETL representation sublangauge.** ACM Transactions on Programming Languages and Systems, 1(1):27, 1979.

82   R M Dixon, C Gaskell. **A Little Knowledge.** Internal deliverable from Hull University Medical Informatics Group Quality Assurance work. www.hull.ac.uk/mig R_M_Dixon@hotmail.com July 1998.

83   R. Dixon, P Grubb, D Camplin, J Ellis, D Ingram, D Lloyd & T Beale, **The Good European Health Record Object Model,** in proceedings Towards an Electronic Patient Record (TEPR'97) 1997.

84   L. Druffel. **Professionalism and the software business.** IEEE Software, 11(4):6, July 1994. This article takes a succinct look at software measurement from a business point of view.

85   E. Dubinsky, S. Freudenberger, E. Schonberg, J. T. Schwatz. **Reusability of design for large software systems: An experiment with the SETL optimizer.** In T. J. Biggerstaff and A. J. Perlis, editors, Software Reusability: Concepts and Models, Chapter 11, pages 275-93. ACM Press/Addison-Wesley, New York, 1989.

86   R H Dunn, **Software Defect Removal,** New York: McGraw-Hill, 1984.

87   T. Durham. **Quality at risk as demand for training soars.** Objects in Europe, 2(1):10-14, Winter, 1995.

88   L. Dusink, P Hall. **Introduction to re-use.** In L. Dusink and P Hall, editors, Proceedings of the Software Re-use Workshop, pages 1-19, 1989.

89 S Easterbrook. **The role of independent V&V in upstream software development processes.** NASA/WVU Software IV&V Facility, Software Research Laboratory. 1996.

90 EHCR-SupA Deliverable 3.5 version 1.1 (Revised Oct '00) **Final Recommendations to CEN for future work.** (documents downloadable from CHIME www.chime.ucl.ac.uk) 2000.

91 J. L. Elshoff. **An analysis of some commercial PL/1 programs.** IEEE Transactions on Software Engineering, pages 113-120, June 1976.

92 M E Fagan, **Design and code inspections to reduce errors in program development**, IBM Systems journal, 15:182-211 1976.

93 R. E. Fairley. **Software Engineering Concepts.** McGraw-Hill, Inc., New York, 1985.

94 **FEAST/2.** Project web site www-dse.doc.ic.ac.uk/~mml/feast. 2001.

95 N.E. Fenton. **Software Metrics: A rigorous approach.** Chapman and Hall, London, 1991.

96 L. Finkelstein. **What is not measurable, make measurable.** Measurement and Control, 15:25-32, January 1982.

97 A. B. Fitzsimmons, L. T. Love. **A review and evaluation of software science.** ACM Computing Surveys, 10:3-18, 1978.

98 N. T. Fletton, M. Munro. **Redocumenting software systems using hypertext technology** In Proceedings of the Conference on Software Maintenance, pages 54-59, 1988.

99 J. Foster. **An industry view on program comprehension.** In Proceedings, 2nd Workshop on Program Comprehension, page 107, Los Alamitos. IEEE Computer Society, 1993.

100 J. R. Foster, A. E. P Jolly, M. T. Norris. **An overview of software maintenance.** British Telecom Technical Journal, 7(4):37-46, 1989.

101 A. Frazer. **Reverse engineering - hype, hope or here?** In P A. V Hall, editor, Software Reuse and Reverse Engineering in Practice, Chapter 10, pages 209-43. Chapman and Hall, London, 1992.

102 T. P Frazier. **Software reuse and productivity: an empirical view.** In P. T. Geriner, T. R. Gulledge, W P Hutzler, editors, Software Engineering Economics and Declining Budgets, pages 69-81. Springer-Verlag, Berlin, 1994.

103 G. W Furnas, T. K. Landauer, L. M. Gomez, S. T. Dumais. **The vocabulary problem in human-system communication.** Communications of the ACM, 30(11):964-71, November 1987.

104 K B Gallagher. **Evaluating Surgeon's Assistant: results of a pilot study.** In proceedings Conference on Software Maintenance. pp 236-255. 1992.

105   K. Gallagher. **Surgeon's Assistant limits side effect**. IEEE Software, 7:64, May, 1990.

106   K. B. Gallagher, J. R. Lyle. **Using program slicing in software maintenance.** IEEE Transactions on Software Engineering, 17(8):751-61, August 1991. This article describes the role of program slicing in software maintenance.

107   P K. Garg, W Scacchi. **A hypertext system to manage software life-cycle documents.** IEEE Software, 7:90-8, May; 1990.

108   C. Ghezzi, M. Jazayeri, D. Mandrioli. **Fundamentals of Software Engineering.** Prentice-Hall International, Inc., New Jersey; 1991. This is one of the few software engineering textbooks that pays more than just lip-service to software maintenance and evolution.

109   T. Gilb. **Software Metrics.** Winthrop Publishers, Inc., Cambridge, Massachusetts, 1977.

110   K. D. Gillis, D. G. Wright. **Improving software maintenance using system-level reverse engineering.** In Proceedings, IEEE Conference on Software Maintenance, pages 84-90, Los Alamitos, CA. IEEE Computer Society; IEEE Computer Society Press, 1990.

111   D. J. Gilmore. **Psychology of Programming**, Chapter 3.2, pages 223-34. Academic Press, London, 1990. This article considers a programming view that asserts that expert programmers have a much wider repertoire of strategies available to them than novices. A number of studies are used to support this stance. Also, a list of programming strategies available to experts – for use in program comprehension and debugging – is described.

112   R. B. Grady, D. L. Caswell. **Software Metrics: Establishing A Company-Wide Program.** Prentice-Hall, Englewood Cliffs, New Jersey; 1987. This book reports on the experience gained from introducing a software metrics programme at Hewlett-Packard. It makes good reading for companies thinking of initiating a similar programme.

113   I. Graham. **Interoperation: Using OOA as a springboard.** Object Magazine, 4(4):66-8, July-August, 1994. In this paper, the author argues that when migrating to an object-oriented paradigm, it is important to find analysis and design methods that support the rich features available in the existing system, for example by using object wrappers, and that facilitate migration. Similarly, when developing a new system, object-oriented analysis should be used as a springboard to analyse and prototype a reversible specification that can be implemented in any language with a view to migrating to an object-oriented language when a suitable one becomes available.

114   I. Graham. **Migration strategies: OT *is* a migration strategy.** Object Magazine, 4(5):20-2, September, 1994.

115   W G. Griswold, D. Notkin. **Automated assistance for program restructuring.** ACM Transactions on Software Engineering and Methodology, 2(3):228-69, July 1993.

116 J. Grumann, P J. Welch. **A graph method for technical documentation and re-engineering of DP-applications.** In P. A. V Hall, editor, Software Reuse and Reverse Engineering in Practice, pages 321-53. Chapman and Hall, London, 1992.

117 T. Guimaraes. **Managing application program maintenance expenditures.** Communications of the ACM, 26(10):739-46, October 1983.

118 R. Gunning. **The Technique of Clear Writing.** McGraw-Hill, 1968.

119 E. Guy, **Co-operative Processing – Cheap**, Computing Canada 1991

120 T. Hall, N. Fenton. **Implementing software metrics – the critical success factors.** Software Quality Journal, 3(4):195-208, December 1994.

121 M. Halstead. **Elements of Software Science.** North Holland, Amsterdam, 1977.

122 M. H. Halstead. **Advances in Computers,** 18:119-72. Academic Press, New York, 1979.

123 J. Han. **Supporting Impact Analysis and change propagation in software engineering environments.** In proc. 8th int. workshop on software technology and engineering practice. STEP97. pp 172-182. 1996.

124 W. Harrison, C. Gens, B. Gifford. **pRETS: A parallel reverse-engineering toolset for fortran.** Journal of Software Maintenance: Research and Practice, 5(1):37-57, March 1993.

125 W. Harrison, K. Magel. **A complexity measure based on nesting level.** ACM SIGPLAN Notices, 16(3):63-74, 1981.

126 D. A. Haworth, S. Sharpe, D. P Hale. **A framework for software maintenance: a foundation for scientific inquiry.** Journal of Software Maintenance: Research and Practice, 4:105-17, 1992.

127 S. Henry, D. Kafura. **The evaluation of software systems' structure using quantitative software metrics.** Software – Practice and Experience, 14:561-73, 1984.

128 J Herbsleb, A Carleton, J Rozum, J. Siegel, D. Zubrow, **Benefits of CMM-Based Software Process Improvement: Initial Results**, Software Engineering Institute, CMU/SEI-94-TR-13, August 1994.

129 D. A. Higgins. **Data Structured Maintenance: The Warnier/Orr Approach.** Dorset House Publishing Co. Inc., New York, 1988.

130 J. -M. Hoc, T. R. G. Green, R. Samurcay, D. J. Gilmore, editors. **Psychology of Programming.** Academic Press, London, 1990.

131 G. F. Hoffnagle, W E. Beregi. **Automating the software development process.** IBM Systems Journal, 24(2):102-20, 1985.

132 R. Holibaugh. **Reuse: Where to begin and why.** In Proceedings, Reuse in Practice Workshop. Software Engineering Institute Pittsburgh, PA, July 11-13 1989.

133 J. W. Hooper, R. O. Chester. **Software Reuse: Guidelines and Methods.** Plenum Press, New York, 1991.

134 E. Horowitz, J. B. Munson. **An expansive view of reusable software.** In T. J. Biggerstaff and A. J. Perlis, editors, Software Reusability: Concepts and Models, 1(2):19-41. ACM Press/Addison-Wesley, New York, 1989.

135 S. Horwitz, T. Reps, D. Binkley. **Interprocedural slicing using dependence graphs.** ACM Transactions on Programming Languages and Systems. 12(1):35-56. 1990.

136 C. A. Houtz, K. A. Miller. **Software improvement program – a solution for software problems.** In R. S. Arnold, editor, Proceedings, Workshop on Software Maintenance, pages 120-24, Silver Spring, MD. IEEE Computer Society Press, 1983. Describes a Software Improvement Programme (SIP), which is an incremental and evolutionary approach that can be used to 'revamp' a legacy system.

137 W S. Humphrey. **The IBM large-systems software development process: Objectives and direction.** IBM Systems Journal, 24(2):76-8, 1985.

138 IEEE **Standard for Software Verification and Validation.** IEEE STD 1012-1998.

139 IEEE **Guide to Software Verification and Validation Plans.** IEEE 1059-1993.

140 D. Ince. **History and industrial applications.** In Software Metrics: A Rigorous Approach, Chapter 14, pages 277-95. Chapman and Hall, London, 1991.

141 D. Ince. **ISO 9001 and Software Quality Assurance.** The McGraw-Hill International Software Quality Assurance Series, McGraw-Hill, Maidenhead, 1994.

142 D. Ingram, D. Lloyd, D. Kalra, T. Beale, S. Heard, P. A. Grubb, R. M. Dixon, D. A. Camplin, J. C. Ellis, A. M. Maskens. **GEHR Deliverables 19, 20, 24 - 'GEHR Architecture', Version 1.0.** (documents downloadable from CHIME www.chime.ucl.ac.uk) 1995.

143 J. Jeng, H. C. Chang. **Using formal methods to construct a software component library.** In I. Sommerville and M. Paul, editors, Proceedings, 4th European Software Engineering Conference, pages 397-417. Springer-Verlag, September 1993.

144 P. Jesty. **The second SCSC (Safety Critical Systems Club) symposium – A personal view.** Safety Systems – the Safety Critical Systems Club Newsletter, 3(3):1-4, May 1994.

145 P. N. Johnson-Laird. **Mental Models: Towards a Cognitive Science of Language, Inference, and Consciousness.** Cambridge University Press, Cambridge, 1983.

146 C. Jones. **How not to measure programming quality.** Computer World, XX(3):82, January 20 1986.

147 J Jones & L Bottaci. **Formal Specification Using Z: A Modelling Approach.** International Thomson Computer Press. 1995.

148 T. C. Jones. **Reusability in programming: A survey of the state of the art.** IEEE Transactions on Software Engineering, SE-10(5):488-94, September 1984.

149 C. Kaner, J. Falk, H. Q. Nguyen. **Testing Computer Software.** 2nd edition. John Wiley & Sons. 1999

150 K. C. Kang. **A reuse-based software development methodology.** In G. Booch and L. Williams, editors, Proceedings of the Workshop on Software Reuse. Rocky Mountain Inst. of Software Engineering, SEI, MCC, Software Productivity Consortium, Boulder, Cob., October 1987.

151 K. C. Kang. **Position paper.** In J. Baldo, C. Braun, editors, Proceedings of the Reuse in Practice Workshop. Software Engineering Institute, July 1989.

152 A. A. Kaposi. **Software Engineer's Reference Book,** Butterworth-Heinemann Ltd, Oxford, 1991.

153 B. W. Kernighan, R. Pike. **The UNIX Programming Environment.** Prentice-Hall, New Jersey, 1984.

154 G. A. Kiran, S. Haripriya, P. Jalote. **Effect of Object Orientation on Maintainability of Software.** In proc. ICSM97, Italy. Pp 114-121. 1997.

155 T. D. Korson, V. K. Vaishnavi. **An empirical study of the effects of modularity on program modifiability.** In E. Soloway and S. Iyengar, editors, Empirical Studies of Programmers, Chapter 12, pages 168-86. Ablex Publishing Corporation, New Jersey, 1986. Describes an empirical study of the effects of modularity on adaptive maintenance. The results suggest that a modular program is faster to modify than a non-modular program.

156 D. Krupinski, D. Vlamis. **Training techniques for the object evolution.** Object Magazine, 4(5):77-81, September 1994.

157 R. G. Lanergan, C. A. Grasso. **Software engineering with reusable designs and code.** IEEE Transactions on Software Engineering, SE-10(5):498-501, September 1984. Reports on a reuse approach that an organisation used for developing and maintaining its business software. The approach capitalised on the fact that 60% of all business application designs and code are redundant and can be standardised and reused. As a result of this approach, there were significant benefits in productivity and reliability, improved end-user relations, and better utilisation of personnel.

158 K. Lano, P. T. Breuer, H. Haughton. **Reverse-engineering Cobol via formal methods**. Journal of Software Maintenance: Research and Practice, 5(1):13-35, March 1993. Describes methods and tools used to reverse engineer Cobol application programs back to design and specification, both of which are captured using the object-based abstractions that the tools create. The program code is first transformed into an intermediate language, Uniform. The result is then transformed into a functional description language and finally to the specification language, Z. Also extracted from the code are data flow diagrams, entity-relationship diagrams, and call-graphs.

159 K. Lano, H. Haughton. **Reverse Engineering and Software Maintenance: A Practical Approach**. McGraw-Hill, London, 1994.

160 S. Lauchlan. **Case study reveals future shock**. Computing, page 9, February 1993.

161 P. K. Lawlis, R. M. Flowe, & J B Thordahl, **A Correlational Study of the CMM and Software Development Performance**, Crosstalk: The Journal of Defense Software Engineering, 8(9):21-25, September 1995.

162 M. J. Lawrence. **An Examination of Evolution Dynamics.** In proceedings 6th int. conference on Software Engineering. Tokyo, Japan. 13-16 Sept. IEEE cat. n.81CH1795-4. pp 188-196, 1982.

163 P. J. Layzell, L. Macaulay. **An investigation into software maintenance: Perception and practices**. In Conference on Software Maintenance, pages 130-140, Los Alamitos, California. IEEE Computer Society. 1990. Reports on a study undertaken to study the perception and practice of software maintenance in five major UK companies. Results of the investigation indicated that maintenance is being perceived in a more positive light; maintenance departments are becoming more accountable to user departments; and it seems existing maintenance tools are not being used as one would expect. The need for technology to support communication between users, developers and maintenance staff was also identified.

164 D. Leblang. **The CM challenge: Configuration management that works**. In W E Tichy, editor, Configuration Management, Chapter 1. John Wiley and Sons, Chichester, 1994.

165 S. Leestma, L. Nyhoff. **Programming and Problem Solving in Modula-2**. Macmillan, New York, 1989.

166 M. M. Lehman. **The Programming Process**. IBM Res. Rep. RC 2722, IBM Research Centre, Yorktown Heights, NY 10594, Sept. 1969.

167 M. M. Lehman & L. A. Belady. **Program Evolution - processes of software change**. Academic Press. London 1985.

168 M. M.. Lehman. **The environment of design methodology,** keynote address. In T. A. Cox, editor, Proceedings, Symposium on Formal Design Methodology, pages 18-38, Essex, STL Ltd. 1980.

169 M. M. Lehman. **Program Evolution**. Academic Press, London, 1985.

170 M. M. Lehman. **Uncertainty in computer application and its control through the engineering of software**. Journal of Software Maintenance:Research and Practice, 1 (1):3-27, 1989.

171 M. M. Lehman & V. Stenning. **FEAST/1: Case for support**. ICSTM. March 1996.

172 M. M. Lehman. **Laws of Software Evolution Revisited**. Position paper, EWSPT96. Oct 1996. LNCS 1149 Springer Verlag. 1997

173 M. M. Lehman, D. E. Perry, J. F. C. Ramil. **Implications of evolution metrics on software maintenance**. In proceedings Int. conf. ICSM98. pp 208-217. 1998.

174 M. M. Lehman, D. E. Perry, J. F. C. Ramil, W. M. Turski & P. Wernick. **Metrics and laws of software evolution**. IEEE CS Press. 1997.

175 S. Letovsky. **Cognitive processes in program comprehension**. In E. Soloway and S. Iyengar, editors, Empirical Studies of Programmers, Chapter 5, pages 58-79. Ablex Publishing Corporation, New Jersey, 1986. Reports on an investigation into the cognitive processes that are involved in understanding programs. The results from the study are then used to derive a computational model of programmers' mental processes, commonly known as the opportunistic model.

176 B. P. Lientz, E. B. Swanson. **Software Maintenance Management**. Addison-Wesley Publishing Company, Reading, Massachusetts, 1980.

177 P. H. Lindsay, D. A. Norman. **Human Information Processing: An Introduction to Psychology**. Academic Press, New York, 1977.

178 D. S. Linthicum. **4GLs: No easy answers**. Object Magazine, 4(5):38-42, September 1994.

179 A. Lister. **Software science – the emperor's new clothes?** Australian Comp. Journal, pages 437-39, May 1982.

180 D. C. Littman, J. Pinto, S. Letovsky, E. Soloway. **Empirical Studies of Programmers**, Chapter 6, pages 80-90. Ablex Publishing Corporation, New Jersey, 1986.

181 A. Lobba. **Automated configuration management**. In proceedings of the 1987 Conference on Software Tools, IEEE, 1987.

182 P. Loucopoulous, P J. Layzell. **Improving information systems development and evolution using rule-based paradigm**. Software Engineering Journal, 4(5):259-67, 1989.

183 J. P. Loyall, S. A. Mathisen. **Using Dependence Analysis to Support the Software Maintenance Process**. Proc. Int. Conf. on Software Maintenance. pp 282-291. 1993.

184 A. Macro. **Software Engineering: Concepts and Management**. Prentice-Hall International Ltd, Hemel Hempstead, 1990.

185 L. Markosian, P Newcomb, R. Brand, S. Burson, T. Kitzmiller. **Using an enabling technology to reengineer legacy systems.** Communications of the ACM, 37(5):58-70, May 1994.

186 J. Martin. **Fourth Generation Languages – Volume II:** Survey of Representative 4GLs, Savant Research Studies, Carnforth, Lancashire, 1984.

187 J. Martin, C. McClure. **Maintenance of Computer Programming, volumes I and II.** Savant Research Studies, Carnforth, Lancashire, 1982. These books cover a wide range of software maintenance issues from an early 1980's perspective.

188 J. Martin, C. McClure. **Software Maintenance – The Problem and Its Solutions.** Prentice-Hall, Inc, Englewood Cliffs, New Jersey, 1983.

189 T. J. McCabe. **Battle Map, Act show code structure, complexity.** IEEE Software, 7:62, May 1990.

190 T. J. McCabe. **A complexity measure.** IEEE Transactions on Software Engineering, SE-2(4):308-20, December 1976.

191 C. L. McClure. **Managing Software.. Development and Maintenance.** Van Nostrand Reinhold, New York, 1981.

192 J. McDermid. **Software Engineer's Reference Book,** Chapter 16. Butterworth-Heinemann, 1991.

193 B. Meek, P. Heath, N. Rushby, editors. **Guide to Good Programming.** Ellis Horwood Publishers, Chichester, 2nd edition, 1983.

194 C. A. Miller. **The magical number seven, plus or minus two: Some limits on our capacity for processing information.** Psychological Review, 63:81-97, 1956.

195 S. B. Sheppard, B. Curtis, P. Milliman, T. Love. **Modern coding practices and programmer performance.** Computer, 12(12):41-9, December 1979.

196 K. H. Moller, D. J. Paulish. **Software Metrics: A Practitioner's Guide to Improved Product Development.** Chapman and Hall, London, 1993. This book presents tutorial and case study material that can be useful to those introducing a metrics programme into software management or those who wish to improve on an ongoing programme.

197 J. C. Munson, S. G. Elbaum. **Code Churn: A Measure for Estimating the Impact of Code Change.** 24. Electronic Edition (IEEE Computer Society DL). 2000.

198 G. J. Myers, **A controlled experiment in program testing and code walkthroughs / inspections.** Communications of the ACM, Sept. 760-768. 1978.

199 G. J. Myers **The Art of Software Testing.** New York: John Wiley and sons. 1979.

200 K. Narayanaswamy, W. Scacchi. **Maintaining configurations of evolving software systems.** IEEE Transactions on Software Engineering, SE13(3):324-34, March 1987.

201 R. J. Miara, J. A. Musselman, J. A. Navarro, B. Shneiderman. **Program indentation and comprehensibility.** Communications of the ACM, 26(11):861-67, November 1983.

202 J. M. Neighbors. **Draco: A method for engineering reusable software systems.** In T. J. Biggerstaff and A. J. Perlis, editors, Software Reusability:Concepts and Models, Chapter 12, pages 295-319. ACM Press/Addison-Wesley, New York, 1989.

203 Object Management Group. **Model-Driven Architecture.** (doc no. ormsc/2001-07-01). OMG, Framingham, MA. 2001.

204 Object Management Group. **Software Process Engineering Metamodel.** (doc no. ptc/2002-05-04). OMG, Framingham, MA. 2002.

205 G. Olander. Chembench: **Redesign of a large commercial application using object-oriented Techniques.** In J. L. Archibald and M. C. Wilkes, editors, Addendum to the Proceedings: 1992 Conference on Object-Oriented Programming Systems, Languages, and Applications, pages 13-16, New York, September-October, ACM Press. 1992.

206 P. Oman. **Maintenance Tools.** IEEE Software, 7:59, May 1990.

207 P. W. Oman, C. R. Cook. **The improved paradigm for improved maintenance.** IEEE Software, pages 39-45, January 1990.

208 P. W. Oman, C. R. Cook. **Typographic style is more than cosmetic.** Communications of the ACM, 33(5):506-20, May 1990.

209 W. Osborne. **Software Maintenance and Computers**, pages 2-14. IEEE Computer Society Press, Los Alamitos, 1990. This article provides answers to 64 key questions about software maintenance. The article addresses a wide range of issues including the feasibility and applicability of software reuse, achieving programmer and software productivity.

210 W. M. Osborne. **Building and sustaining software maintainability.** In Proceedings of Conference on Software Maintenance, pages 13-23, Austin Texas, 21-24 September 1987.

211 W M. Osborne, E. J. Chikofsky. **Fitting pieces to the maintenance puzzle.** IEEE Software, 7:11-12, January 1990.

212 A. Padula. **Use of a program understanding taxonomy at Hewlett-Packard.** In Proceedings, 2nd Workshop on Program Comprehension, pages 66-70, Los Alamitos. IEEE Computer Society, 1993.

213 G. Parikh. **Making the immortal language work.** International Computer Programs Business Software Review, 7(2):33, April 1986.

References

214 G. Parikh, N. Zvegintzov. **Tutorial on Software Maintenance**. IEEE Computer Society Press, Silver Spring, Maryland, 1983.

215 D. Parnas. **Software aspects of strategic defense systems**. Communications of the ACM, 28(12):1328, December 1985.

216 R. J. Paul. **Why users cannot 'get what they want'**. SIGSOIS Bulletin, 14(2):8-12, 1993.

217 M. C. Paulk, C. V. Weber, B. Curtis, & M. B. Chrissis, **The Capability Maturity Model: Guidelines for Improving the Software Process**, ISBN 0-201-54664-7, Addison-Wesley Publishing Company, Reading, MA, 1995.

218 D. Pearce. **It's a wrap**. Consultant's Conspectus, pages 35-6, March 1995.

219 N. Pennington. **Stimulus structures and mental representations in expert comprehension of programs**. Cognitive Psychology, 19(3):295-341, July 1987.

220 N. Pennington, B. Grabowski. **Psychology of programming.** In J. -M. Hoc, T. R. G. Green, R. Samurcay and D. J. Gilmore, editors, Psychology of Programming, Chapter 1.3, pages 45-62. Academic Press, London, 1990.

221 A. Perlis, F. Sayward, M. Shaw, editors. **Software Metrics: An Analysis and Evaluation**. The MIT Press, 1981.

222 M. Petre. **Expert programmers and programming languages**. In J. -M. Hoc, T. R. G. Green, R. Samurcay, D. J. Gilmore, editors, Psychology of Programming, Chapter 2.1, pages 103-15. Academic Press, London, 1990.

223 M. M. Pickard, Carter. **Maintainability**. ACM SIGSOFT Software Engineering Notes, 18(3) :A36-A39, July 1993. In this paper the authors argue that there exists a relationship between design metrics and the maintainability of operational systems. Results of a reverse engineering study on 57 Cobol programs revealed that there exists a correlation between design metrics, such as function points and other information flow-based metrics, and maintainability.

224 A. Podgurski, L. Pierce. **Retrieving reusable software by sampling**. ACM Transactions on Software Engineering and Methodology, 2(3):286-303, July 1993.

225 R. Poston. **T test-case Generator**. IEEE Software, 7:56, May 1990.

226 B. Potter, J. Sinclair, D. Till. **An Introduction to Formal Specification and Z**. Prentice-Hall International (UK) Ltd, Hemel Hempstead, 1991.

227 J. Poulin, W. Tracz. WISR'93: **6th annual workshop on software reuse summary and working group reports**. ACM SIGSOFT Software Engineering Notes, 19(1):55-71, January 1994.

228 R. E. Prather. **The axiomatic theory of software complexity measure**. The Computer Journal, 27:340-47, 1984.

229   R. S. Pressman. Software Engineering: **A Practitioner's Approach**. McGraw-Hill, New York, 1987.

230   R. Prieto-Diaz. **Domain analysis: An introduction**. ACM Software Engineering Notes, 15(2):47-54, April 1990.

231   R. Prieto-Diaz, P. Freeman. **Classification of reusable modules**. IEEE Software, 4(1):6-16, January 1987.

232   F. A. Rabhi. **A parallel programming methodology based on paradigms**. In P Nixon, editor, Transputer and Occam Developments, pages 239-51. LOS Press, Amsterdam, 1995.

233   V. Rajlich. **Vifor transforms code skeletons to graphs**. IEEE Software, 7:60, May 1990.

234   S. R. Ratikin. **Software Verification and Validation for Practitioners and Managers**. 2nd ed. Artech House. 2001.

235   C. Rich, R. C. Waters. **The Programmer's Apprentice**. ACM Frontier Series. ACM Press, New York, 1990.

236   F. S. Roberts. **Encyclopaedia of Mathematics and its Applications**. Addison-Wesley, Reading, Massachusetts, 1979.

237   J. M. Roche. **Software metrics and measurement principles**. ACM SIGSOFT Software Engineering Notes, 19(1):77-85, January 1994. This article provides a tutorial review of current Software Engineering measurement and points out problems with existing measurement processes. It concludes by suggesting that some of these problems could be overcome by including sound measurement principles into Software Engineering measurement processes.

238   H. D. Rombach. **A controlled experiment on the impact of software structure on maintainability**. IEEE Transactions on Software Engineering, SE-13(3):344-54, March 1987.

239   S. Rugaber, S. B. Omburn, R. J. LeBlanc Jr. **Recognising design decisions in programs**. IEEE Software, 7(1):46-54, January 1990. This paper argues that an important aspect of design recovery is being able to recognise, understand and represent design decisions present in a given source code. It contends further that program constructs such as control and data structures, variables, procedures and functions, definition and implementation modules, and class hierarchy serve as indicators of design decisions.

240   J. Rumbaugh, M. Blaha, W. Premerlani, F. Eddy, W. Lorensen. **Object-Oriented Modelling and Design**, Prentice-Hall International, Englewood Cliffs, New Jersey, 1991.

241   P. Samuelson. **Reverse-engineering someone else's software: Is it legal?** IEEE Software, 7:90-6, January 1990.

242   S. R. Schach. **The economic impact of software reuse on maintenance**. Journal of Software Maintenance: Research and Practice, 6(4)185-96, July-August 1994.

243 D. R. Schatzberg. **Total quality management for maintenance process management**. Journal of Software Maintenance: Research and Practice, 5(1):1-12, March 1993.

244 A. L. Schmidt. **Effects of experience and comprehension on reading time and memory for computer programs**. International Journal of Man-Machine Studies, 25:399-409, 1986.

245 N. F. Schneidewind. **The state of software maintenance**. IEEE Transactions on Software Engineering, SE-13(3):303-10, March 1987.

246 H. E. Sengler. **The Psychology of Computer Use**, pages 91-106. Academic Press, London, 1983.

247 B. A. Sheil. **The psychological study of programming**. In R. M. Baecker and W A. S. Buxton, editors, Readings in Human-Computer Interaction: A Multidisciplinary Approach, pages 165-74. Morgan Kaufman, Los Altos, California, 1987.

248 V. Y. Shen, S. D. Conte, H. E. Dunsmore. **Software science revisited: A critical analysis of the theory and its empirical support**. IEEE Transactions on Software Engineering, SE-9(2):155-65, March 1983. Shen and his colleagues present a critique of Halstead's Software Science measures and also review experimental results of studies that were undertaken to test the validity of these measures. They point out some theoretical shortcomings.

249 B. Shneiderman. **Measuring computer program quality and comprehension**. International Journal of Man-Machine Studies, 9:465-78, 1977.

250 B. Shneiderman. **Software Psychology**. Winthrop, Cambridge, Massachusetts, 1980.

251 B. Shneiderman, R. Mayer. **Syntactic semantic interactions in programming behaviour: a model**. International Journal of Computer and Information Science, 8:219-38, 1979.

252 F. Shull, F. Lanubile, V. R. Basili. **Investigating Reading Techniques for Object-Oriented Framework Learning**. IEEE Transactions on Software Engineering. 26(11):1101-1118. Nov 2000.

253 M. A. Simos. **The domain-oriented software life cycle: Towards an extended process model for reusability**. In G. Booch and L. Williams, editors, Proceedings of the Workshop on Software Reusability. Rocky Mountain Inst. of Software Engineering, SEI, MCC, Software Productivity Consortium, Boulder, Cob., 1987.

254 H. M. Sneed, A. Kaposi. **A study on the effect of reengineering upon software maintainability**. In Proceedings, IEEE Conference on Software Maintenance, pages 91-9, Los Alamitos, CA, IEEE Computer Society, IEEE Computer Society Press. 1990. The data collected from this study indicated that reengineering can decrease complexity and increase maintainability, but that restructuring has only a minor effect on maintainability.

255 I. Sommerville. **Software Engineering**, 3rd edition. International Computer Science Series. Addison-Wesley, Workingham, England, 1989.

256 I. Sommerville, R. Thomson. **An approach to the support of software evolution.** The Computer Journal, 32(8):386-98, 1989.

257 J. Stikeleather. **What's a client, what's a server?** Object Magazine, 4(5):94-5, September, 1994.

258 J. P. Strickland, P. P. Uhrowczik, V. L. Watts. **Ims/vs: An evolving system.** IBM Systems Journal, 21(4):490-513, 1982. Discusses the evolutionary development history of IMS/VS (a Management Information System) since its inception in 1969, highlighting some of the reasons for this evolutionary tendency.

259 Sun Microsystems. **Java 2 Enterprise Edition Specification v1.3.** Sun, Palo Alto, CA. 2001.

260 E. B. Swanson. **The dimensions of maintenance.** In Proceedings, 2nd International Conference on Software Engineering, pages 492-97, San Francisco, October 1976.

261 A. A. Takang, P. A. Grubb. **The effects of comments and identifier names on program comprehensibility: An experimental investigation.** Research 95/1, Department of Computer Science, University of Hull, UK, 1995.

262 A. A. Takang, P. A. Grubb, R. M. Dixon. **Post-delivery evolution of general practice software systems.** In Proceedings, Primary Health Care Specialist Group Annual Conference, pages 158-68, Cambridge, 17-19 September 1993.

263 T. Tamai, Y. Torimitsu. **Software lifetime and its evolution process over generations.** In Proceedings, Conference on Software Maintenance, 8th Conference, pages 63-69, Orlando, Florida, IEEE Computer Society Press, November 1992.

264 R. C. Tausworthe. **Standardised Development of Computer Software.** Prentice-Hall, Englewoods Cliffs, New Jersey, 1977.

265 B. E. Teasley. **The effects of naming style and expertise on program comprehension.** International Journal of Human-Computer Studies, 40:757-70,1994. Describes a study aimed at investigating the effect of naming style and expertise on understanding. It was concluded that naming style in high-level procedural language programs affects the understanding of novice programmers but not experienced programmers.

266 P. Thomas, R. Weedon. **Object-Oriented Programming in Eiffel.** Addison-Wesley, Wokingham, England, 1995.

267 W. Tracz. **Where does reuse start?** ACM Software Engineering Notes, 15(2):42-6, 1990.

268 W. M. Turski. **Reference Model for Smooth Growth of Software Systems.** University of Warsaw, June 1996

269 W. M. Turski. **The Reference Model for Smooth Growth of Software Systems Revisited.** IEEE Transactions on Software Engineering 28:8 814-815 2002.

270 S. R. Vallabhaneni. **Auditing the Maintenance of Software.** Prentice-Hall, Englewood Cliffs, NJ, 1987.

271 A. van Deursen, P. Klint, A. Sellink. **Validating year 2000 compliance.** Software Engineering (SEN) R9713. 1997.

272 D. van Edelstein. **Report on the IEEE STD 1219-1993 – Standard for Software Maintenance.** ACM SIGSOFT – Software Engineering Notes, 18(4):94-95, October 1993.

273 E. C. Van Horn. **Software Engineering,** Chapter 12, pages 209-26. Academic Press, New York, 1980.

274 H. van Vliet. **Software Engineering: Principles and Practice.** John Wiley, Chichester, 1993.

275 L. Vanek, L. Davis. **Expert dataflow and static analysis tool.** IEEE Software, 7:63, May, 1990.

276 A. von Mayrhauser. **Maintenance and evolution of software products.** In M. C. Yovits, editor, Advances in Computers, Chapter 1, pages 1-49. Academic Press, Boston, 1994.

277 A. von Mayrhauser, A. M. Vans. **From program comprehension to tool requirements for an industrial environment.** In Proceedings, 2nd Workshop on Program Comprehension, pages 78-86, Los Alamitos, California, IEEE Computer Society Press. 1993.

278 O. Walcher. **Reengineering legacy systems using GUI and client/server technology.** In J. L. Archibald and M. C. Wilkes, editors, Addendum to the Proceedings: Conference on Object-Oriented Programming Systems, Languages, and Applications, pages 37-8, New York, ACM Press. September-October 1993.

279 D. R. Wallace & R. U. Fujii. **Software Verification and Validation: its role in computer assurance and its relationship with software project management standards.** National Technical Information Service. 1989.

280 B. L. Wang, J. Wang. **Is a deep class hierarchy considered harmful?** Object Magazine, 4(7):33-40, November-December, 1994.

281 R. Warden. **Re-engineering – a practical methodology with commercial applications.** In P. A. V. Hall, editor, Software Reuse and Reverse Engineering in Practice, Chapter 14, pages 283-305. Chapman and Hall, London, 1992.

282 R. C. Waters, E. Chikofsky. **Reverse engineering: progress along many dimensions.** Communications of the ACM, 37(5):23-4, May 1994. This article is a guest editorial which reflects on the wave of changes attributable to reverse engineering issues over the years. The paper points out that reverse engineering

is not just a peripheral concern but arguably the most important part of software engineering.

283   P. Wegner. **Capital-intensive software technology**. IEEE Software, 1(3):7-45, July 1984.

284   G. M. Weinberg. **The Psychology of Computer Programming**. Van Nostrand Reinhold Company, New York, 1971. This book makes good reading for anyone interested in the psychology of programming.

285   M. Weiser. **Program slicing**. IEEE Transactions on Software Engineering, SE-10(4):352-57, July 1984.

286   G. Welchman. **The Hut Six Story**. Classical Crypto Books. 1997.

287   J. White. **Object lessons**. Consultant's Conspectus, pages 2-5, March, 1995.

288   S. Wiedenbeck. **Processes in computer program comprehension**. In E. Soloway and S. Iyengar, editors, Empirical Studies of Programmers, Chapter 4, pages 48-57. Ablex Publishing Corporation, New Jersey, 1986. This article reports on an experiment which used memorisation and recall method to study the role of 'beacons' in program comprehension. Analysis of the results indicated that experienced programmers recalled key lines or beacons better than other parts of the program, whereas no such results were observed for novices.

289   S. Wiendenbeck. **Beacons in computer program comprehension**. International Journal of Man-Machine Studies, 25:697-709, 1986.

290   N. Wilde. **Dependency analysis tool set prototype**. IEEE Software, 7:65, May 1990.

291   D. G. Wildes, E. J. Nieters. **RUTE real-time Unix simulator for PS OS**. IEEE Software, 7:54, May 1990.

292   C. Withrow. **Error density and size in Ada software**. IEEE Software, 1:26-30, January 1990.

293   S. N. Woodfield, H. E. Dunsmore, V. Y. Shen. **Effect of modularization and comments on program comprehension**. In Proceedings, 5th International Conference on Software Engineering, pages 215-23, Los Alamitos, California, IEEE Computer Society Press. March 1981.

294   C. M. Woodside. **Program Evolution,** Chapter 16, pages 339-54. Academic Press, London, 1985.

295   M. R. Woodward, M. A. Hennel, D. Hedley. **A measure of control flow complexity in program text**. IEEE Transactions on Software Engineering, SE-5:45-50, March 1979.

296   A. Yamashiro, H. Nakano, K. Yoshida, E. Saito. **Comparison of OOA and Real-Time SA – From the experiment of analysing an image filing system**. In J. L. Archibald and M. C. Wilkes, editors, Addendum to the Proceedings:

Conference on Object-Oriented Programming Systems, Languages, and Applications, pages 41-4, New York, ACM Press. September-October 1993.

297   E. Yourdon. **Techniques of program structure and design.** Englewood Cliffs: Prentice Hall. 1975.

298   E. Yourdon. **Structured Systems Analysis**, Prentice-Hall International, Englewood Cliffs, New Jersey, 1989.

299   H. Zuse. **Software Complexity: Measures and Methods.** Walter de Gruyter, Berlin, 1991.

300   N. Zvegintzov, editor. **Software Management Technology Reference Guide: 1994/95** European Edition. Software Maintenance News, Inc., Los Alamitos, California, 1995.

Index

Abd-El-Hafiz 60
Abstraction 24, 101, 103, 105, 110, 134, 139, 144, 146, 151
Abstraction Engineering 291
Acceptance Test Plan 239
Acme Health Clinic 21, 39, 40, 61, 77, 88, 82, 86, 125, 170, 187, 227, 236, 274
Adaption-Driven Restructuring 145
Adaptive Change 33, 36, 40
Aharonian 153, 178, 179
Air Traffic Control 12
Alternative Views 137, 138, 139
Analysts 104
ANSI C 274
ANSI/IEEE 193
Application Domain 19, 25, 28, 118, 141, 142, 162, 164, 177, 214, 216, 284
Application Generator Systems 162
Application-Specific 284
Application-Type 216
Ariane 201
Arnold 271
Assessment 253, 237
Assignment Patterns 207, 208
Assimilation Process 110, 115
Automatic Documentation 283

Baecker 125
Baseline 39, 141, 225, 226
Basic Concepts 5
Basili 60, 85, 115, 169, 203, 256
Beginner's Guide/Tutorial 239
Belady 144
Bennett 235
Bernstein 48, 55

Biggerstaff 150, 159, 162, 177, 178
Black Box Testing 190
Black-Box Reuse 161
Boehm 49, 80, 82, 155, 261, 263
Boehm's Model 80
Bohner 271
Boldyreff 150
Booch 289
Book Paradigm 125
Bott 178
Bottom-Up 98, 110, 114, 129
Bottom-Up/Chunking Model 113
Briand 203
Brooks 29, 30, 111, 120, 124, 242
Brooks' Model 111, 120
Budget Reallocation 54
Building 234
Building and Sustaining Maintainability 269
Building Better Systems 265
Butterworth-Hayes 13, 14

Capability 300, 309
Capability Maturity Model® 88
Career Structure 208
Carrying out the Change 92
Carter 133
Categorising Software Change 14
Category of Customer 240
Cause-Effect Relation 101
Change Control 235, 236
Change Control, Management Responsibilities 236
Change in Policies 19, 21
Change Ownership 215
Change Requirements 23
Change, When to Make a Change 86

Changes, Classification of 34
Chapin 313
Chembench 294
Chester 173, 175, 177
Chikofsky 103
Choi 141, 144
Chronological Data, Clinical 77
Chunking 99, 110, 113, 114, 121
Classification 313
Classification Problem 169
Cocomo 49, 155, 206, 261, 263
Code-and-Fix Model 66
Cognitive Process 99, 109, 110, 111, 130
Cognitive Structure 99, 109, 110, 111, 130
Cohesion 159, 167, 181
Colbrook 146
Combined Development and Maintenance 214
Comments 113, 118, 120, 121, 122, 124, 150, 239
Commercial Interest 179
Communication 208
Competition 19, 21, 301
Complexity 255
Complexity Assessment 308
Components Engineering 166
Components, Classification of 85
Components-Based Processes 171
Composition-Based Reuse 160
Comprehension 28, 92, 98, 99
Comprehension Process Models 107
Comprehension Strategies 110, 114
Comprehension Support Tools 125
Comprehension Theories and Studies, Implications of 128
Comprehension, Aims of 100
Configuration 225

Configuration Management 223, 226
Conradi 89, 313
Consistency 23, 124, 131, 159, 228, 244, 260, 294
Constraints 2, 10, 45, 69, 82, 99, 165, 230, 306
Context of Maintenance 1
Continuity of Service 11
Control 253
Control Abstractions 168
Corbi 97
Corrective Change 34, 35, 52, 143, 147, 213
Correctness 274
Cost 5, 261, 283, 300
Cost and Benefits 300, 309
Cost Estimation 261
Cost Reduction 283
Coupling 159, 167, 181
Critical Appraisal 65
Cross 103, 147
Cross-Referencer 304
Current Problems 149
Cyclomatic Number 256, 257, 308

Damsté 33
Data 156
Data Abstraction 135
Data Dictionaries 239
Data Flow Analyser 304
Davis 269, 300
Dead Paradigms 25
Decision-Support Features 103
Decomposition 24, 105, 118, 149, 286, 287, 289
Decomposition Mechanism 121
Decomposition to Aid Comprehension 286
DeMarco 59, 253
Dependency Analyser 305

Design 156
Design for Reuse 166
Design Principles 129
Design Recovery 141
Designers 105
Development Methodology 240, 295
Diminishing Returns 81
Documentation 122, 238, 308
Documentation, Categories of 238
Documentation, Classification of 240
Documentation, Producing and Maintaining Quality 242
Domain Analysis 164
Domain Knowledge 209
Dusink 170
Dynamic Analyser 304

Ease of Understanding 283
Ease of Use 262, 263, 284, 301
Economic Constraints 55
Economic Implications 2, 47, 48
Education 179
Education and Training 129
Education and Training Strategies 213
Effecting Change 24, 42, 95, 98, 130, 261
Efficiency 277
Effort Reallocation 54, 56
Empirical 23, 27, 55, 110, 119, 121, 122, 128, 129, 130, 155, 245, 248, 249, 258, 282
Encodable 249
Enhancement Booklet 239, 241
Enigma Codes 194
Entity 248
Environment 20
Environment Management 234
Environmental Factor 17, 20
E-Type System 34, 45, 315

Evaluation 253
Evolving Requirements 126
Example Measures 254
Execution Effect 101
Expertise 118

FDA 198, 199
FEAST 55, 315
Features 7, 23, 69, 100, 110, 160, 300
Finkelstein 249
Fitness for Purpose 273
FORTRAN 77 274
Forward Engineering 144
Fourth-Generation Languages 279
Fourth-Generation Languages, Impact on Maintenance 282
Fourth-Generation Languages, Properties of 281
Fourth-Generation Languages, Weaknesses 283
Framework 2, 17, 18
Framework for Software Maintenance 18
Framework, Components 20
Freeman 169, 173
Fritz Hager 200
Function Abstraction 135
Functional Requirements 10, 99, 104
Fundamentals of Software Change 33
Future 311

Generality 167, 181
Generation-Based Reuse 162
Generator-Based Systems, Evaluation 164
Generic Reuse/Reusability Model 173
Ghezzi 167
Gilb 103

Gordon Symonds 196
Guidelines and
    Recommendations 129
Guy 47

Hall 170
Halstead 255, 256, 257, 258, 260,
    262, 263
Halstead's Measures 257
Han 272
Hands-On Experience 214
Haughton 142
Hidden Benefit 221
Higgins 53
High Level Language 270
High Payoff 81
Hooper 173, 175, 177

IEEE 9, 193, 213, 273
Image 47
Image Filing System 295
Image Problems 52
Impact Analysis 271
Impact Analysis in Creating
    Maintainable Systems 272
Implementation 8, 89
Implementation Issues 118
Improvement 254
Ince 272
Increased Productivity 282
Incremental Release 41
Inertia 51
Information Gap 18, 23
Information Needs 103, 109, 130
Initial Capital Outlay 178
Innovation 19, 20
Insight II 293
Installation Guide 239
Integration Testing 191
Integrity 277
Integrity In Measurement 249
Interaction 29, 31, 167

Interoperability 278
Investment 81, 166
ISO 170, 277, 292
Iterative Enhancement Model 84

Jane's Air Traffic Control Special
    Report 13
Jones 10

Kaner 183, 193
Kang 173, 175, 176
Keeping Track of the Maintenance
    Process 219
Kim 203
Knowledge Acquisition and
    Performance 128
Knowledge Base 56, 115, 124,
    291
Krupinski 292

Lano 142
Leblang 232, 234
Legal Issues 179
Lehman 5, 25, 27, 28, 33, 39, 44,
    46, 93, 144
Lehman's Laws 44
Letovsky 115
Level of Awareness 212
Levels of Reverse
    Engineering 138
Lientz 48, 81, 216
Life-Cycle 6, 59, 60
Limitations and Economic
    Implications 2, 47
Limitations to Software
    Change 50
Linthicum 284, 285
Lord Kelvin 247
Lost Information 136, 138, 151

Machiavelli 292
Macro 239

Maintainability 260
Maintainers 103, 129
Maintainers and Their Information Needs 103
Maintaining Systems 11, 15, 48, 127, 266
Maintaining Systems Effectively 11
Maintenance 146, 91
Maintenance Challenge 18, 19, 25, 54
Maintenance Crisis 18, 56, 265, 270
Maintenance Department 216
Maintenance Factors 29
Maintenance Framework 17
Maintenance Measures 247
Maintenance Measures, Guidelines for Selection 261
Maintenance of the Existing System 56
Maintenance Personnel 28
Maintenance Process 23, 59
Maintenance Process Models 71
Maintenance Productivity 206
Maintenance Teams 210
Maintenance Tools 299
Management 95, 203, 205, 236
Management and Organisational Issues 203
Management Responsibilities 205
Managers 104
Mandatory Upgrades 11
Marcus 125
Martin 210, 280, 281
Maturity 19, 25, 87, 88
McCabe 103, 256, 257, 260, 262, 263, 308
McCabe's Cyclomatic Complexity 256
McClure 210, 281
McDermid 7

Measurement 248, 249, 250, 253, 314
Measurement, Integrity 249
Melo 203
Mental Models 109
Metric 249, 251
Migration Between Platforms 136, 138, 151
Migration to Object-Oriented Platforms 290
Military Standards 193
Mobile2OOO 292
Model 60, 110, 271
Models and Strategies 271
Module Ownership 214
Moller 255
Motivating Maintenance Personnel 206
Myers 186

Naming Style 118
Narayanaswamy 232
Need for Change 17, 91, 94, 312
Need for Software Maintenance 10
New Development, Difference from Maintenance 9
Nomenclature 48, 52, 241
Nomenclature and Image Problems 52
Non-Functional Requirements 99, 104
Non-Technical Factors 178
Not Invented Here Factor 179

Object Management Group 171
Object Oriented Programming 270
Objectives 212
Object-Oriented Paradigm 285
Object-Oriented Paradigm, Impact on Maintenance 288

Object-Oriented Platforms, Migration 290
Object-Oriented Techniques in Software Maintenance 292
Ongoing Support 42
Openness of Architecture 301, 309
Operating Environment 20
Operational Environment 8, 19, 29, 45
Opportunistic 99
Opportunistic Model 115
Organisation and Presentation of Programs 122
Organisational Culture 302
Organisational Environment 21
Organisational Modes 214
Organisational Strategy 51
Osborne 82, 83, 86, 90, 92, 242, 243
Osborne's Model 82

Paper Trail 220
Paradigm Shift 19, 24, 142, 310
Past and Present 312
Patient Identification 170
Paulish 255
People 206
Perfective Change 36
Perlis 177
Permanent Team 211
Personnel 156
Personnel Education and Training 211
Petre 118
Pickard 133
Pierce 169
Podgurski 169
Poor Design 284
Portability 274
Post-Delivery Evolution 34, 53

Potential Solutions to Maintenance Problems 54
Prather 256
Prediction 254
Preventive Change 39
Prieto-Diaz 164, 169, 173
Problem Domain 100
Process 155
Process Abstraction 135
Process Control 235
Process Maturity 87
Process Model 2, 60, 65, 71, 89, 107, 172, 174, 176
Process Quality 259
Product 156
Product Quality 259
Product-Environment Relation 103
Program 157
Program Comprehension 314
Program Comprehension Strategies 110
Program Slicer 303
Program Understanding 97
Programmers 105
Programming Languages 177
Programming Practice 19, 23, 103, 116, 130, 195, 261
Project Co-ordination 179
Proof 184
Property of an Entity 249
Proprietary 284

Quality 259
Quality Assessment 243
Quality Assurance 272
Quality Documentation 242
Quality of the Existing System 51
Quick Reference Card 239
Quick-Fix Model 76

Ratcliffe 178
Ratikin 192
Reading Techniques 115
Recognition 110, 208, 213
Recognition Enhancement 213
Redocumentation 139
Reduction in Cost 283, 289
Reduction in Workload 283
Reengineering 146
Reference Guide 239
Regression Testing 191
Reliability 276
Replacement of the System 55
Representation of Information 177
Requirements Analysis/Specification 239
Research Areas 313
Residual Errors 35, 55, 147, 158, 182
Resource Limitations 50
Resources 15, 54, 209
Responsibilities 205, 236
Restructuring 144
Retraining Personnel 291
Reusability 278
Reusable Components 137, 138, 151, 159, 162, 166, 169, 178, 291
Reusable Components, Characteristics 166
Reuse 147, 153, 155, 158, 159, 160, 162, 166, 168, 172, 173, 176, 177, 178, 313
Reuse and Reusability 153
Reuse Libraries 178
Reuse Libraries, Problems 168
Reuse Process Model 172, 176
Reuse, Approaches to 159
Reuse, Factors that Impact 177
Reuse, Objectives and Benefits 158
Reuse, Targets 155

Reuse/Reusability Model, Generic 173
Reuse-Maintenance Vicious Cycle 178
Reuse-Oriented Model 85
Reverse Engineering 133, 169
Reverse Engineering and Associated Techniques in Practice 147
Reverse Engineering, Conditions 143
Reverse Engineering, Purpose and Objectives 135
Rewards 207
Ripple Effect 10, 29, 34, 39, 51, 67, 100, 186, 265
Risk Assessment 70
Role of Software Documentation 241
Rugaber 141
Rumbaugh 295
Rushby 35

Safety-Critical 18, 27
Safety-Related 18, 27
Scacchi 141, 144, 232
Schach 159
Schneidewind 53
Seaman 203
Sheil 121
Sheppard 121
Shneiderman 121
Side Effects 136, 137, 151
Simos 172, 175
Simulator 305
Size 255
Software Airbag 27
Software Change 34
Software Change Control 225
Software Change Fundamentals 2
Software Changes, Categorising 40

Software Configuration 225
Software Configuration
 Management 225, 231, 232
Software Documentation 226, 238
Software Documentation, Role
 of 241
Software Evolution 34, 53
Software Experience Bases 88,
 313
Software Maintenance
 Framework 18, 19, 31
Software Maintenance
 Process 315
Software Maintenance Process 53,
 60, 83, 315
Software Maintenance Tool 266,
 300
Software Measure 251
Software Measurement 250, 314
Software Measurement,
 Objectives 253
Software Metric 251
Software Product 25
Software Production Process 60
Software Reuse 147, 313
Software Tester 184, 186
Software Tester's Job 186
Source Code 8, 94, 107, 115, 122,
 124, 125
Source Code Book 126
Source Code Control System 307
Specification/Design 239
Specification Recovery 142
Spiral Model 69
Stability of Vendor 301, 319
Staff, Attracting and Retaining 52
Standardisation 168, 171
Standards 54, 118, 129, 158, 168,
 170, 240, 270, 272
Static Analyser 303
Strategies, Education and
 Training 213

Strategies, Impact Analysis 271
Strategies, Program
 Comprehension 110
Structured Testing 190
S-Type System 34
Supervision 207
Support Tools 314
Supporting Techniques 143
Swanson 48, 81, 216
System Administration 239
System Documentation 101, 107,
 110, 115, 122, 193, 238, 239,
 240
System Overview 239
System Rationale 239
System Test Plan 239

Tamai 55
Targets for Reuse 155
Taxonomy of Tools 302
Team Working 205
Teasley 314
Technical Factors 177
Temporary Team 211
Test 184
Test Case Generator 306
Test Data, Who Chooses it 187
Test Paths Generator 306
Test Plans 192
Testability 275
Testing 183
Testing Code 190
Testing Software 184
Testing, Points to Note 193
Testing, What to Test and
 How 187
Tests, Categorising 189
Therac 25 194
Threesome Marriage 315
Tool 300
Tools for Comprehension and
 Reverse Engineering 302

Tools to Support
  Comprehension 125, 302
Tools to Support Configuration
  Management 306
Tools to Support Reverse
  Engineering 302
Tools to Support Testing 305
Tools, Criteria for Selecting 300
Top-Down 99, 100
Top-Down Model 111
Torimitsu 55
Traditional Process Models,
  Critical Appraisal 65
Transformation Tool 305
Transformation-Based
  Systems 163
Turski 256

Understandability 260
Understanding 94, 116, 283
Understanding the Current
  System 108
Understanding, Factors that
  Impact 116
Uniformity 168
University Education 213

Usability 275
User 20
User Documentation 238, 239,
  242
User Requests 11
User Requirements 19, 31

Van Vliet 167
Variant 226
Verification and Validation 192
Version 226
Version Control 232
Version of the System 241
Vlamis 292
Vocabulary Problem 99, 119, 120

Waterfall Model 67
Weinberg 104, 243
White Box Testing 190
White-Box Reuse 161, 162, 169
Workload Reduction 283
Work-Type 215

Zhang 150
Zuse 249, 253, 255, 256
Zvegintzov 309